IMAGES
of America

WOODWARD COUNTY

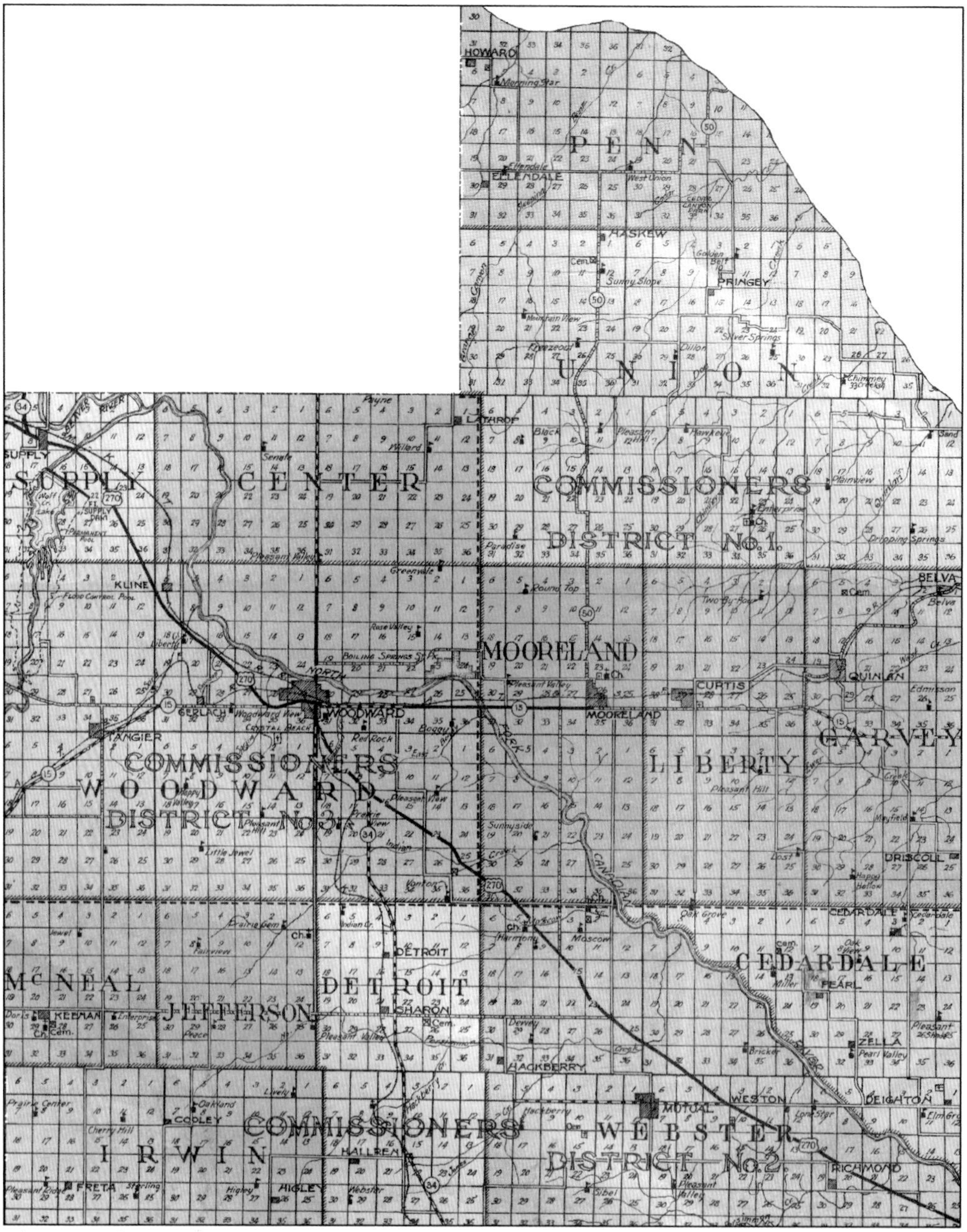

This map depicts the current boundaries of Woodward County. These county lines became effective at Oklahoma's statehood on November 16, 1907.

On the cover: This photograph is of the Atchison, Topeka and Santa Fe Railway depot in Woodward around 1910. The depot was built in 1909 near Ninth Street and was destroyed by the April 9, 1947, tornado. The Santa Fe railway brought Woodward into existence in 1887 and continues to operate in this vibrant community with almost 70 freight trains passing through the city each day. (Courtesy of the Plains Indians and Pioneers Museum.)

IMAGES
of America

WOODWARD COUNTY

Ian D. Swart

ARCADIA
PUBLISHING

ISBN 978-0-7385-6115-8

Published by Arcadia Publishing
Charleston, South Carolina

Printed in the United States of America

Library of Congress Catalog Card Number: 2008935439

For all general information contact Arcadia Publishing at:
Telephone 843-853-2070
Fax 843-853-0044
E-mail sales@arcadiapublishing.com
For customer service and orders:
Toll-Free 1-888-313-2665

Visit us on the Internet at www.arcadiapublishing.com

This volume is dedicated to all Woodward County pioneers, especially R. W. and Lizzie. Their efforts have transformed the virgin prairie into a civilization.

Contents

ACKNOWLEDGMENTS

Firstly, I would like to express my gratitude to the Plains Indians and Pioneers Museum Board of Directors for the charge to create this volume. A special thank-you goes to museum staff members Robert Roberson, Tammy Hawbaker, Courtney Jones, and volunteer Wade Lambel for exhibiting patience while I created this book.

This publication would not have been possible without the passion of many photographers, especially Frank Saunders, Woodward's first photographer. He captured the essence of early day Woodward County with the lens of his camera. A large number of his photographs are included in this book.

Thanks also to my friend Marcella Fuller Plank Bynum. She is Woodward County through and through. I sincerely appreciate you taking the time to share the many stories that were passed down to you by your forebears. My knowledge of Woodward County would not be what it is without you.

My love of the great state of Oklahoma is due to the many lessons learned from my grandparents. Thank you for sharing your lives and memories with me. The blood of Oklahoma pioneers courses through my veins, and you have taught me never to forget it.

The passion I have for learning and preserving history stems from my fifth-grade history teacher, the late Nancy Cunningham. I credit her for planting the seed of history in my heart. Thank you, Mrs. Cunningham.

I would also like to thank my wife, Ashley, for believing in me and encouraging me to pursue this project. Thank you for your unfailing devotion. I love you.

All photographs included herein are used with permission from the Plains Indians and Pioneers Museum in Woodward, Oklahoma, unless otherwise noted.

INTRODUCTION

Woodward County, originally known as N County, was 60 miles square. It was composed of present-day Woodward County and portions of Harper, Ellis, and Woods Counties. The county was the westernmost county of the Cherokee Outlet. It bordered Texas and the Oklahoma Panhandle on the west and Kansas to the north. Political pressure applied by William H. Murray during the Oklahoma Constitutional Convention resulted in the reduction of the size of Woodward County to its present boundaries.

Before its designation as a county of Oklahoma Territory, the U.S. Cavalry had established Camp Supply in 1868 during the Indian Wars at the confluence of the Wolf Creek and Beaver River, about 13 miles northwest of present-day Woodward. It played a large part in the settlement of natives on reservations in western Oklahoma. George Armstrong Custer was stationed for a short time in what would become Woodward County. The post closed in 1894 after the area was settled by nonnatives.

The lush grasslands of the Cherokee Outlet provided ample fodder for Texas cattle en route to railheads in Kansas during the 1870s and 1880s. The Cherokee Strip Livestock Association was created in 1883 in an effort to lease the prairie lands in the possession of the Cherokee Nation. They were successful until the federal government decided to open the Native American land for settlement.

It was on September 16, 1893, that thousands of hopeful pioneers rushed into the territory to claim prime locations for the chance of a new beginning. Not only did settlers rush in on horses, mules, wagons, and bicycles, but they also rode trains into the territory and ran on foot to claim prime town lots.

These hardy pioneers built northwest Oklahoma from the ground up. As no trees were readily available, they dug into the virgin soil to build homes and crude shelters until lumber could be shipped in by rail for frame houses. The railroad served as the lifeblood of the area. A town's success depended on its proximity to the rail. Those fortunate enough to lie close to the railroad were given a chance to survive with a steady supply of visitors and traders passing through. Rail lines were so important that towns might even pick up and literally move to a track that bypassed them. It was the railroad that brought life to the open prairie and created the town of Woodward in 1887.

Soon after the opening of the outlet, business centers along wide main streets sprang up across the prairie landscape. With the creation of new towns came general merchandise stores, banks, post offices, and lawyers' offices.

Before statehood, Woodward city was home to 15 brothels and 23 saloons. They provided a never-ending source of excitement, especially when disagreements led to gunplay, such as the 1895 shoot-out of John E. (Jack) Love and Temple Houston against brothers Ed and John Jennings.

The disagreement began in the courtroom the morning of October 8. On trial were several men accused of stealing a keg of beer from a railroad car near the Atchison, Topeka and Santa Fe Railway (Santa Fe) depot. Houston, the famous son of Texas revolutionary Sam Houston, appeared with county attorney Smith for the prosecution. The Jennings brothers appeared for the defense. During examination of evidence, an argument over minor points occurred, and Houston suggested Ed Jennings of being "grossly ignorant of the law." Slamming his fist on the table, Ed declared Houston to be a "damned liar" and attempted to slap his face. Guns were drawn, but those present in the courtroom intervened. Court was adjourned until the next morning so the men would have an opportunity to cool off. But this was not to be. While Houston and exsheriff Love were having a friendly drink in one of Woodward's saloons, the brothers Jennings walked in.

A Woodward dispatch to the territorial press on October 9 gave this account of Woodward's most famous gunfight:

> Last night about 10 o'clock, this town was aroused by a fusillade of shots in one of the principal saloons here, known as the "Cabinet," and owned by Jack Garvey. Hastening there the spectators beheld lawyer Ed Jennings weltering in blood, his brain oozing from a bullet hole in the left side of his head, his hand still clinging to a smoking revolver, half concealed by his prostrate form.
>
> Lawyer John Jennings was fleeing up the street with one arm limp and dangling by his side from which the blood poured in streams.
>
> Lawyer Temple Houston and ex-Sheriff Jack Love were on their way to the sheriff's office to surrender their persons to his custody.
>
> Neither Love nor Houston were wounded, although several bullets passed through their clothes and hats.

Love and Houston later stood trial on the second floor of Peter Martinson's building (known as the Opera House) for the murder of Ed Jennings. They were acquitted as it was found they acted in self-defense.

By the dawn of the 20th century, women in Woodward County had put up with enough of the rowdy cow towns they found themselves living in. In order to make Woodward more civilized, they established literary societies and other social organizations in which they could nurture refinement. They also hoped to have Woodward's red-light district dismantled. This sentiment was evident by the 1899 indictment of Minnie Stacie, a hopelessly guilty brothel madam, in Woodward County Court. Attorney Houston, who had been away on business, returned home on the morning Stacie's trial began. Realizing she had no one to defend her, Houston rushed to the courtroom and stated that he would come to her aide. After a 10-minute recess, Houston defended her, and convinced the jury to let her go. The "Soiled Dove Plea," as it was later called, became known as the perfect defense and is still taught to Harvard Law School students.

In the decade after the land run, Woodward County farmers were harvesting bumper crops. The economy of the county was booming and more people were moving in to make their fortunes in northwest Oklahoma.

In a special souvenir edition of the *Woodward News* in 1903, editor William Ezra Bolton proclaimed the greatness of the "Empire County of Oklahoma" as he called his home.

He writes, "The most advanced ideas of thought predominated and made Woodward superior to most counties in any country, new or old."

Bolton continued to describe the current development of the county seat:

> Three splendid elevators at Woodward are kept busy handling the enormous wheat crop of this year, and the big stockyards are not idle by any means. An important fact in the Commercial life of Woodward is that in addition to being the seat of government in the "Empire County," it is also the center of a land district for the government, a Unites States Land Office being located here. Added to this is the big pay roll of the Santa Fe [railroad], this point being the

terminal as well as the connection of the A. T. & S. F. Railway and the S. K. of T. Railway, the latter being a Santa Fe System line extending from here southward through Texas and New Mexico . . .

The city of Woodward is also preparing to build a water works system of the latest and best kind and when this is done the town will lack nothing to make it a modern and up-to-date city of prosperous commercial lines and hundreds of happy homes.

And what of the future? No one may estimate that which is hidden by the veil of oncoming years, but it is safe to say that in ten years from now, the town of Woodward will contain not less than 5,000 people, perhaps double that number even. The other towns of the county, the live hustling ones, will become important trading centers. The population of the county will advance along the line of general development of the rich resources of fertile uplands and valleys until the general feeling of unrest and change is substituted by content coupled with conditions which will make Woodward county famous as one of the choicest and fairest portions of the earth, in which to live and enjoy all the happiness of good government.

Now that citizens in the territory were settled in this new land, minds turned to statehood, and Woodward County was not without a voice. E. O. McCance of Mutual was elected as a delegate to the constitutional convention in Guthrie in 1906.

On September 7, 1907, William Jennings Bryan, a leading figure in the Democratic Party, spoke to 20,000 people gathered in Woodward and urged the ratification of Oklahoma's proposed constitution and the election of a democratic ticket. Two months later, the proclamation admitting Oklahoma as a state was signed by Pres. Theodore Roosevelt on November 16, 1907, with the quill from an American golden eagle captured near Woodward.

With statehood came a sense of permanence for Oklahomans. The first-generation wooden buildings were soon replaced by grand structures of brick and stone as family roots were planted deeper and deeper in the red Oklahoma soil.

Along with statehood came prohibition, thus ending Woodward's rough and tumble social scene. The dozen or so saloons and the red-light district north of the tracks in Woodward were no longer in business. "Uncle Jack" Garvey, owner of the Cabinet saloon, turned his establishment into a bank.

Gone too was one of the loudest voices of Woodward County. Temple Houston died in 1905 from a cerebral hemorrhage. The silver-tongued devil, the son of Sam, was dead. He was laid to rest in the newly created Elmwood Cemetery southwest of Woodward. A few months before his death, he allowed his name to be added to a short list of candidates for Oklahoma's first governor. His widow, Laura, remained in Woodward and became postmistress. Although Temple Houston died at the young age of 45, he left an indelible mark on Woodward and the rest of the county.

The decade after statehood was one of much growth and development in Woodward. A second rail line entered the Woodward city limits in 1912. The Wichita Falls and Northwestern Railway, later the Missouri-Kansas-Texas Railway (Katy), sealed the county seat's place as an extensive shipping point. The first train on this line rolled into town on May 9, 1912. Railroad officials joined with county residents in celebrating this achievement with much pomp and circumstance as they drove in the final golden spike. The U.S. Department of Agriculture Great Plains field station opened southwest of town in 1913. It still operates in Woodward under the name Southern Plains Range Research Station.

The Woodward Commercial Club, predecessor of the chamber of commerce, was organized in 1916. The Woodward Elks came to be in 1919. Ten years later, the Woodward Elks Rodeo was established to tie the town more closely with the cattle industry of the area. The rodeo quickly became one of the top contests in the United States. The annual event led to Trego's Westwear, one of the first western clothiers in the country. The Elks rodeo still attracts thousands of visitors to Woodward each summer.

Drilling for oil in the county started in about 1917. Throughout the 1920s, people in the oil business tried their luck in Woodward County with little to show for their efforts. Others stuck with the cotton and wheat farming they had always known, barely making a living year after year.

The Woodward Theatre was built in 1929 in the 800 block of Main Avenue. Financed by J. O. Selman, he insisted that a stage and green rooms be included in the construction. He believed that "talking picture shows" would not last. In 1981, Selman's thoughts became true, in a way, when the theater reopened as a strictly performing arts venue.

The drought and dust storms of the 1930s proved to be an even greater test of the tenacity of Oklahoma pioneer families. Although many left for greener pastures in California, almost two-thirds of the population stayed to see better days in Oklahoma. Crystal Beach Park was created on the east side of Woodward during the 1930s. It remains an important location for recreation in Woodward County.

As if Woodward had not suffered enough from the effects of the Great Depression and dust bowl, another wave of destruction was to come into the lives of county residents. April 9, 1947, brought terror from the sky as the deadliest tornado in Oklahoma's history touched down in Woodward at 8:42 p.m. Over 200 city blocks were destroyed, and at least 107 people were killed. Although the city was dealt a huge blow, the prevailing spirit of the pioneer ancestors proved the resiliency of Oklahomans as they began to rebuild the little town they called home. With help from the Red Cross and other organizations, the disheveled county seat was rebuilt. Woodward was here to stay and prosper.

On May 18, 1956, Charlie Pappe, a local Woodward grocer, opened the second Top-Hat Drive-In Restaurant in the United States, which was the precursor to Sonic Drive-In.

In late November 1956, Woodward renewed its relationship with petroleum. The McCormick No. 1 well was drilled on the farm of Hugh and Iva McCormick. This led to the first real boom the area had seen, which lasted almost 20 years. As residents celebrated Oklahoma's semicentennial in 1957, drought was plaguing the county. In January 1957, Pres. Dwight D. Eisenhower arrived in Woodward County to see drought-stricken farms during a tour of dry western states. He visited the farm of Carl and Frances Peoples west of Tangier.

The boom brought the High Plains Vocational-Technical School, a new Woodward High School building, a new post office, a hospital, and two agriculture-related industries, Oklahoma Nitrogen in 1976 and Woodward Iodine in 1977. Since then, numerous companies have explored for and produced crude iodine in Woodward County.

The boom crashed in 1982, as the result of poor agricultural markets and the collapse of the oil and gas industry.

In 1987, residents of the county seat celebrated its first century on the prairie. Events held across the city lauded the achievements of Woodwardites through the last 100 years. A new exhibit was opened at the Plains Indians and Pioneers Museum, and a parade was held downtown. Oklahoma governor Henry Bellmon came to Woodward to dedicate a new monument in Centennial Park.

The decade of the 1990s ushered in a new era for higher education in Woodward County. Northwestern Oklahoma State University in Alva created a satellite campus in Woodward in 1996. The first structure on its new campus was recently completed at 2007 Thirty-fourth Street.

In 2003, Florida Power and Light's subsidiary, FPL Energy, and the Oklahoma Municipal Power Authority began commercial production of electricity generated from wind turbines constructed 12 miles northeast of Woodward.

At the time of this writing, Woodward County is once again enjoying another boom. New hotels and restaurants are being constructed, profits from sales taxes are increasing, and new residents are making the county home.

The county of Woodward has grown to a population of nearly 19,000 and the county seat serves as a commercial hub for 50,000 area residents. Although Woodward County has endured tornadoes, blizzards, dust storms, economic decline, an oil boom and bust, floods, and fires, there is no better place to call home. The enduring spirit of the pioneers lives on in those who continue to make Woodward County a better place for posterity.

One

N COUNTY
1893–1906

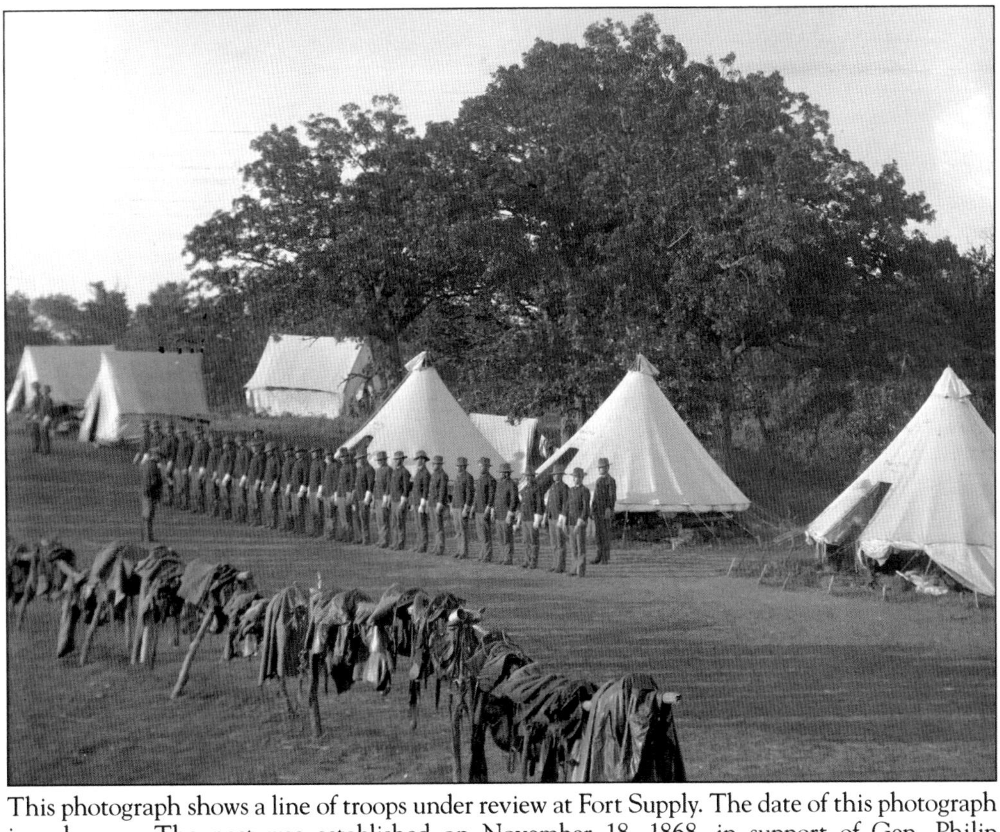

This photograph shows a line of troops under review at Fort Supply. The date of this photograph is unknown. The post was established on November 18, 1868, in support of Gen. Philip Sheridan's campaign against the southern Plains Indians. George Armstrong Custer led the Seventh Cavalry south from here and destroyed the village of the Cheyenne Chief Black Kettle in what became known as the Battle of the Washita.

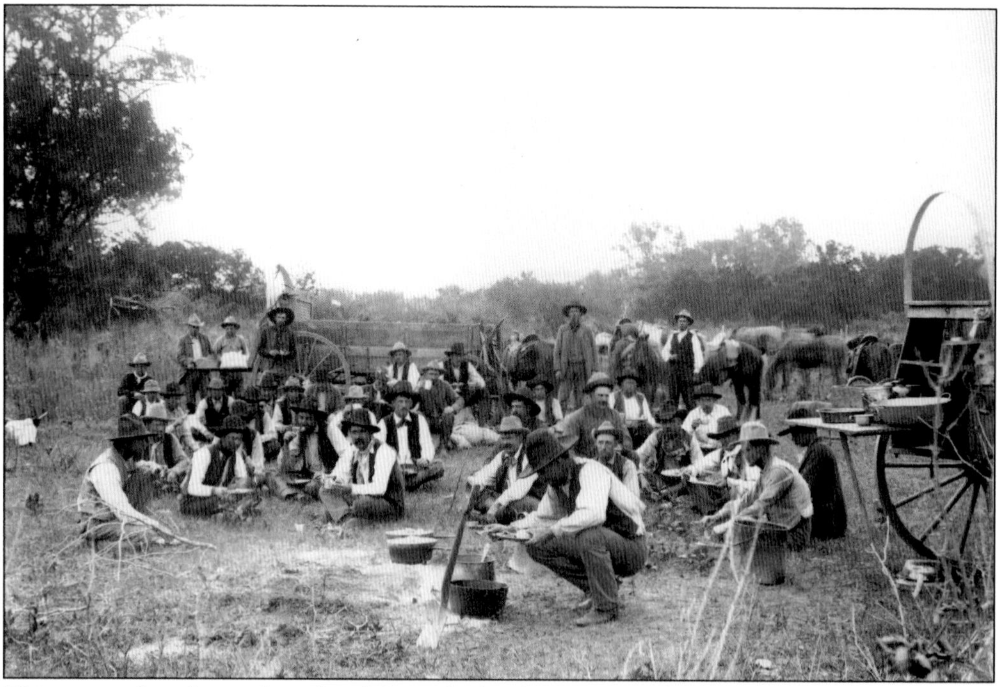

This group of cowboys takes a break from the herd to eat a meal on the open range. Cattlemen, who had been able to graze cattle in all parts of the Cherokee Outlet, were soon pushed out by settlers.

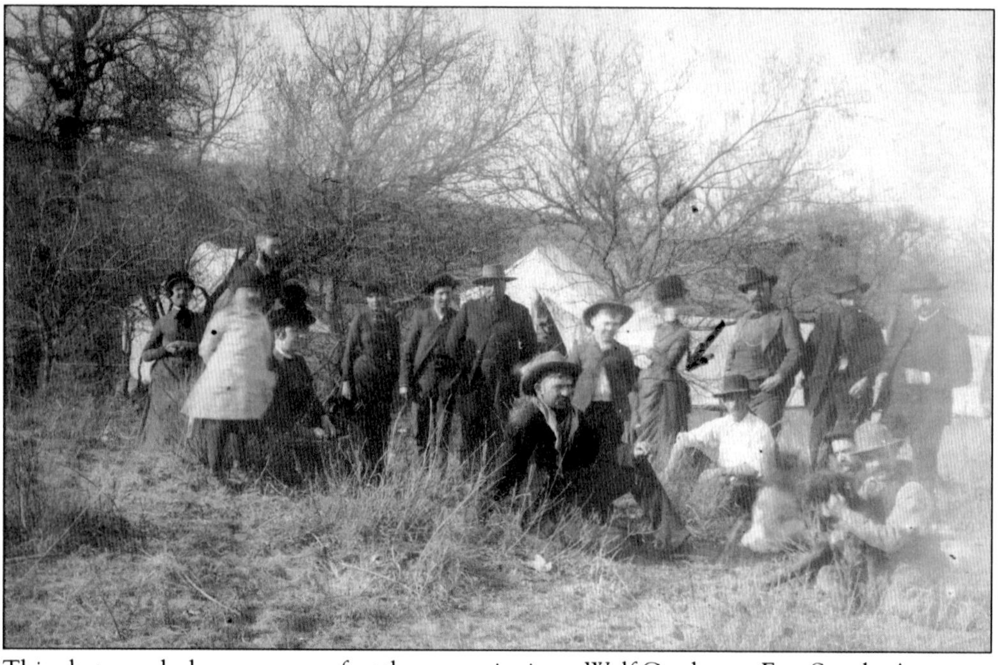

This photograph shows a group of settlers on a picnic on Wolf Creek near Fort Supply. An arrow drawn on the image points to Elizabeth Turnbull Monahan. New settlers to Woodward County enjoyed pleasure trips to the old post. They held dances, bonfires, and other types of recreational activities on the grounds of old Fort Supply.

Woodward has had many photographers, but none have left such a legacy as Frank Saunders, shown here in 1899. His lifelong love of the camera has preserved a rich photographic history of the community and beyond. Born in 1863 in Illinois, he studied photography in Puget Sound, Washington. After the opening of the Cherokee Outlet in 1893, he moved to Woodward and established a photography studio near the corner of Sixth Street and Texas Avenue.

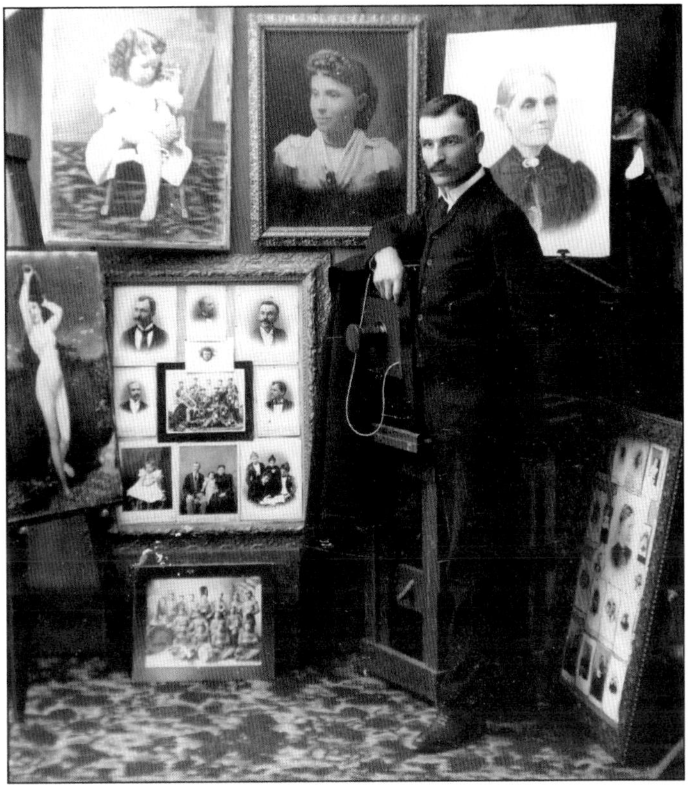

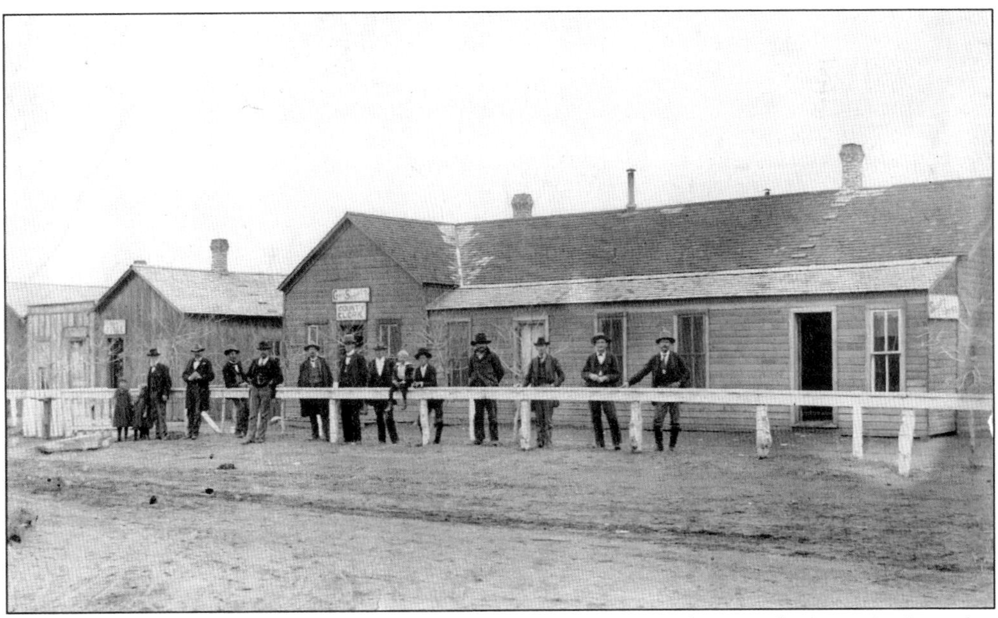

These Woodward County offices predate the original county courthouse, which was built on this site in 1901 on the northwest corner of Tenth Street and Texas Avenue. This photograph dates to 1899 and includes the offices for county superintendent, county clerk, and probate judge.

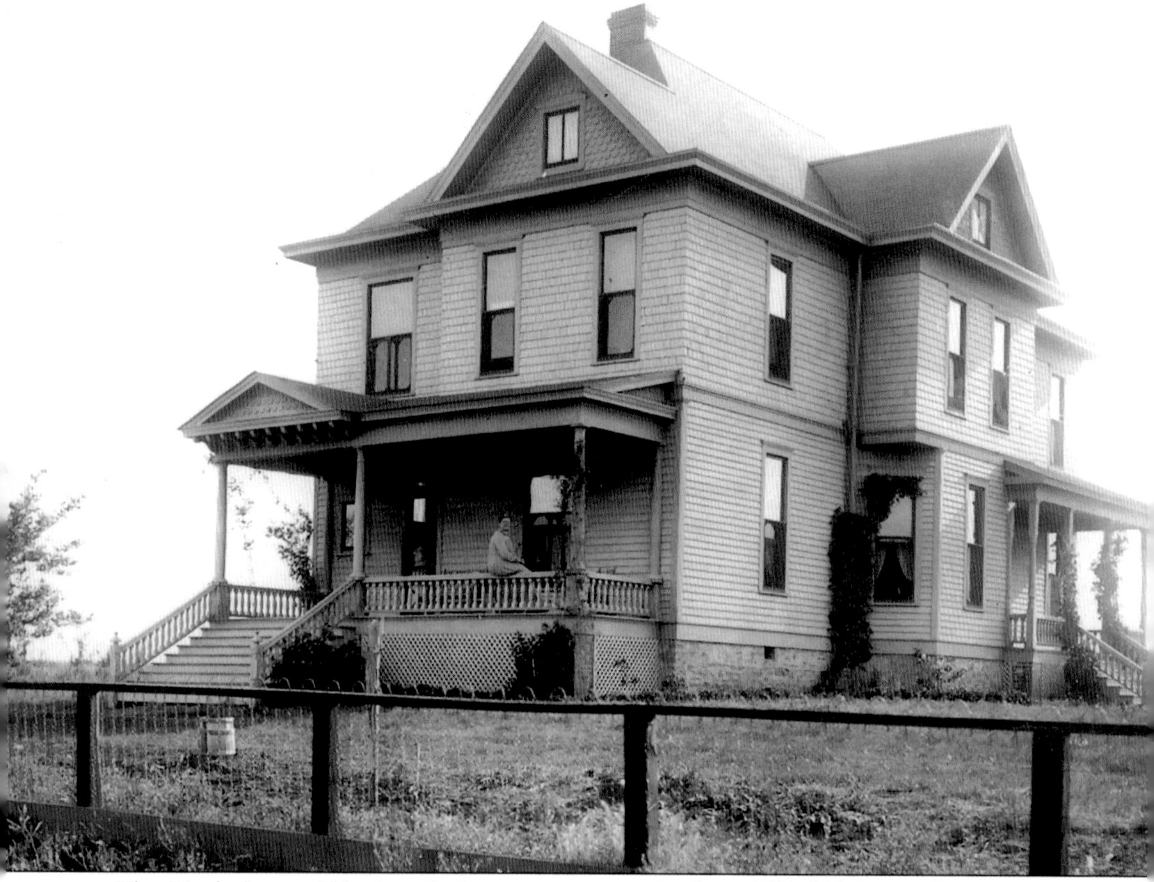

The Tandy house, Woodward's first mansion, was built at 1417 Oklahoma Avenue in 1899. Archibal H. Tandy was born in Kentucky on September 16, 1850. After his 1875 marriage to Zaffrine Lacy, they moved to Haskell, Texas, where he became a rancher. He was soon known for his large land holdings of nearly 100 sections in Roberts and Ochiltree Counties in Texas. His ranch in Woodward County was located nearly 10 miles north of the county seat, and it is not known why he decided to build his palatial home in Woodward. The house contained 14 large rooms, which were decorated with custom-made wallpapers and imported French tile. The house was said to have contained a barred room for sobering up the Bar Z cowboys. By the time his family moved into the impressive structure, small ranchers and farmers were already intruding on his ranges. In 1904, he sold most of his Oklahoma ranchland; however, he remained a citizen of Woodward until his death in 1929. He and his wife are buried in Woodward's Elmwood Cemetery.

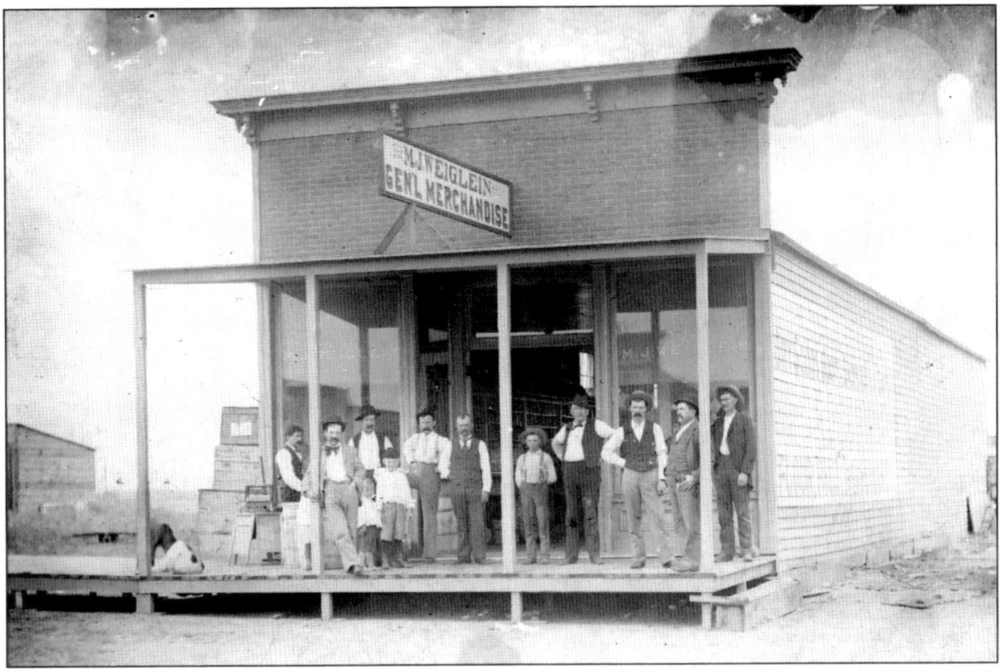

This photograph from about 1895 depicts the M. J. Weiglein General Merchandise Store, which was located at Fort Supply.

William Ezra Bolton (center), shown here with his newspaper staff in 1897, came to Woodward in 1894 and established the *Woodward News*. The first issue was printed on June 1 of that year. Bolton became a large supporter of Woodward County and used his editorial voice to sing its praises to the rest of the country. After the establishment of the Oklahoma Livestock Association in Woodward in 1895, he created the *Live Stock Inspector*, which served as the official publication of the organization.

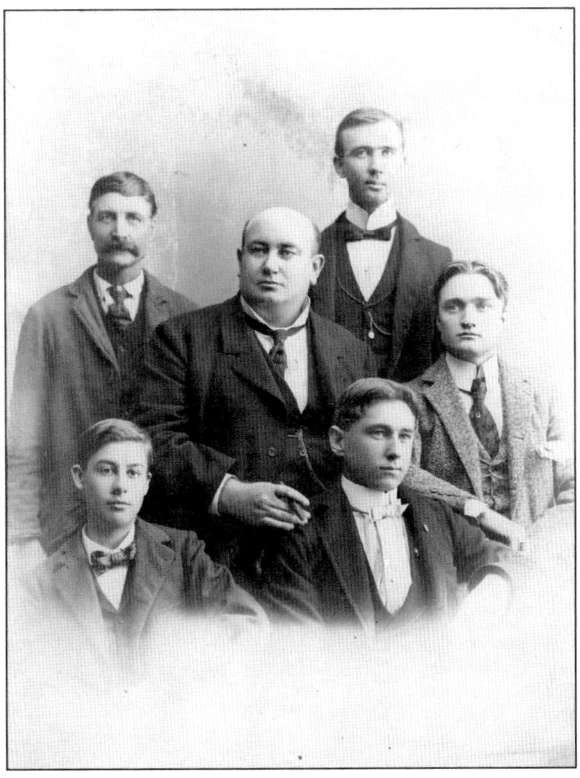

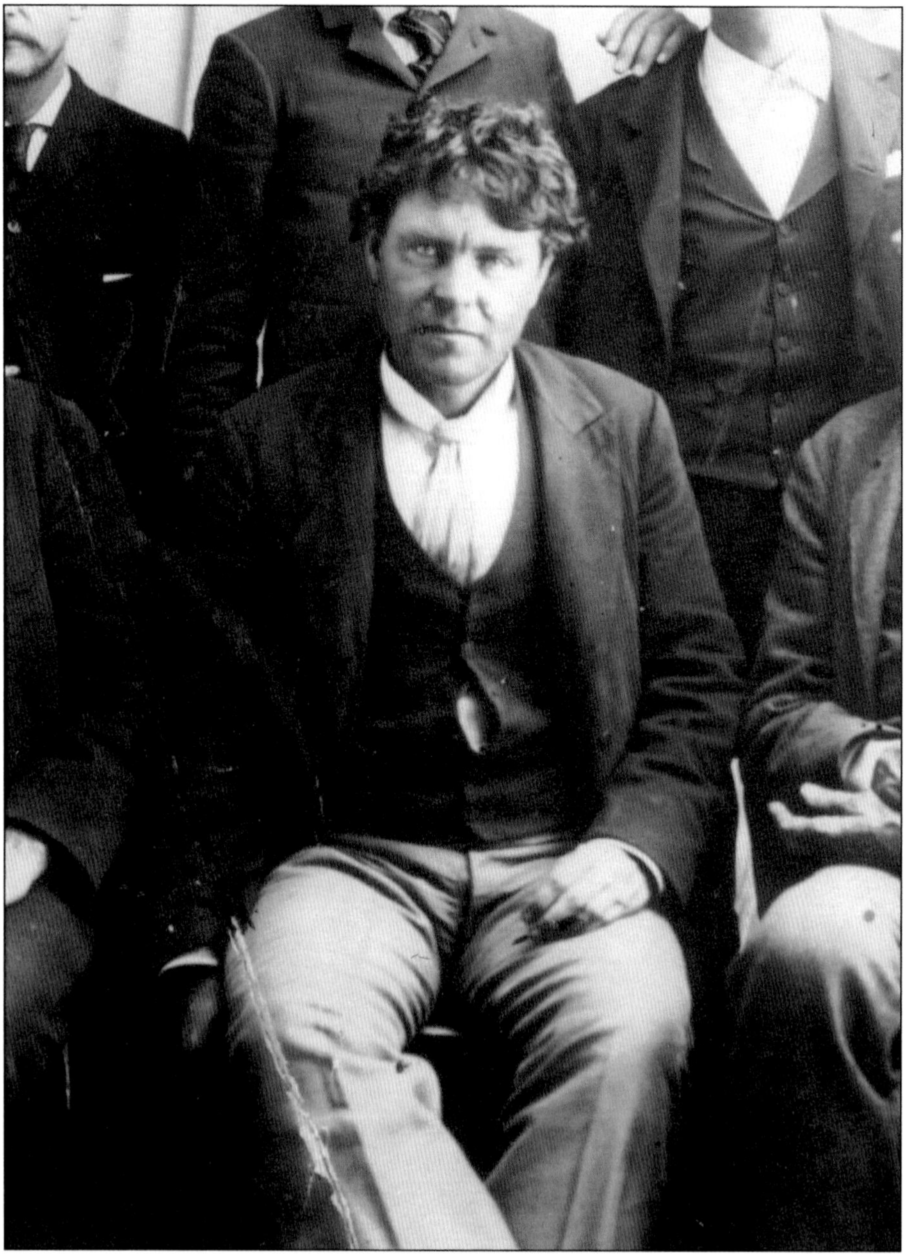

Temple Houston, shown in this 1894 photograph by F. M. Steele, is known as Woodward's favorite son. He was born on August 12, 1860, in the Texas governor's mansion. Houston was considered by many to be one of the country's most brilliant trial lawyers and was noted for his flamboyant dress and behavior. Houston was well educated and spoke French and Spanish fluently as well as seven Native American languages. After serving in the Texas state legislature, Houston moved his law practice to Woodward in 1893 and became involved in the movement for Oklahoma statehood. Houston was equally known as a dead-shot gunfighter. He died of a cerebral hemorrhage on August 15, 1905, at age 45. He is buried in the Elmwood Cemetery outside Woodward. Shortly before his death, Houston allowed his name to be added to a short list of candidates for Oklahoma's first governor.

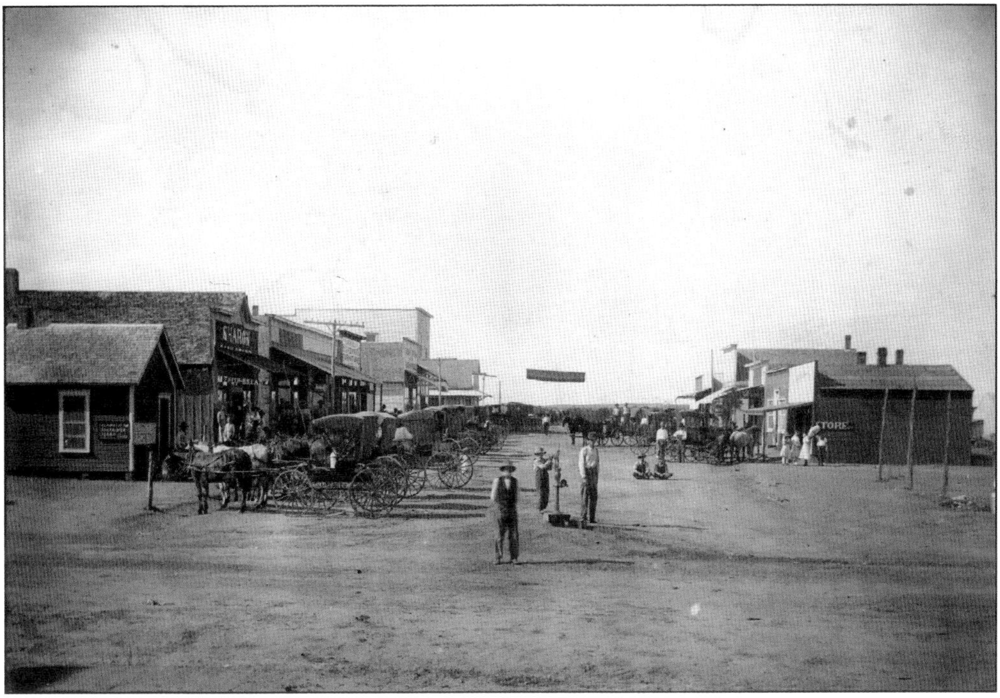

Sharon, located 12 miles south of Woodward, was formerly known as Hackberry. The name changed on February 24, 1912. This photograph of Main Street was taken in about 1914.

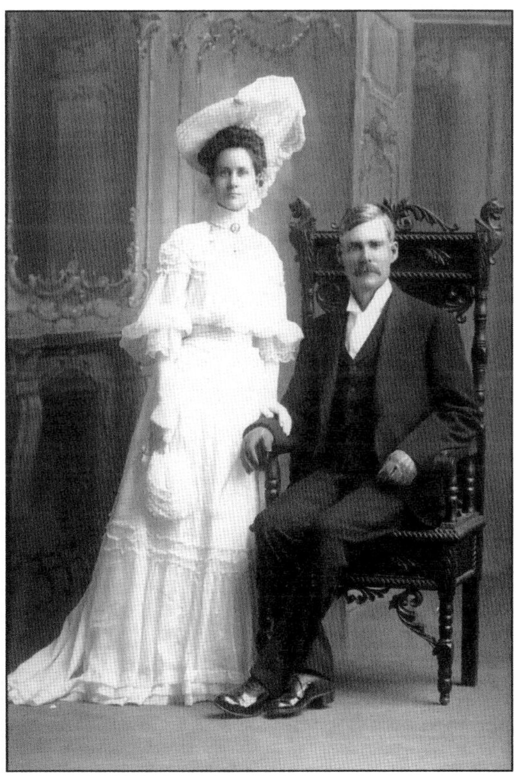

This is a wedding photograph of Joseph Allen and Etha C. Innis from 1900. He was the Woodward County surveyor for 30 years. He also surveyed townships and county lines of Dewey, Harper, Ellis, Beaver, Texas, Cimarron, and Woodward Counties. The Innis family moved into the Tandy mansion in the 1930s.

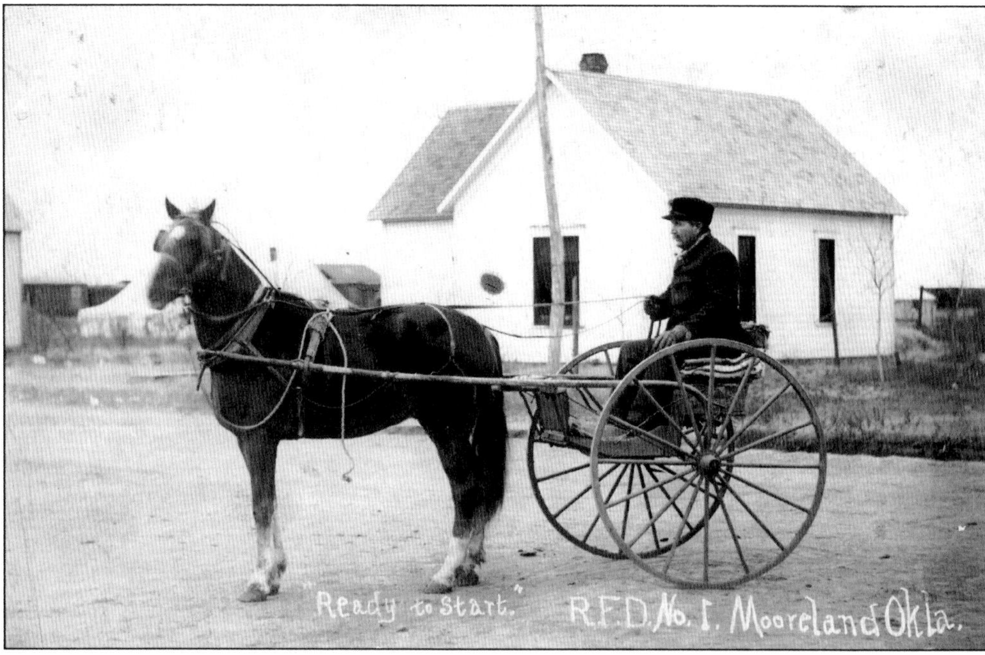

A Mr. Syms was Mooreland's first mail carrier. He is shown here riding in his horse-drawn mail hack.

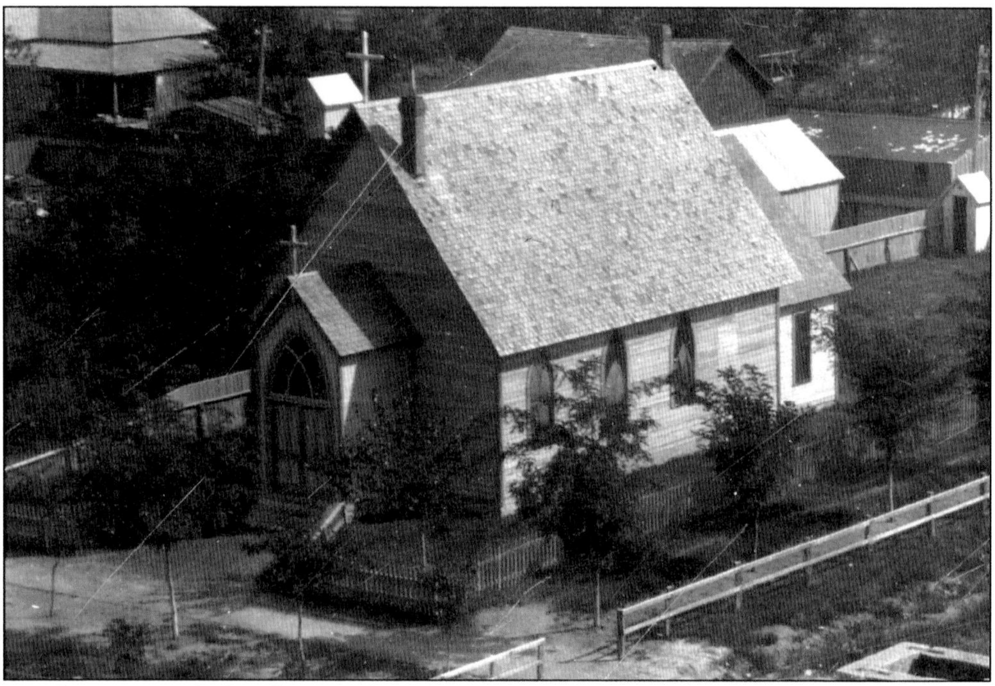

St. John's Episcopal Church, located on the southeast corner of Tenth Street and Texas Avenue, is shown in this 1906 photograph taken by J. R. Boyle. The church, likely the oldest in the Cherokee Outlet, is still in use today. Construction began in 1893 on east Main Avenue, where it stood until 1901. It was moved to its present location to open up prime downtown lots for businesses.

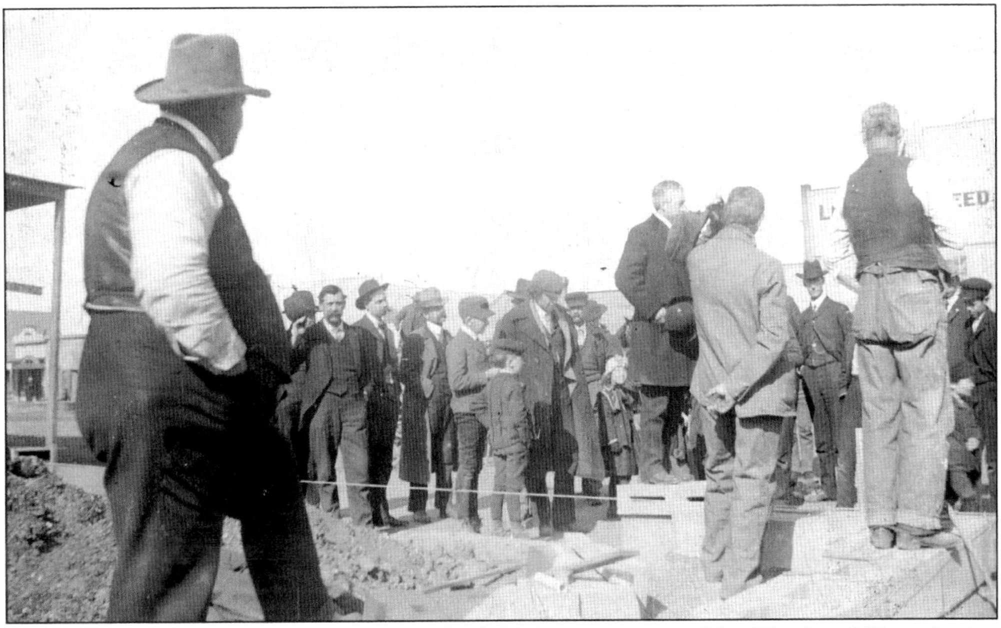

William (Billy) Bolton, the large man on the left who was owner of the *Woodward News,* built a new printing office and post office for Woodward. This photograph shows the dedication of the cornerstone of the building on January 29, 1904. A time capsule, which contained hair, stationery, and current newspapers, is said to have been placed inside. Temple Houston is wearing a cap in the center of the photograph. His three children are with him.

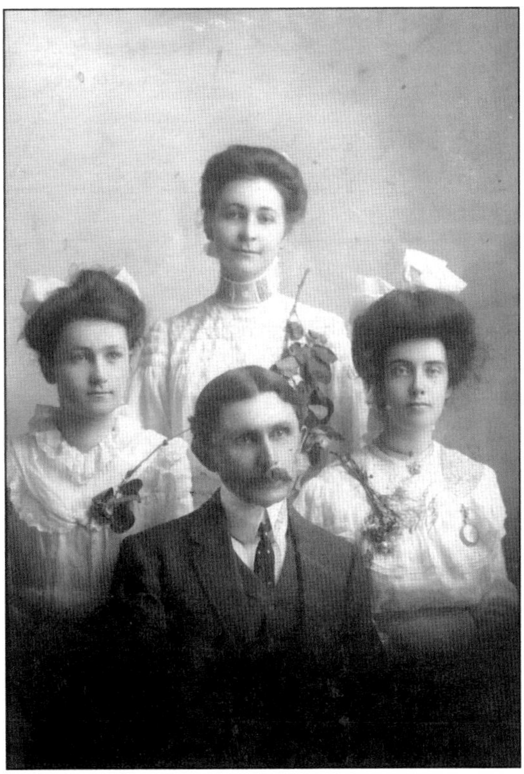

Woodward High School, although established several years before, did not have a graduating class until 1904. The three female students who make up the first graduating class are, from left to right, Ivy Coombs, Florence Chapman, and Mable Gray. The man in front is Prof. Guy M. Lisk, superintendent of the school. The first graduation was held in the Opera House, located over Peter Martinson's store on Main Avenue.

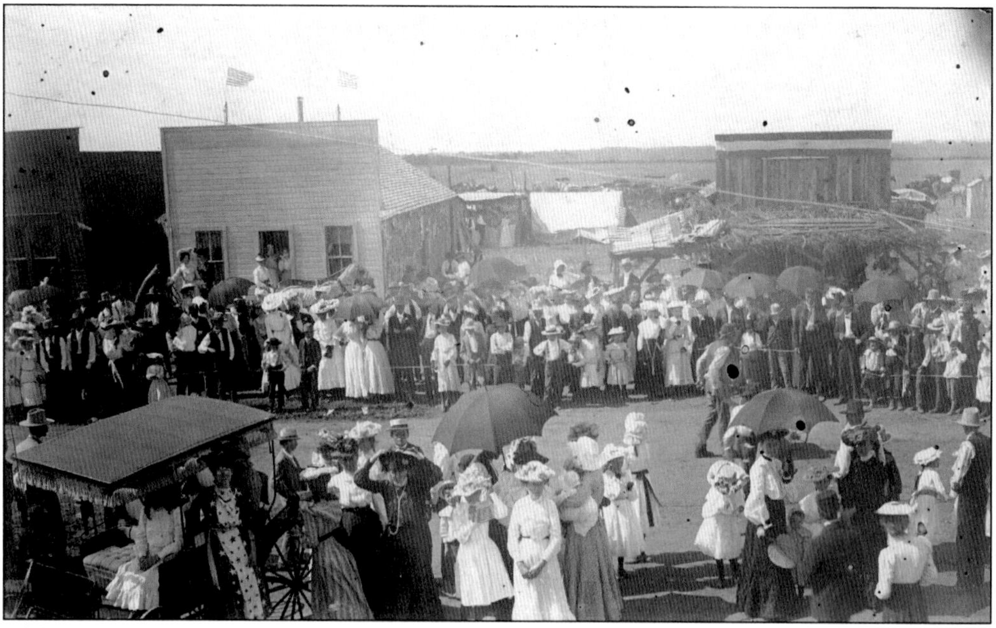

Oklahoma settlers looked for almost any reason to have a celebration. However, no event held as much excitement as did Independence Day. This photograph shows a Fourth of July celebration in Mutual in 1905.

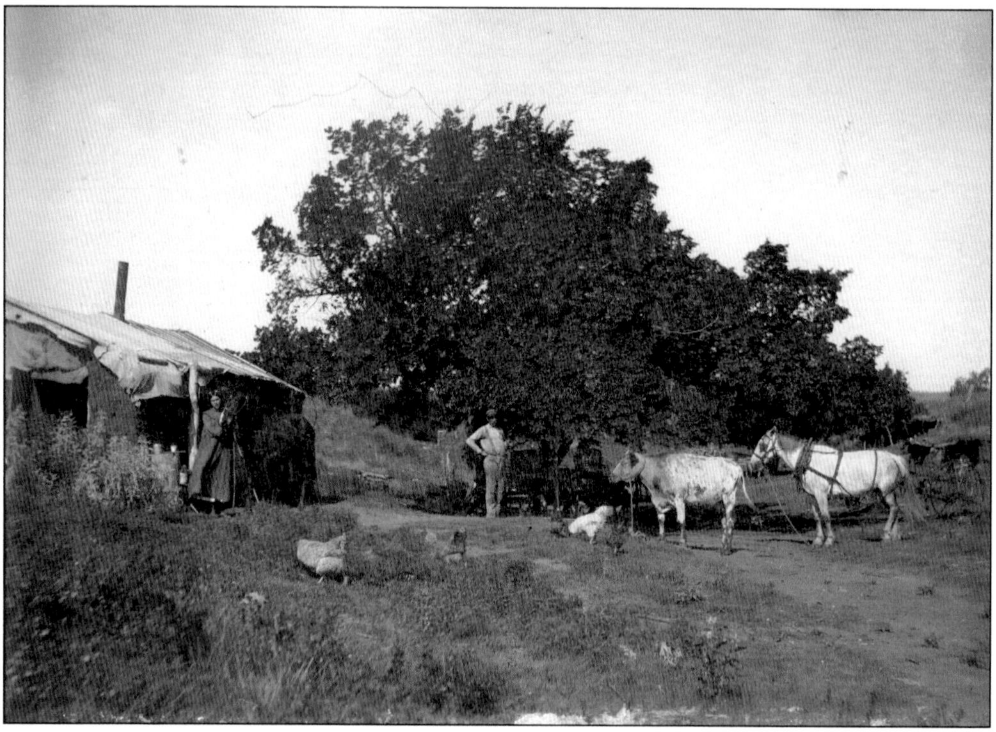

This photograph was taken on the Scovel homestead, which was located between Woodward and Mooreland. The woman on the left is likely Eunie Scovel Williams, wife of Garrett Williams. The names of the horses are Charlie and Barnie. The cow was named Ol Kansas.

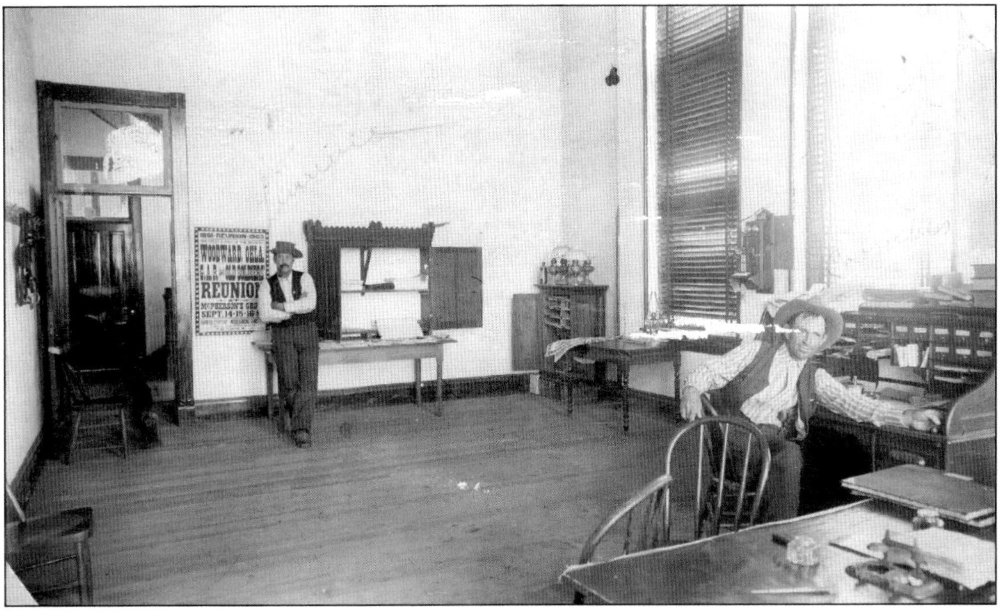

These gentlemen are seated in the Woodward County sheriff's office, which was located in the newly constructed county courthouse. The poster in the background, which is advertising the Grand Army of the Republic and Old Settlers Reunion, dates the photograph to 1903. The poster states that the reunion was to be held at McPherson's Grove September 14–16.

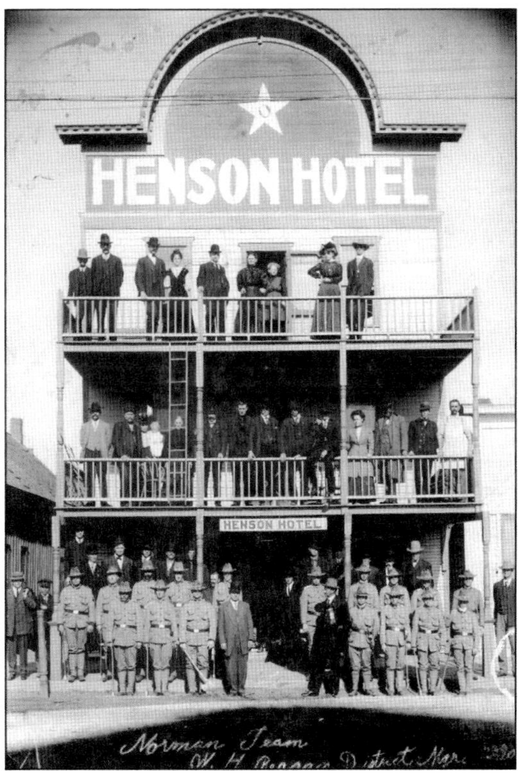

This photograph shows the Henson Hotel, which was located in Woodward between Sixth and Seventh Streets on the north side of Main Avenue. The caption at the bottom of the photograph reads "Norman Team. W. H. Reagan District Mgr. Okla." To whom this reference specifically refers is unknown. The group of soldiers is wearing what appears to be Spanish-American War–era uniforms. The hotel was in operation from 1913 to 1922. The Henson was a multistory brick structure with a wooden front facade.

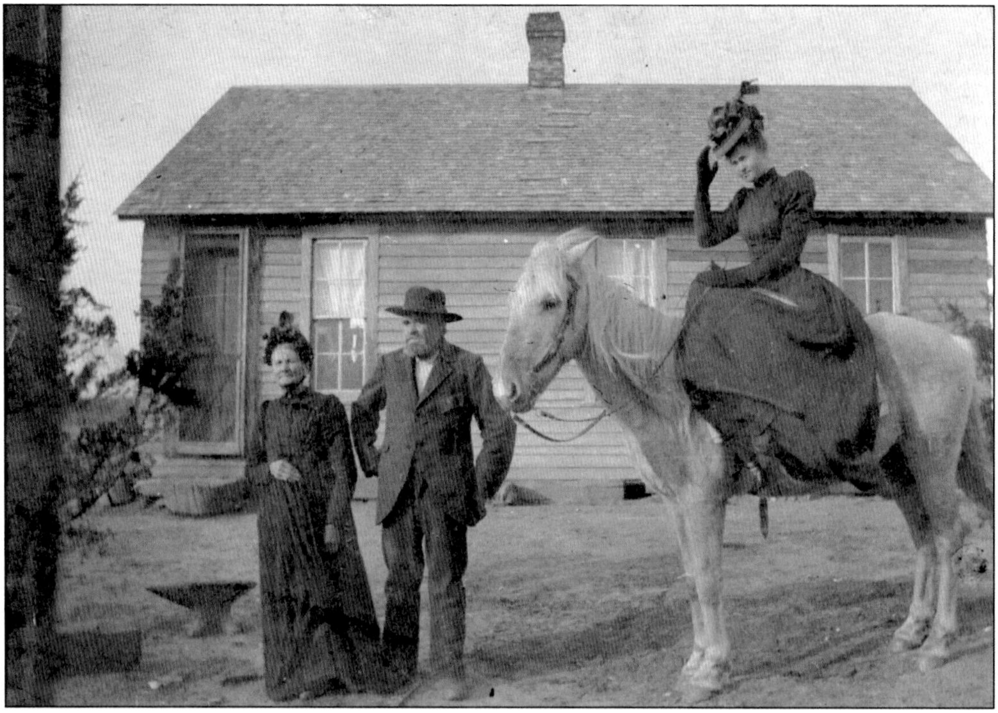

Mr. and Mrs. C. A. Tingler pose for this photograph in about 1895 on their homestead, which was located near Mutual. Their daughter Emma Kinney is riding sidesaddle on her horse Dunnie. The Tingler's wood-frame house is also visible in the photograph.

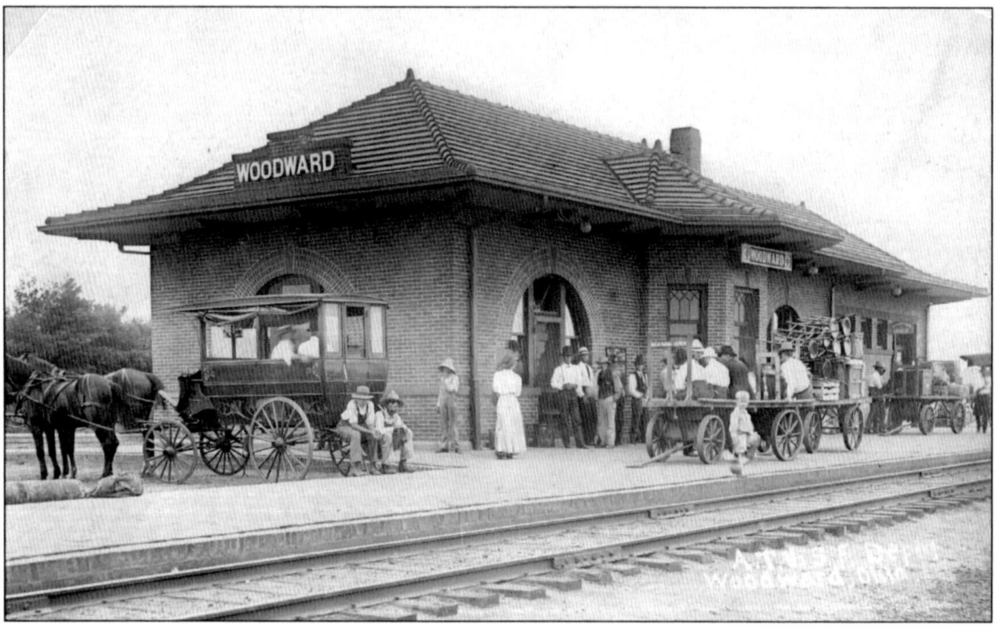

This photograph is of the Atchison, Topeka and Santa Fe Railway (Santa Fe) depot in Woodward around 1910. The depot was built in 1909 near Ninth Street and was destroyed by the April 9, 1947, tornado. The Santa Fe brought Woodward into existence in 1887 and continues to operate in this vibrant community with almost 70 freight trains passing through the city each day.

Jerry R. Dean was an early day Woodward lawyer and judge. He made the run for his town lot by arriving on the train from Higgins, Texas. Other Texans arriving in Woodward in this fashion were Sidney Benton Laune (who was later Dean's law partner), John Gerlach, and Charles Cutter. Dean served as a judge in Deaf Smith County, Texas, before coming to Woodward.

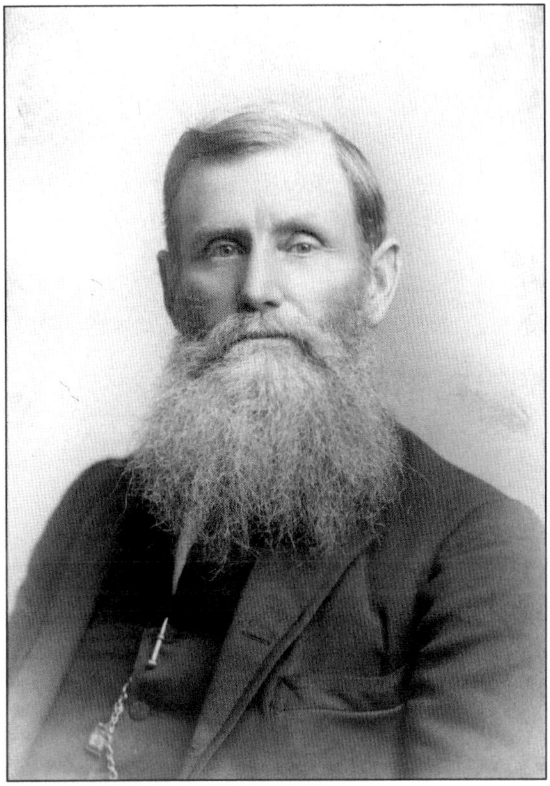

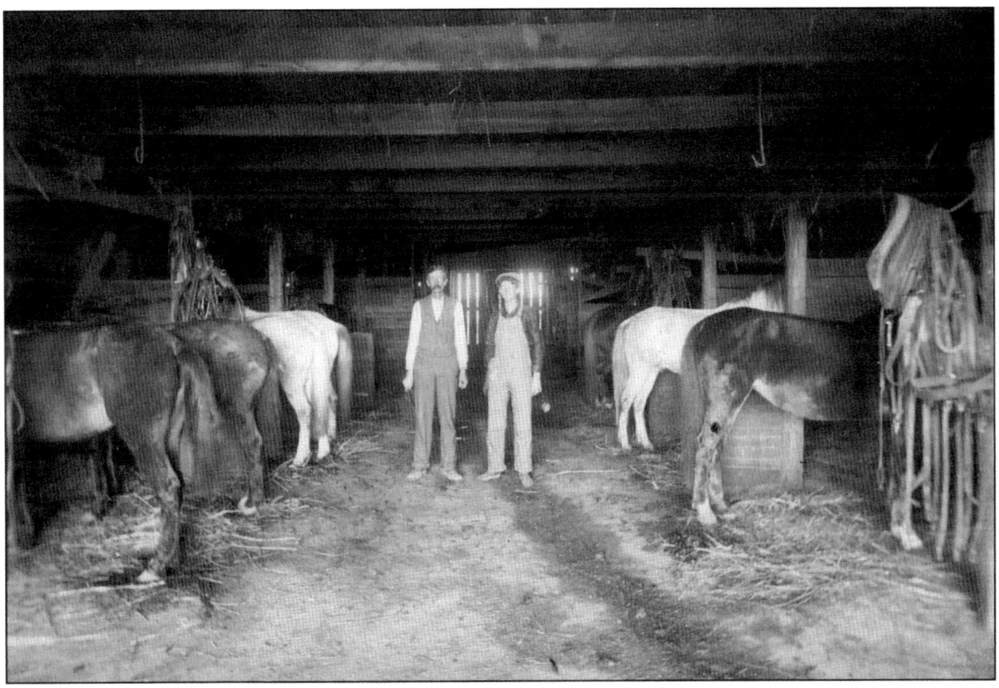

This interior photograph from about 1905 was taken in the livery stables owned by D. N. and Dan Davis in Mooreland.

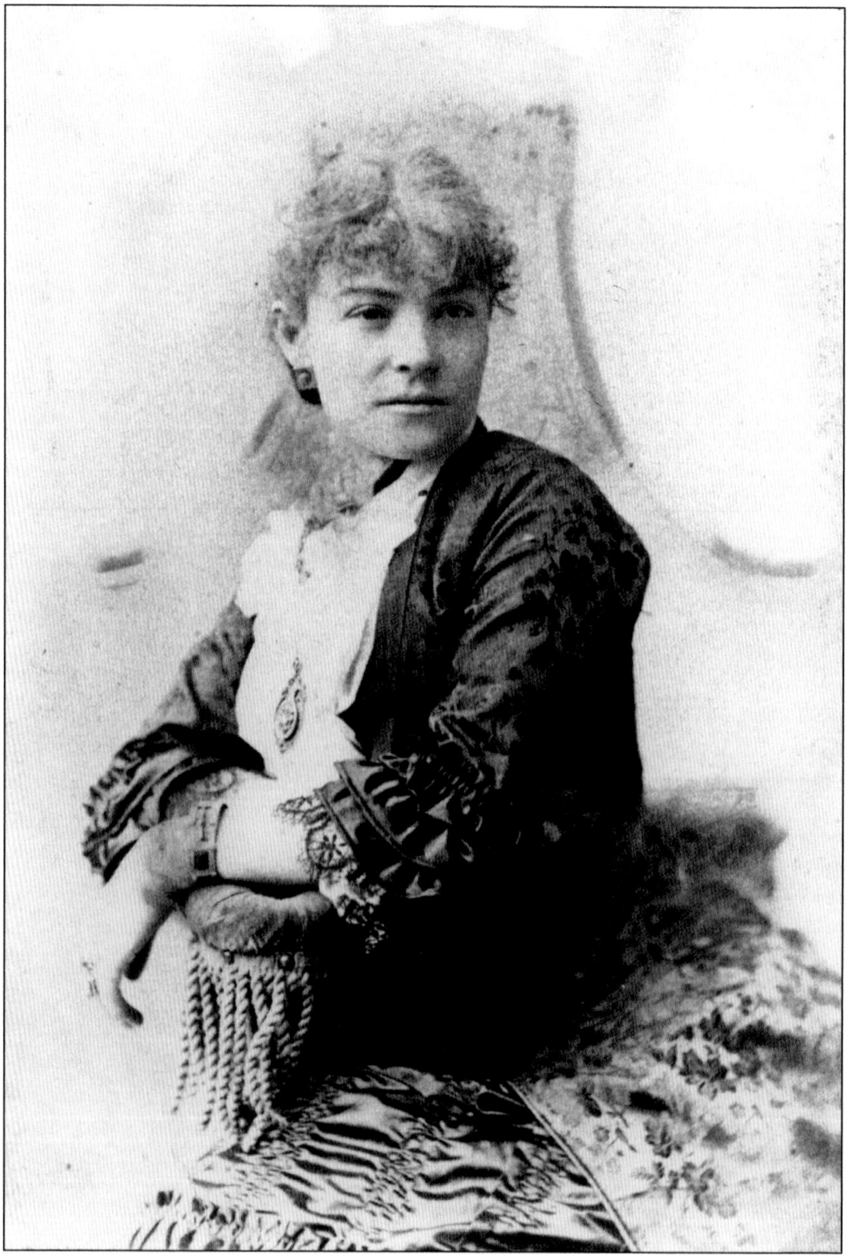

In 1894, Mary Eliza "Miss Dolly" Kezer applied for a job as a dance hall madam in Woodward. She moved here from Denver, Colorado, where she was a high-society escort for men who became rich in the area's silver mines. She was 36 years old when she arrived in the dusty town and soon realized just how much her surroundings had changed. Woodward's small red-light district was located north of the railroad tracks along Ninth Street. In about 1900, Kezer washed her hands of the red-light life and filed on an unclaimed piece of land southwest of Woodward. She lived on the farm until her death by the Woodward tornado of April 9, 1947. She was buried in an unmarked grave in Woodward's Elmwood Cemetery. In about 1979, her relatives raised money to purchase a tombstone for her. Kezer posed for this photograph in about 1880, when she was living a fine life as mistress to an editor of a Denver newspaper.

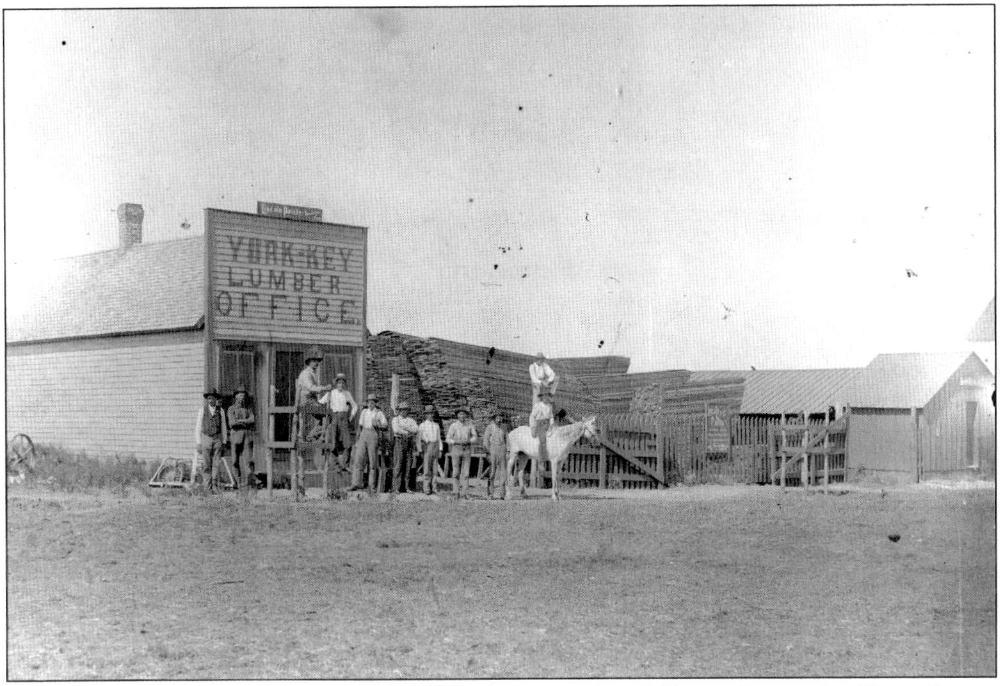

This photograph shows 11 men outside the York-Key Lumber Office in Curtis. Ben Key, a Kansas lumberman, established York-Key lumberyards across Woodward County. He owned a home in Woodward on Texas Avenue near the Episcopal church.

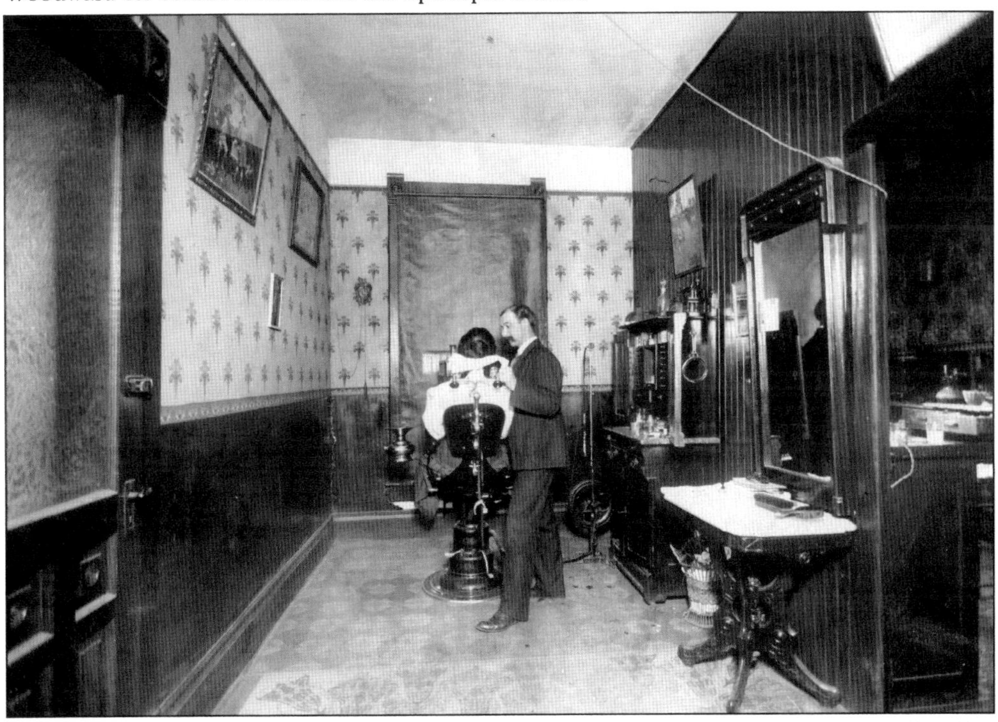

This is a photograph of Dr. Adam Turnbull, an early day dentist in Woodward. Turnbull's office was located on the second floor of 805 Main Avenue.

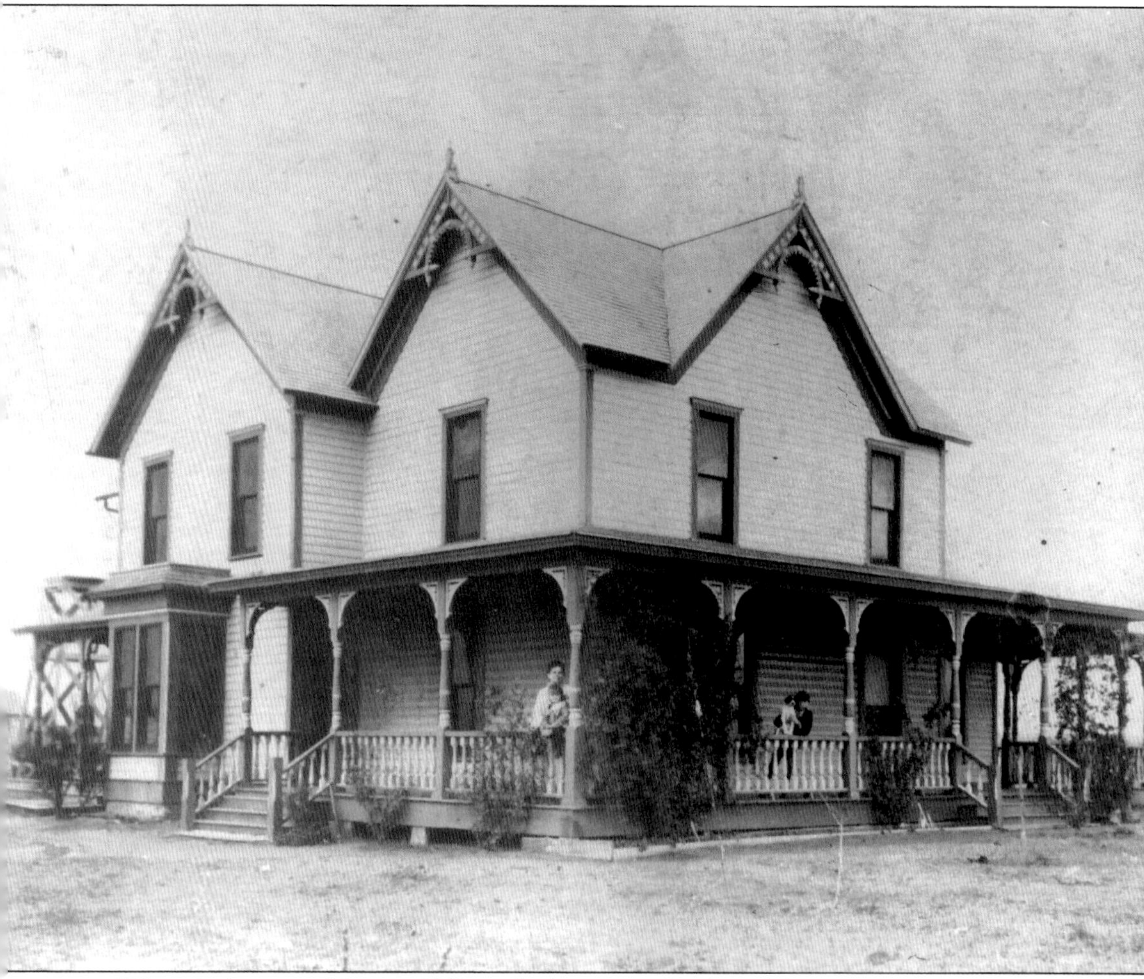

When the house on Houston Hill was built in 1898, locals said there was a peak in the roof for every man Temple Houston had shot. In this photograph, his wife, Laura, holds their daughter Mary, and their son Sam and the family dog pose together, while son Richard hides behind a porch post. The house, which sat at 1415 Texas Avenue, was torn down during the 1970s and replaced by a modern grocery store.

Two

Brand New State
1907–1914

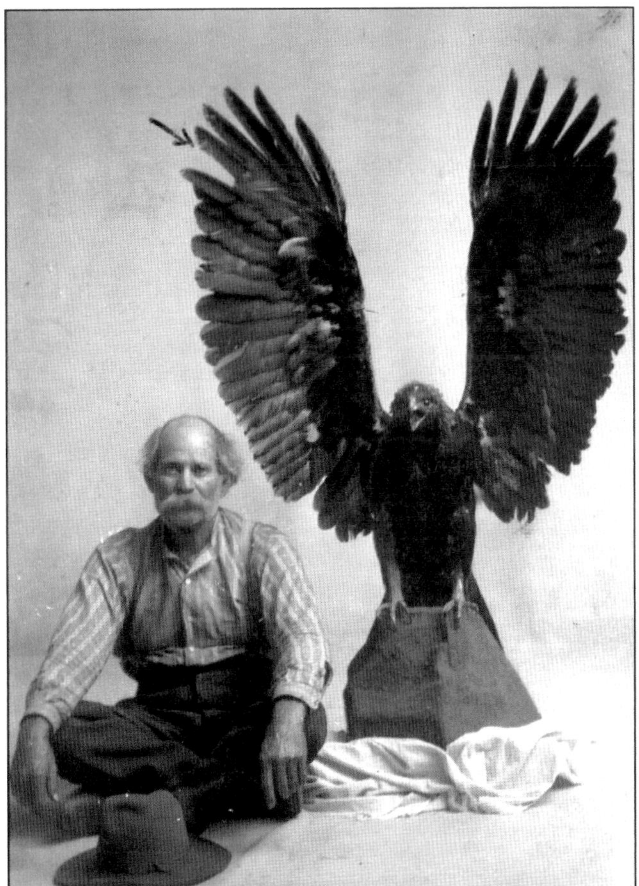

On November 16, 1907, the president of the United States, Theodore Roosevelt, signed the proclamation that made Oklahoma the 46th state in the Union. On the same day, Charles Haskell was sworn in as governor of Oklahoma. The proclamation was signed with a quill plucked from this golden eagle named Old Statehood, which was captured near Woodward. The owner of the creature was L. B. "Dad" Nall, a Woodward merchant.

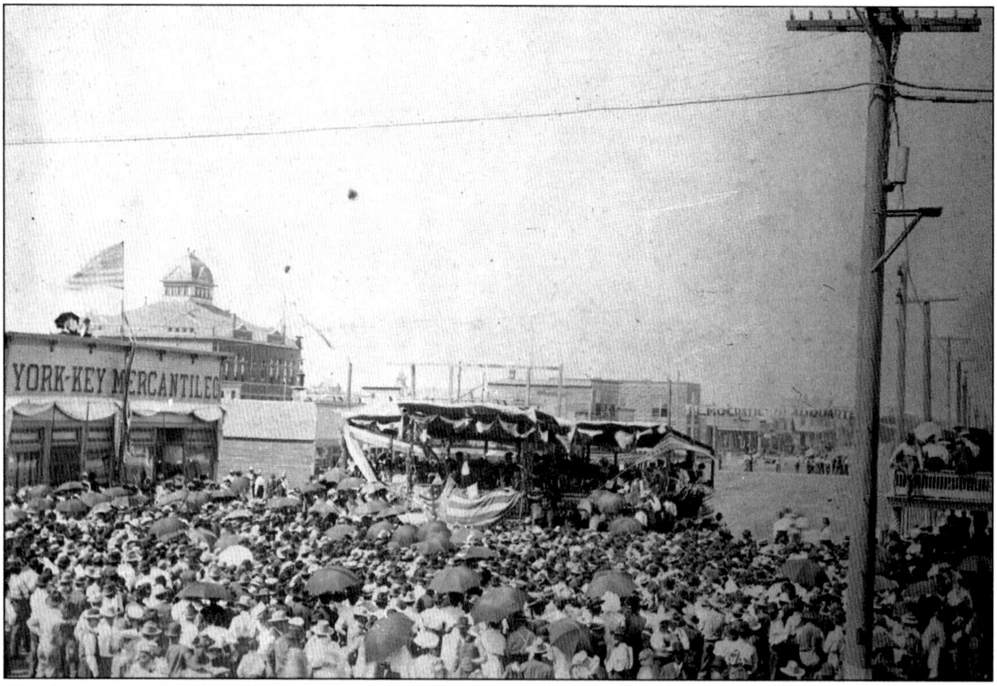

On September 7, 1907, William Jennings Bryan spoke to 20,000 people gathered in Woodward and urged the ratification of Oklahoma's proposed constitution and the election of a democratic ticket. The Woodward County Courthouse, with its unique cupola, is visible in the background.

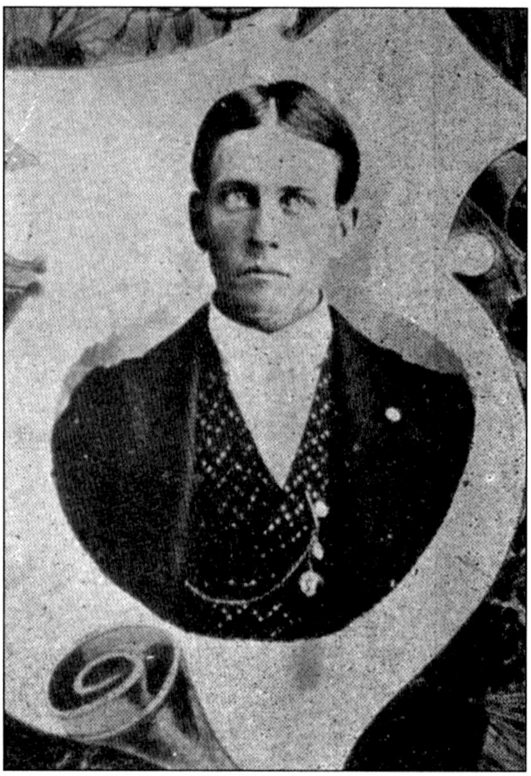

Edward O. McCance of Mutual was elected as a delegate to the Oklahoma Constitutional Convention in 1906. This photograph was taken from a card, which was a press pass or was possibly connected with the convention. McCance was the proprietor of the *Oklahoma Enterprise*, a newspaper published at Persimmon.

On Statehood Day in 1907, a mock wedding of Mr. Oklahoma and Miss Indian Territory took place in Guthrie to signify the union of the twin territories. This photograph was taken at Mutual in 1908. Harry Patton, dressed as Uncle Sam, sits with two girls representing the territories. One of the two girls is Verla Patton (left) and the other is unidentified.

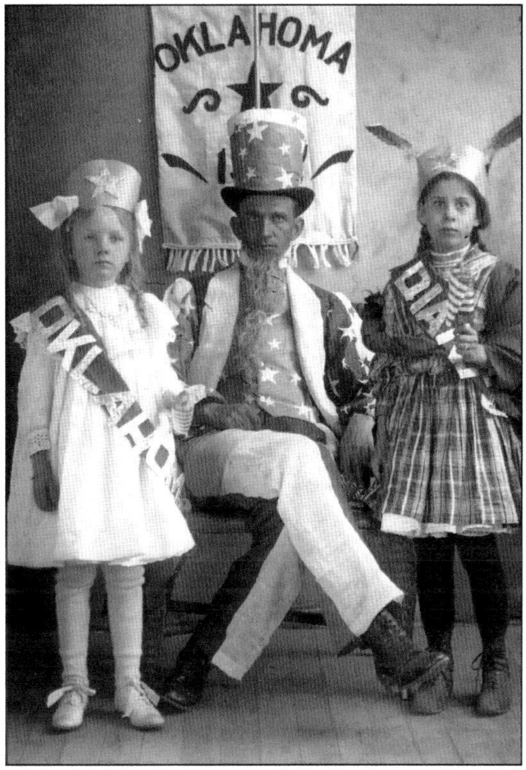

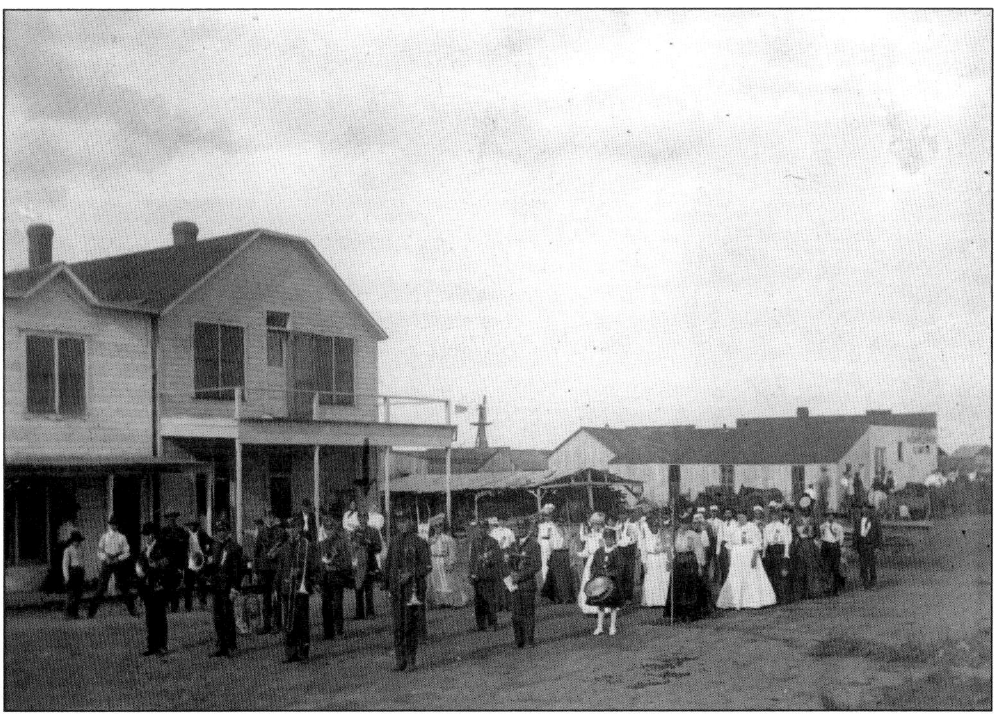

Oklahoma's admission into the Union was celebrated across the county with festivals and parades in almost every town. This parade was held in Quinlan on November 16, 1907.

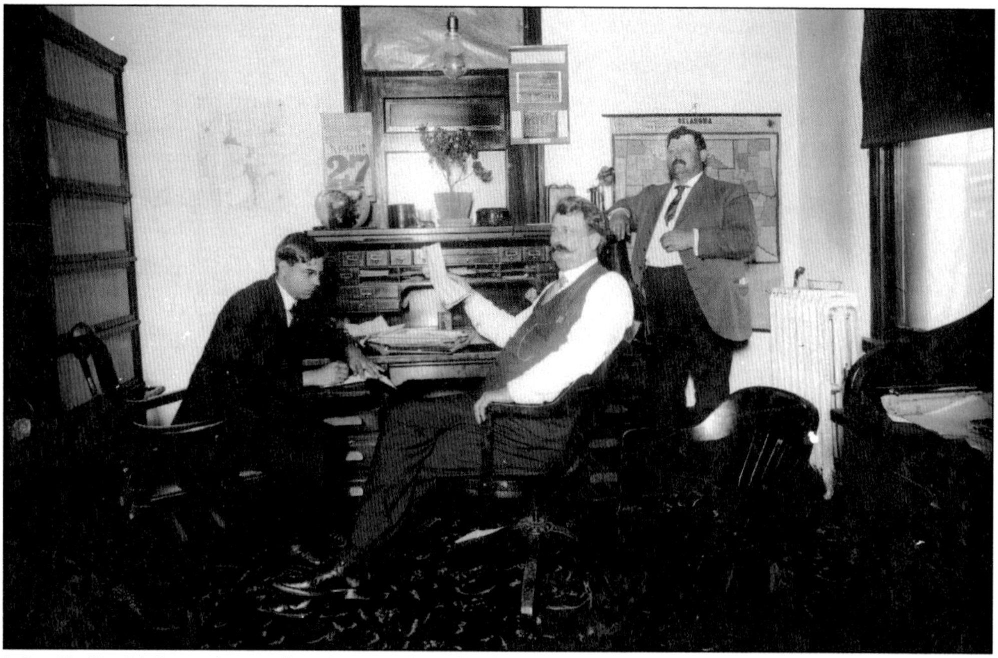

John E. (Jack) Love (center), a former sheriff of Woodward County, became the first chairman of the corporation commission for the State of Oklahoma. He is pictured here in his office in Guthrie on April 27, 1908. Love is remembered for taking 100 Woodward County girls on a train to Guthrie for statehood day in 1907.

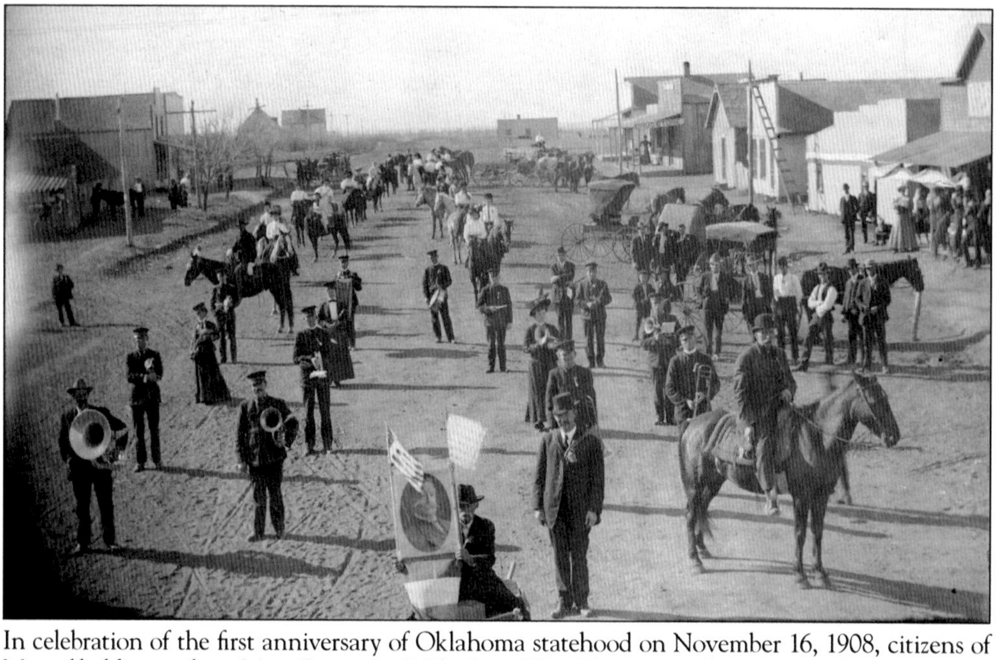

In celebration of the first anniversary of Oklahoma statehood on November 16, 1908, citizens of Mutual held a parade on Main Street. L. G. Plank and Doc Thomas made a wager on the presidential election in which the loser was to push the winner through Mutual streets in a wheelbarrow. Plank is seated in the wheelbarrow carrying a photograph of winning presidential candidate William Howard Taft. The young women on horseback represent each state in the union.

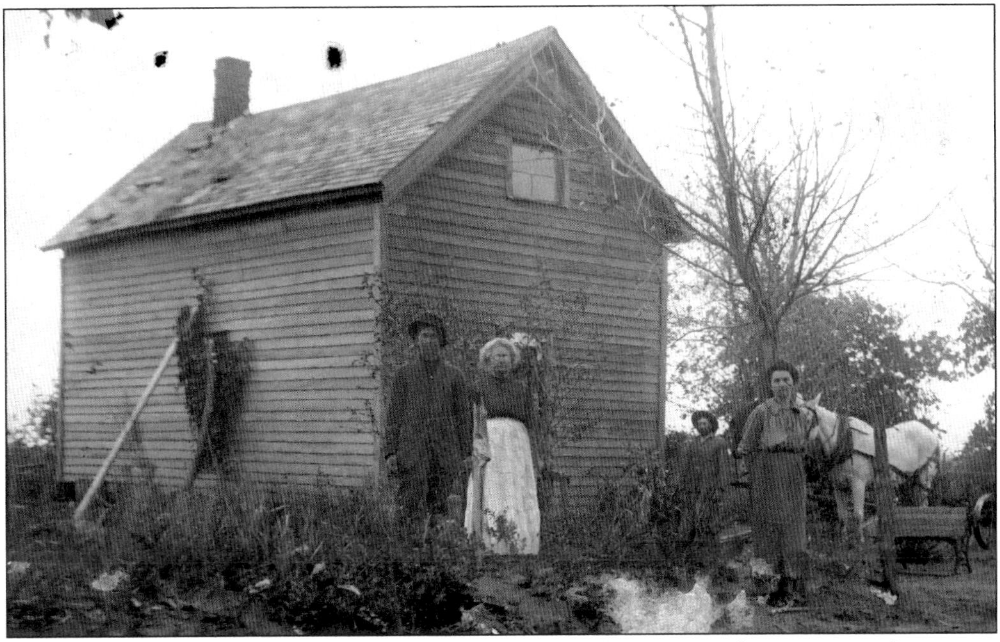

This homestead near Curtis was photographed in October 1909. Information on the reverse reads, "Settled here April 6, 1901 from Labette Co., Kans. Photo by Jesse E. Messenger. Old claim shack near Curtis, Woodward Co., Okla. Size 14 x 24 - 12 ft. to eaves. Built of native cottonwood & weather boarded. Team - Old Dick & Edd. Dogs - Bunkum & Rover." Oddly, the writer neglected to record the names of the people in the photograph.

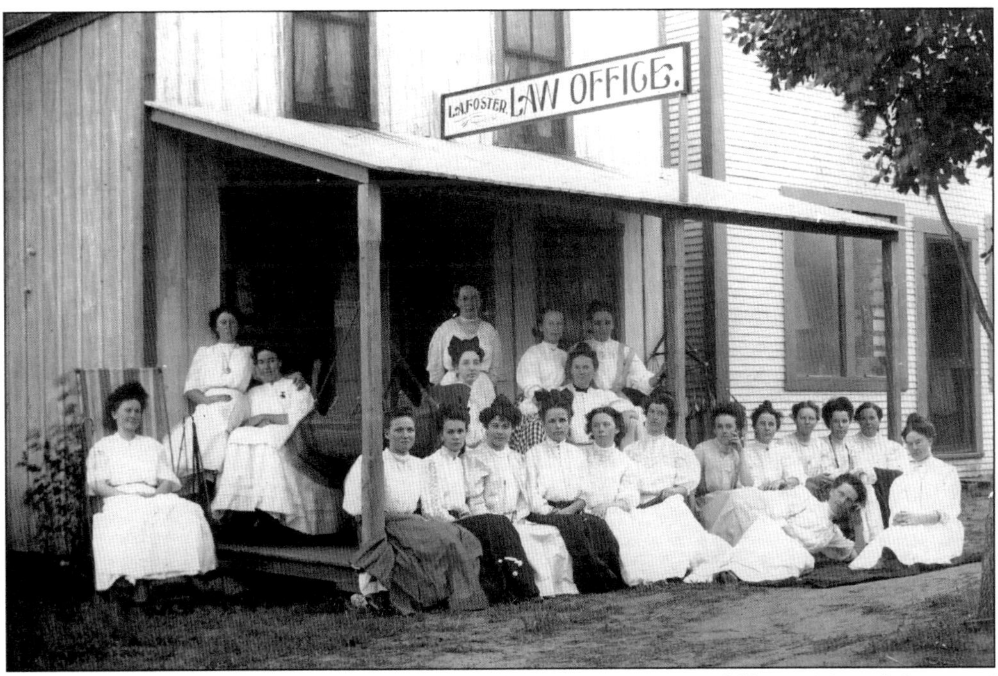

These women are seated on the front porch of the L. A. Foster Law Office in Mutual. It existed from 1907 to 1914.

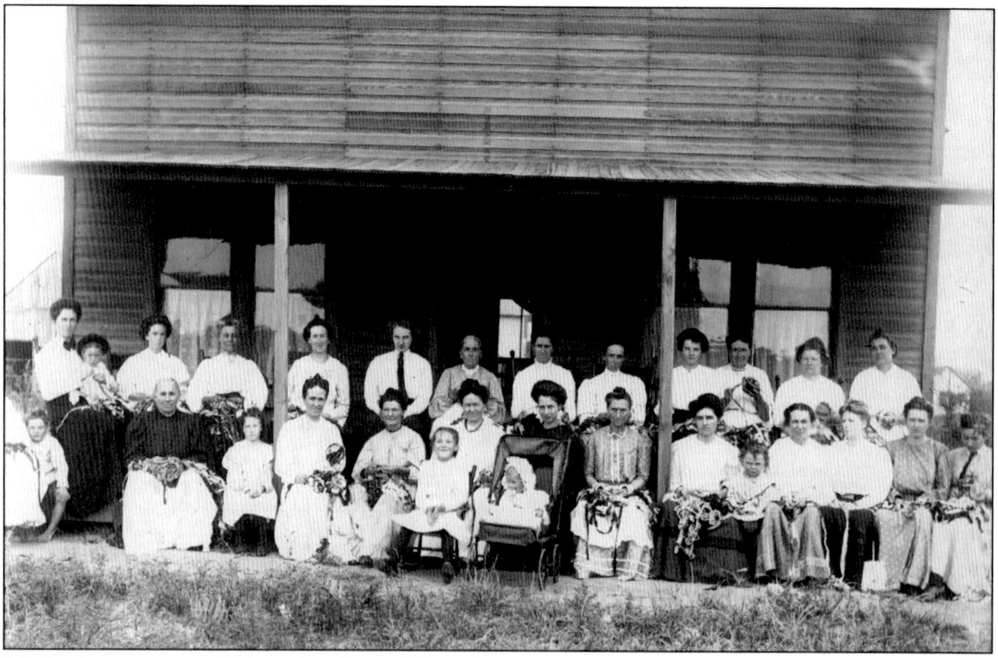

Methodist women of Mooreland posed for this photograph during the second decade of the 20th century. The Ladies Aid Society made sure that the minister was paid and that the expenses of the church were covered. They raised money through various fund-raisers. Sunday school and Bible school were also important missions.

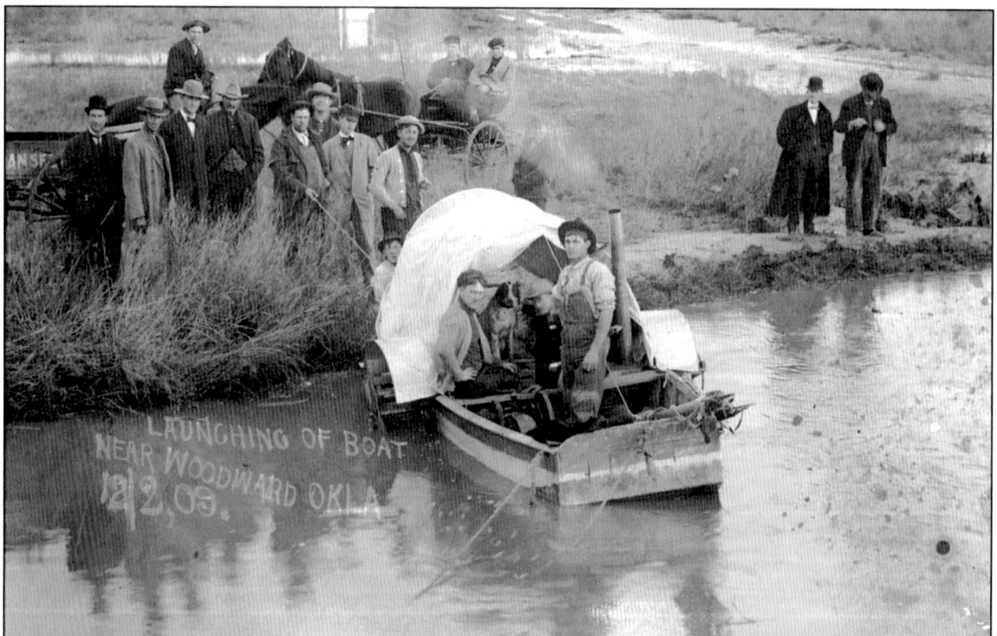

Spectators lined the bridge over the North Canadian River on Eighth Street in Woodward to watch the launching of a steam-powered boat on December 2, 1908. Others watched from the riverbank, as seen in this photograph.

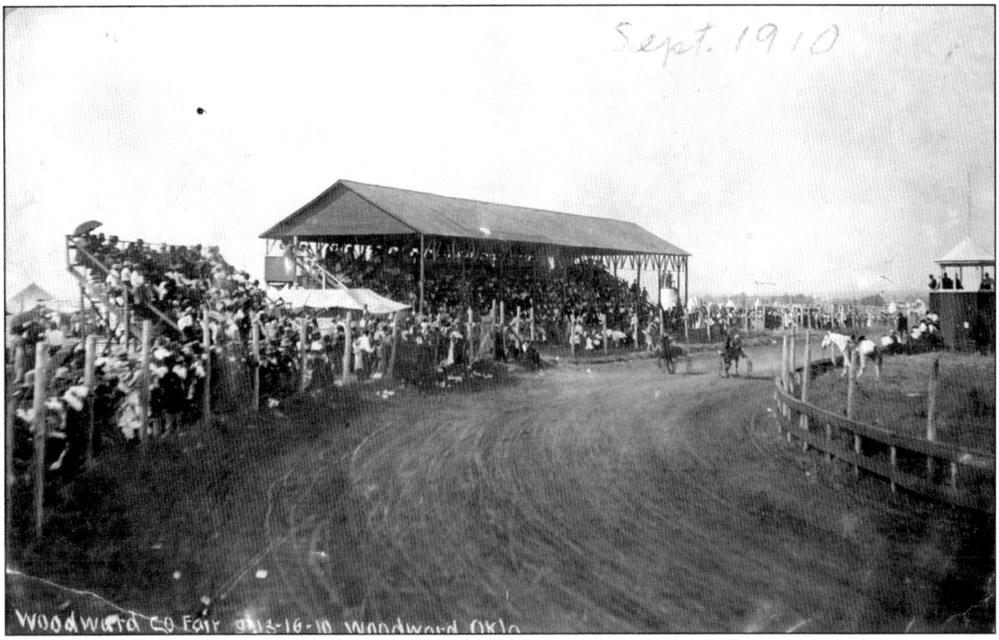

This photograph shows the horse-and-buggy races held September 13–16, 1910, during the Woodward County Fair in Woodward. The image contains hundreds of spectators watching as the racers come around the track.

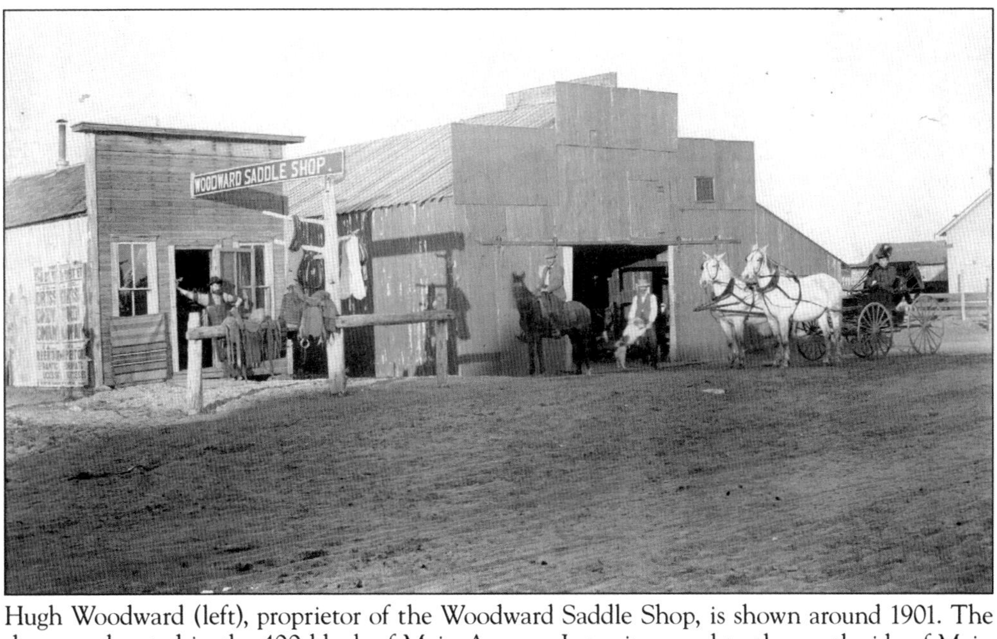

Hugh Woodward (left), proprietor of the Woodward Saddle Shop, is shown around 1901. The shop was located in the 400 block of Main Avenue. Later it moved to the north side of Main Avenue between Eighth and Ninth Streets. The man with the dog is G. A. Champion; his wife sits in the buggy. The man on the horse is unidentified.

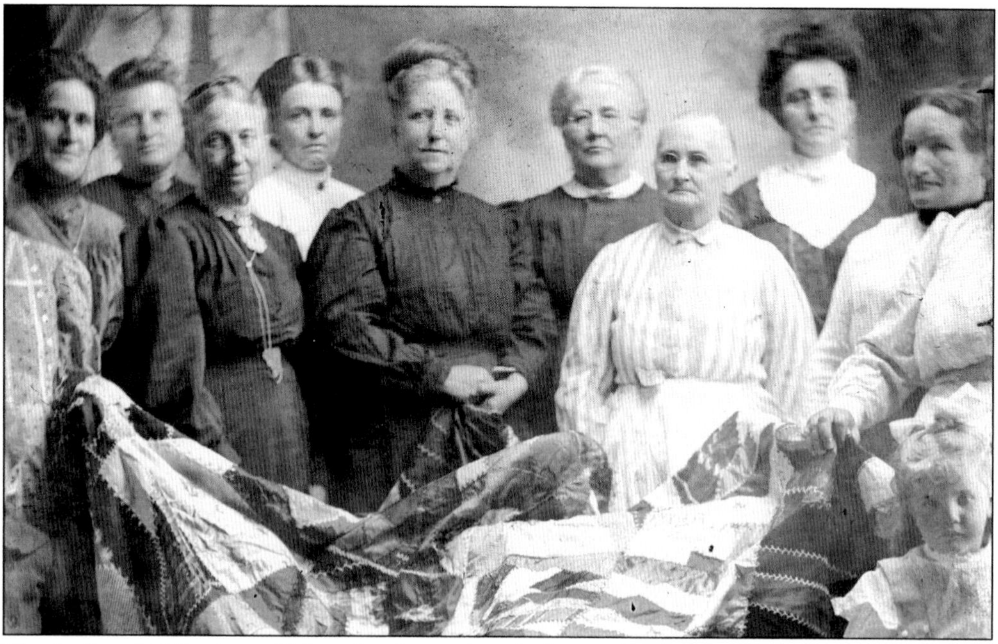

The Ladies Aid Society of Mooreland posed with this quilt in about 1907. From left to right are Mrs. Clark Hagan, Mrs. T. C. Van Frank, Mrs. J. P. Davis, Mrs. Gore, Mrs. J. C. Laudewalk, Grandma Hagan, Grandma Young, Mrs. Henry Wyckoff, Mrs. Alph Hampton, Mrs. Isreal, and the daughter of Mrs. Isreal. An unidentified woman is standing at the far left.

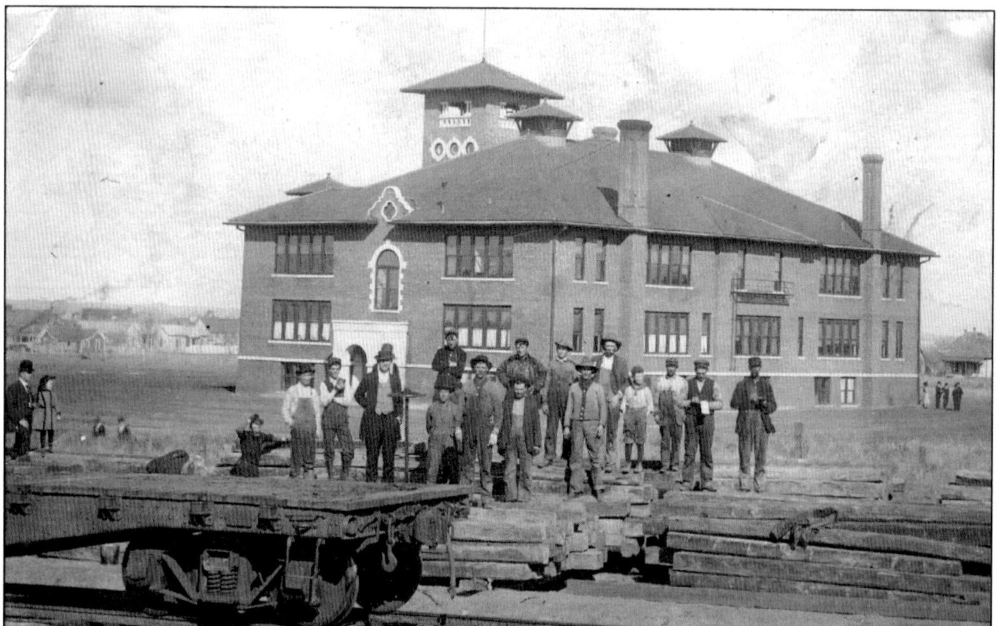

This 1912 photograph shows local men who were part of the crew to lay track through Woodward for the Wichita Falls and Northwestern Railway. The large building in background was the Woodward High School, which was built in 1910 and dubbed "Old Central." It was heavily damaged in the 1947 tornado and was torn down after the storm.

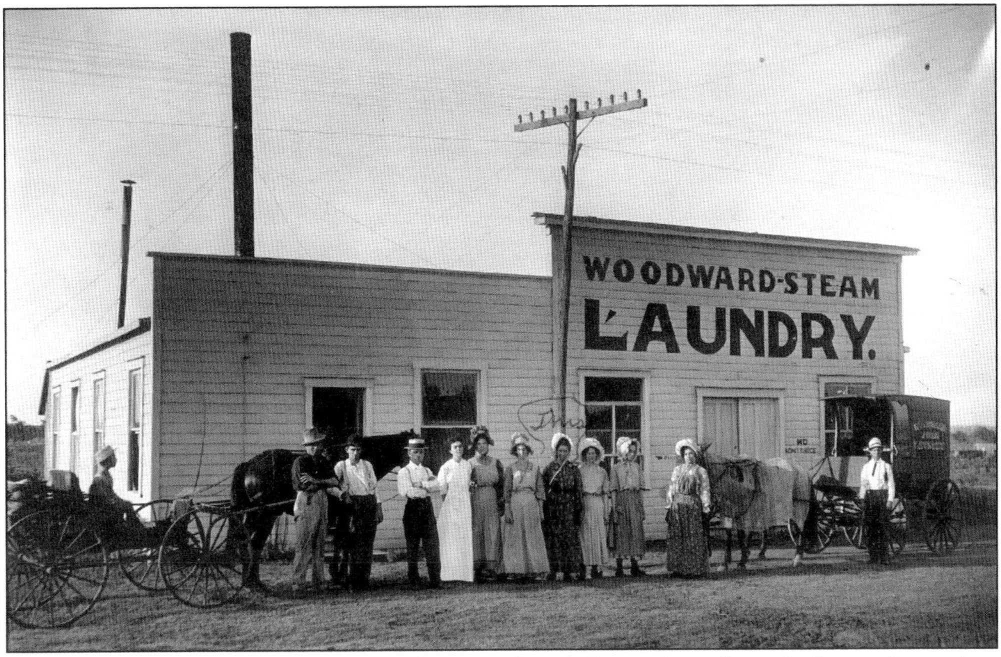

This image captures the exterior of the Woodward Steam Laundry, which was located at 901 Eighth Street in Woodward. This business later became the Woodward Electric Sanitary Laundry. The name was changed from Woodward Electric Sanitary Laundry to Henry Hunter's in 1927 when it was purchased by Henry Hunter of Elk City.

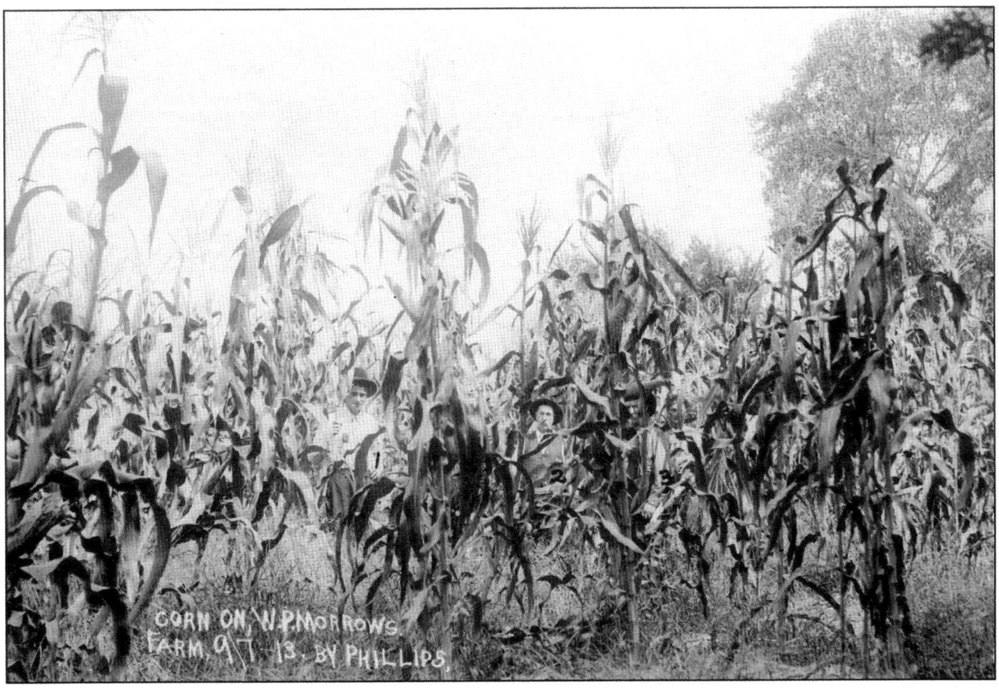

The cornstalks grew taller than these men in 1913 on the William P. Morrow farm north of Woodward. His farm later became part of Boiling Springs State Park. Morrow invented a number of agricultural devices, including a cultivator and harness snap.

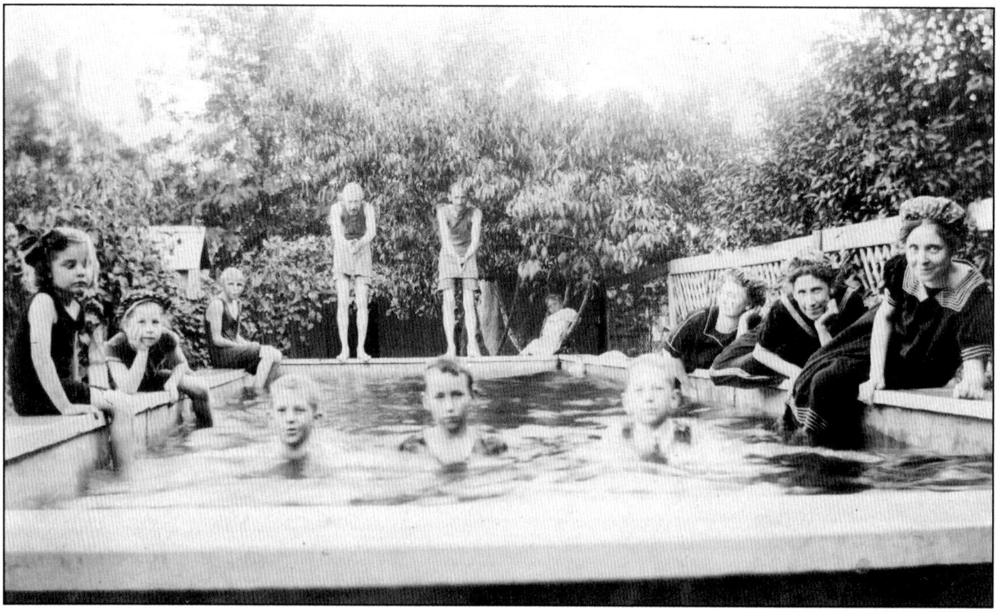

This pool, built at the home of H. H. Stallings, was a first in Woodward. It began as a family pool but was later opened up to the public. Shown in the pool from left to right are Webster H. Sharp, Harry Stallings, and Eugene Sharp. Shown on the edge of the pool from left to right are Reba Saunders, Anna Mae Sharp, unidentified, Charles E. Sharp, H. H. Stallings, Mrs. Stallings, Mabel Sharp, and Mamie Saunders.

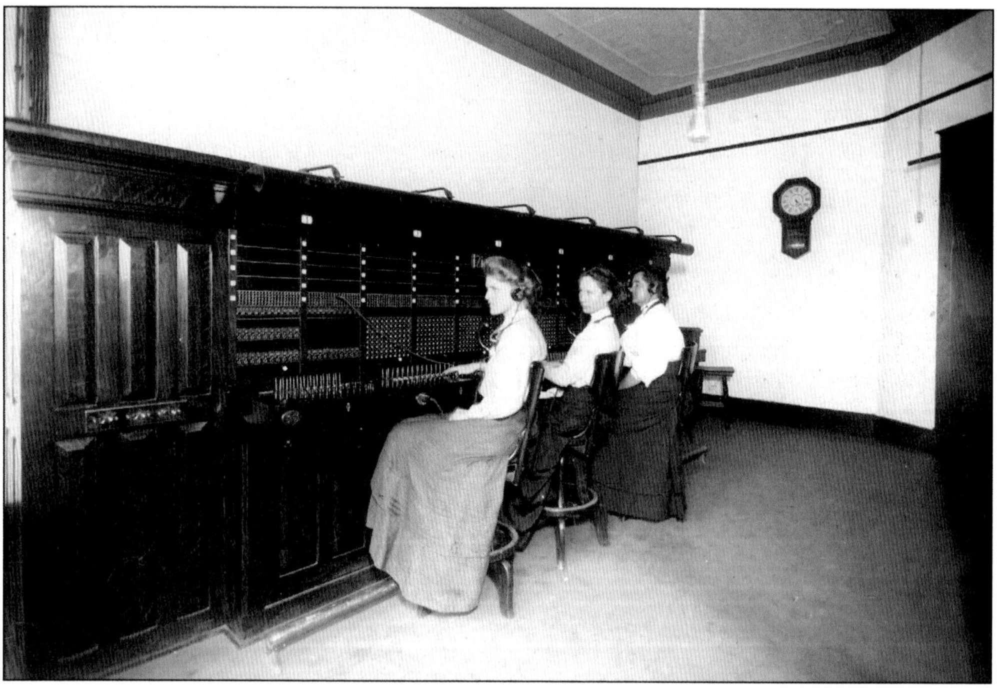

The first telephone office in the county seat was located above the Boehm Meat Market (now the Josie Adams Cultural Centre) on Main Avenue. Myrtle McCarty Martinson is the woman seated at left.

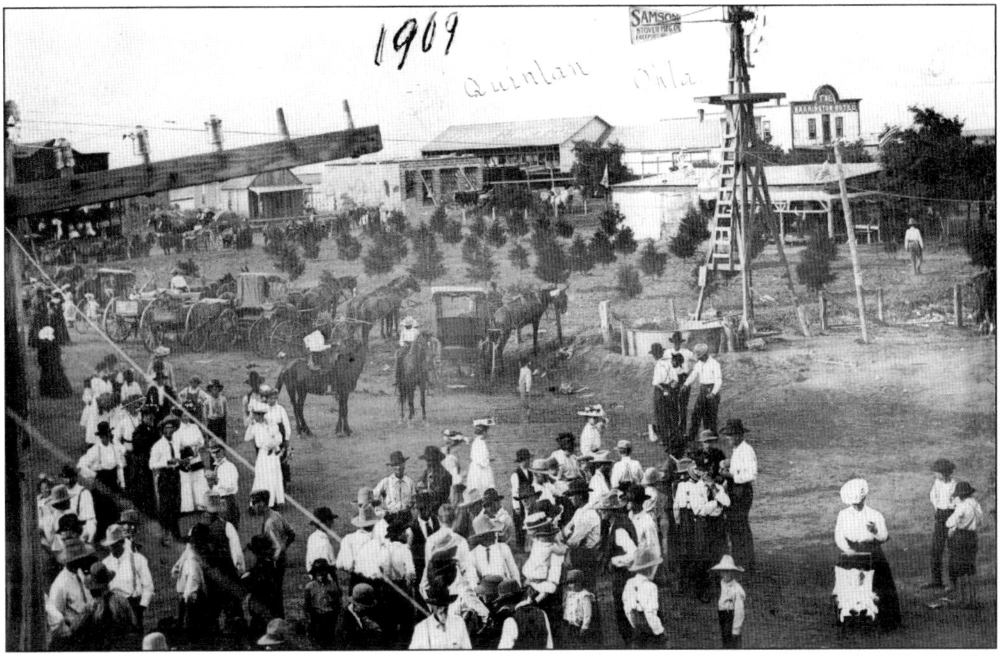

This photographic postcard captures the scene of events on July 4, 1909, in Quinlan. The Harrington Hotel can be seen in the background.

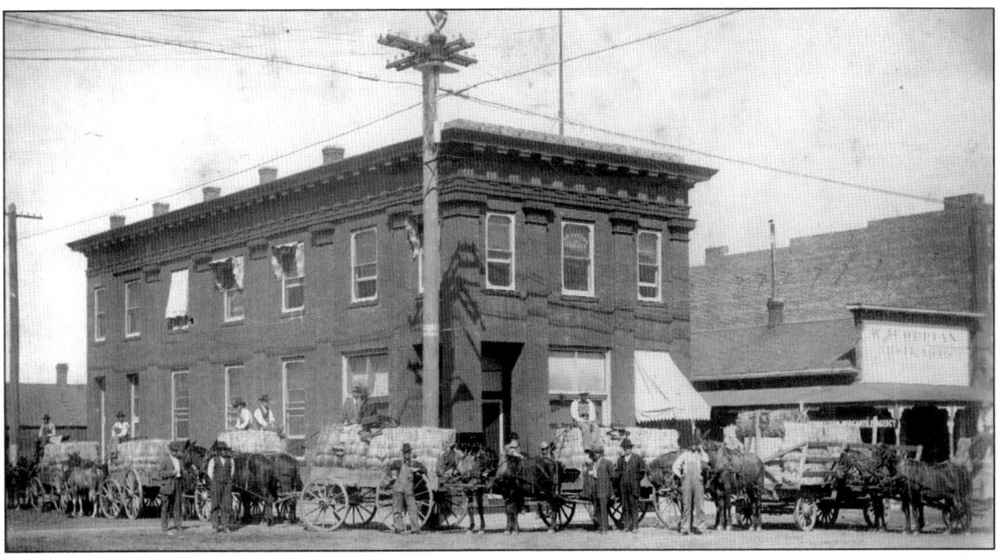

The northeast corner of Ninth Street and Main Avenue was the location of Woodward's first chartered bank, the Exchange Bank. In 1905, John Gerlach bought this location and built the present-day building. He moved his bank from the south side of the street to this location. Goetzinger Abstract Company has been in this location since 1948. The wagons in the foreground are loaded with broomcorn, which was a cash crop in Woodward County. In 1906, over $1 million worth of the crop was shipped from Woodward in 380 railcars.

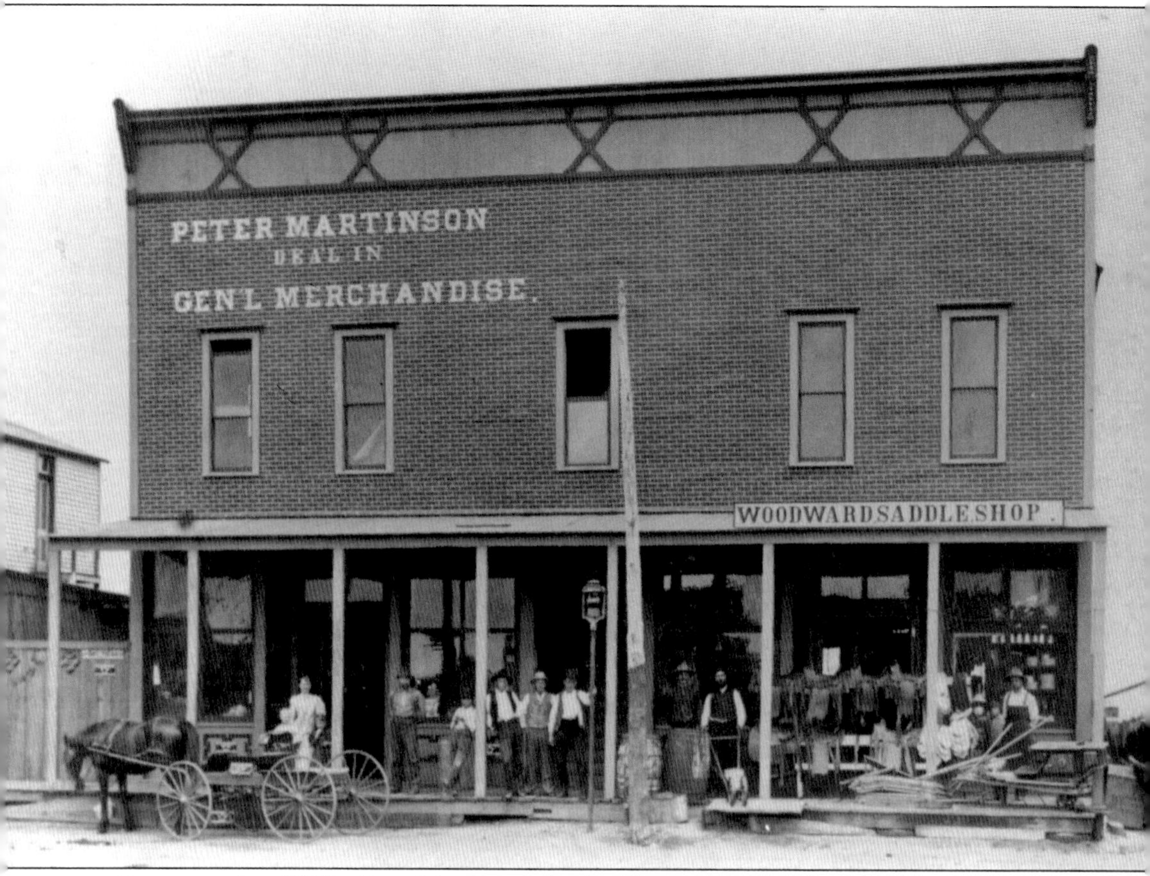

Constructed in 1895 by Peter Martinson, this building is Woodward's oldest brick structure. The first floor housed Martinson's General Merchandise on the left and Dick Woodward's saddle shop on the right. Herman Brockhaus, Martinson's business partner, later ran his own store from this location after Martinson's Grocery opened a few doors to the west. The second floor of the building was known as the Opera House, which was the venue for Woodward's earliest community events. The funeral for Ed Jennings and later the 1896 trial of Temple Houston and Jack Love for his murder took place upstairs. Houston also delivered his famous "Soiled Dove Plea" in May 1898 in the Opera House in defense of Minnie Stacie, a local brothel mistress. Once the new courthouse was built in 1901, the Opera House ceased to be such an important community venue.

This two-story wooden schoolhouse was constructed in Woodward about 1909. It sat on the block where Centennial Park is now. It was used for about a year before it was totally destroyed by fire. A new brick high school was constructed in 1910 behind the current Woodward Middle School-South.

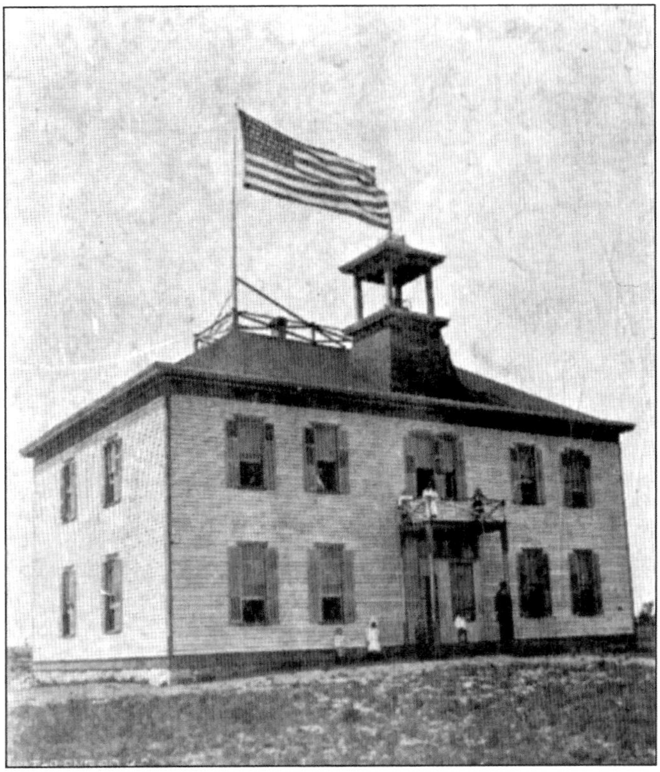

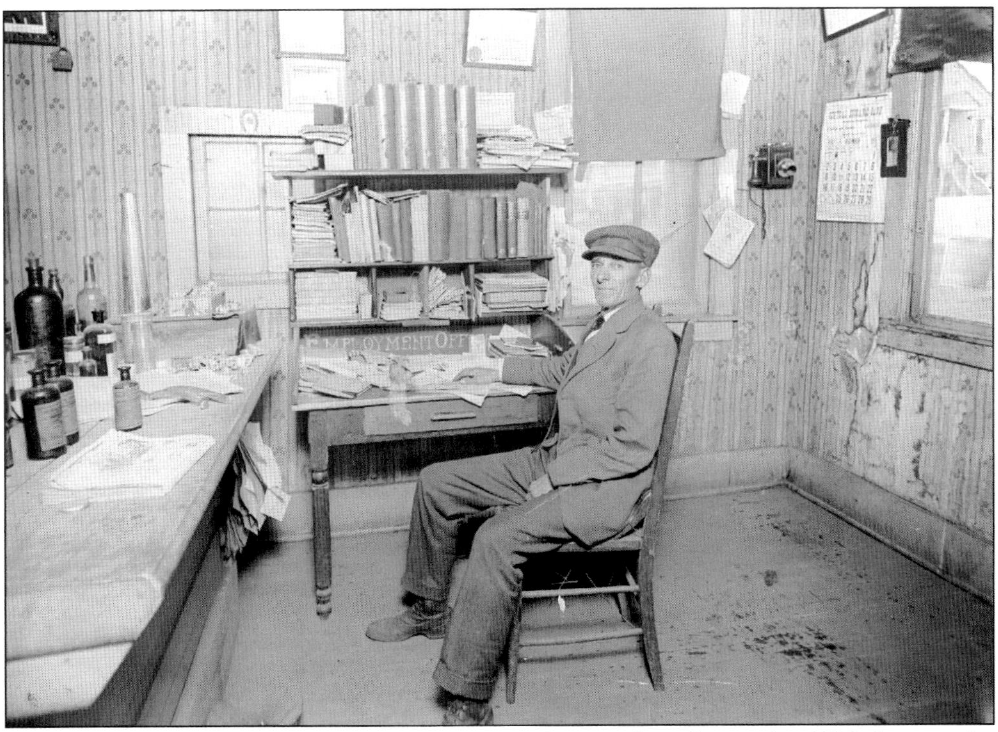

Dr. C. E. Miller was Woodward's first veterinarian. He sits in his office in this 1906 photograph.

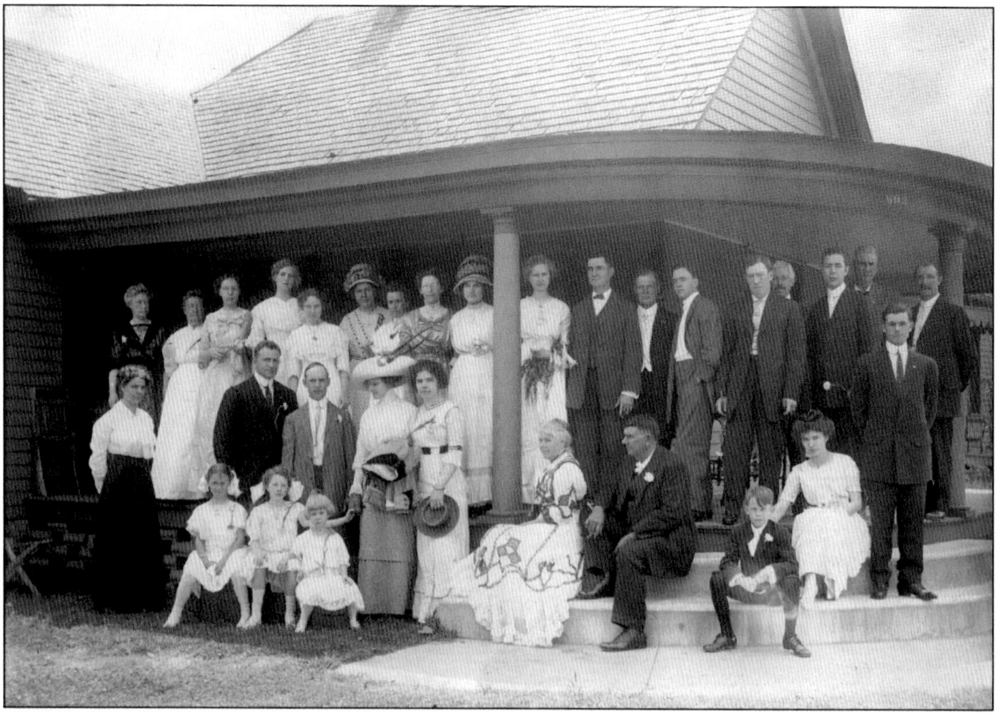

Connie Beatte's wedding party poses on the front porch of the Beatte home in June 1913. No other information is known about this occasion.

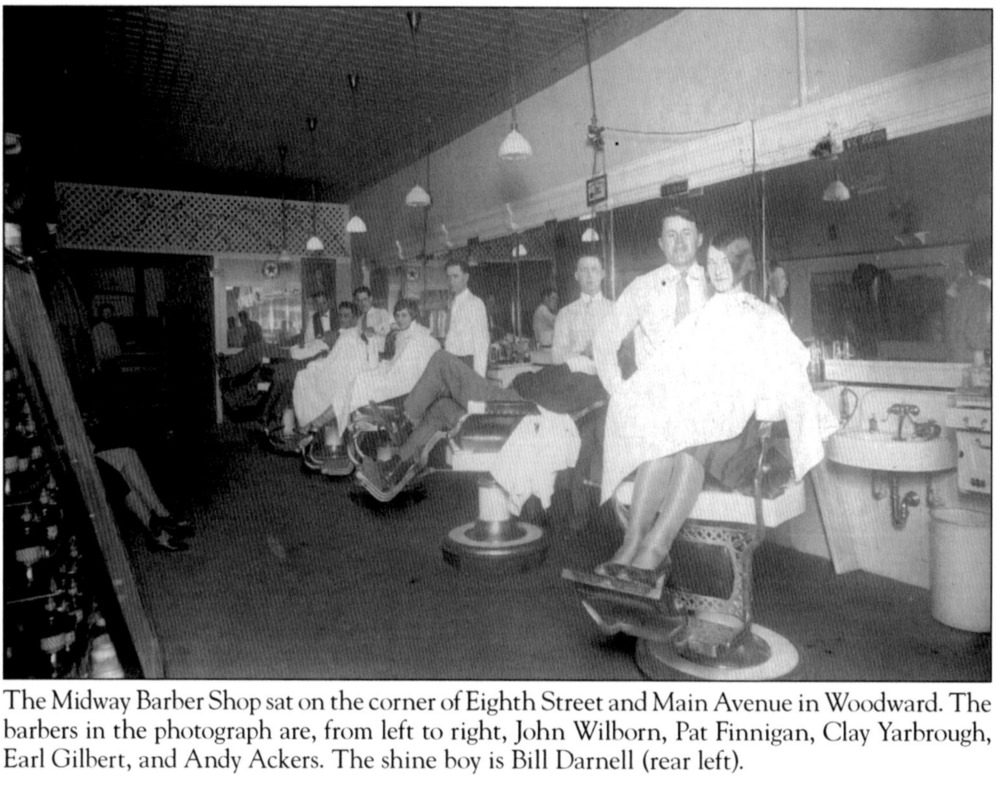

The Midway Barber Shop sat on the corner of Eighth Street and Main Avenue in Woodward. The barbers in the photograph are, from left to right, John Wilborn, Pat Finnigan, Clay Yarbrough, Earl Gilbert, and Andy Ackers. The shine boy is Bill Darnell (rear left).

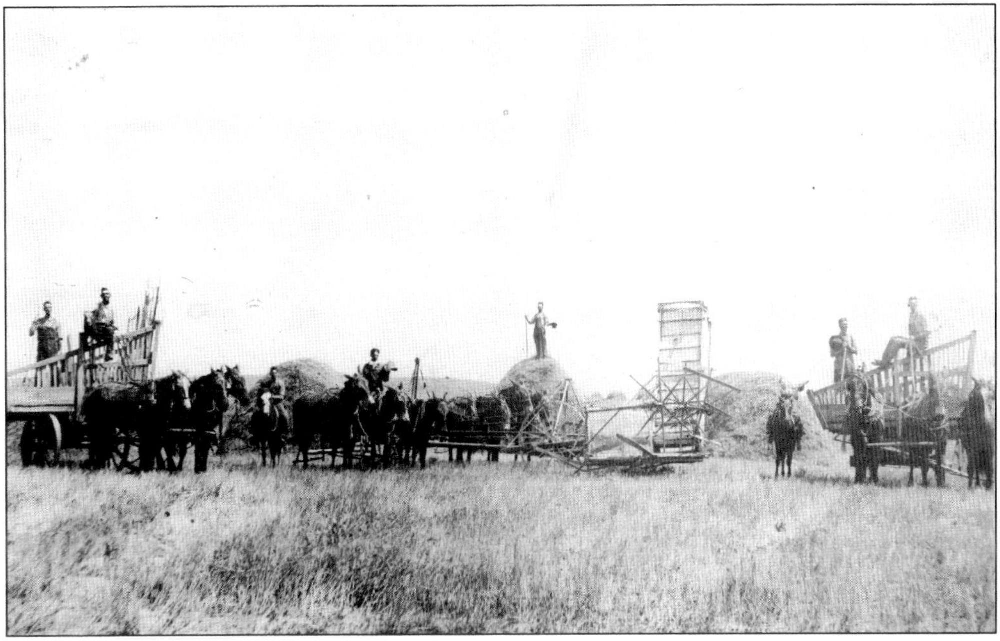

A break from the 1914 wheat harvest allowed the Geddes family to pose for this photograph near the Willard community in the northern part of the county.

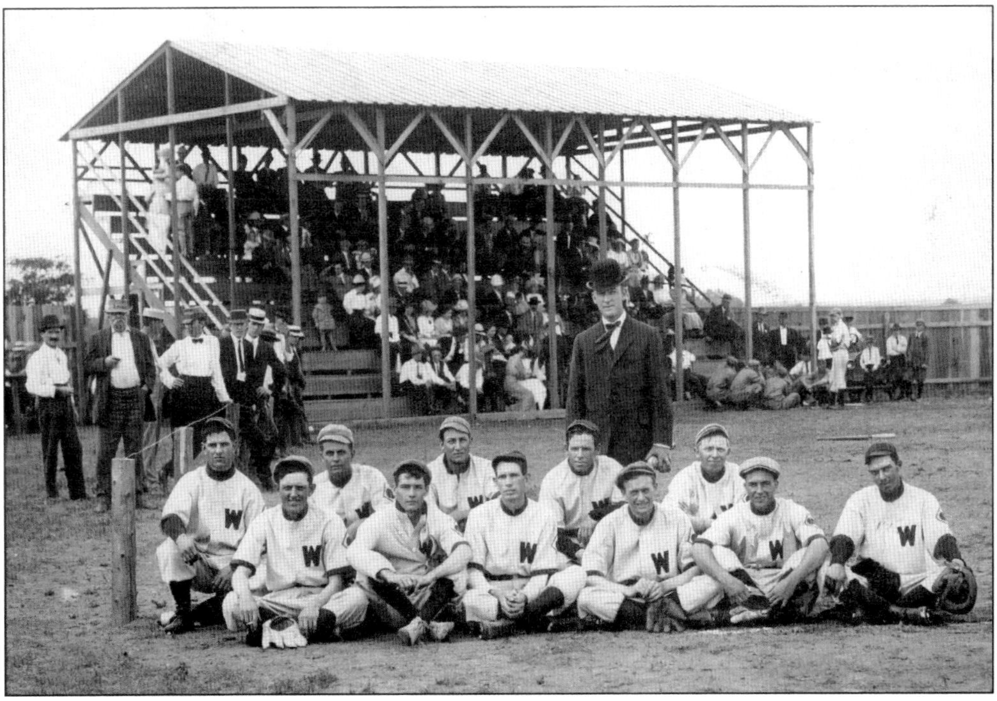

This photograph shows the Woodward baseball team of 1912 and the old baseball park, which was located west of the Oklahoma Gas and Electric building on Ninth Street in Woodward. From left to right, the roster includes (first row) John Young, Abe Heath, Art Fuller, Curt Weiglin, Stewart (the cousin of Curt Weiglin), and Uncle Fuller; (second row) Chester Martinson, Otto Stallings, Pat Patterson, Arthur "Smithy" Smith, and an unidentified player.

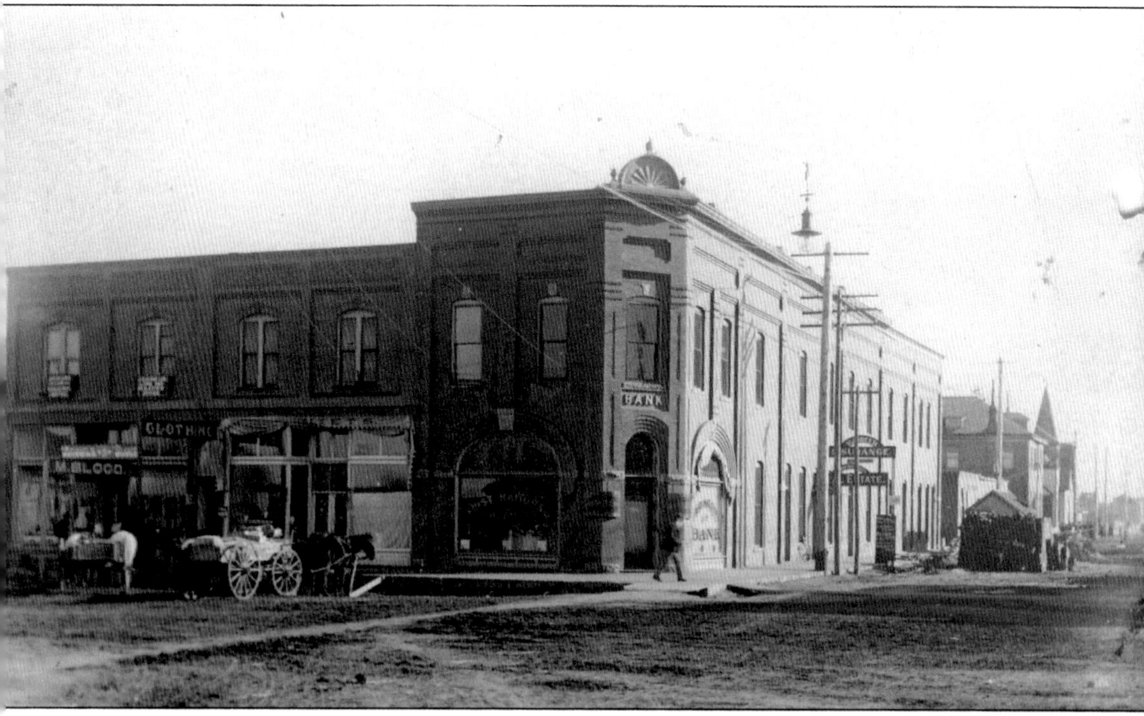

This image shows the First National Bank building, located on the southeast corner of Eighth Street and Main Avenue in Woodward. It opened for business in 1900 with Len L. Stine as its owner. It was a fitting name for his bank since he seemed to be a man of many firsts. He bought the first band instruments for Woodward, installed the first telephone system in the county seat, and purchased the first automobile in the growing city. Other Woodward County banks had trouble during the 1920s. The Farmer's Bank in Mutual folded in 1924, and the Quinlan State Bank closed its doors in 1929. Stine's bank was just fine—for another decade. On Monday, January 18, 1932, Stine's small empire collapsed. By 11:00 a.m., depositors had relieved him of all cash on hand. It seems Stine had invested in German bonds, which the public thought were no good. They made a run on the bank and forced him to close it for good. He lived out the rest of his life a pauper.

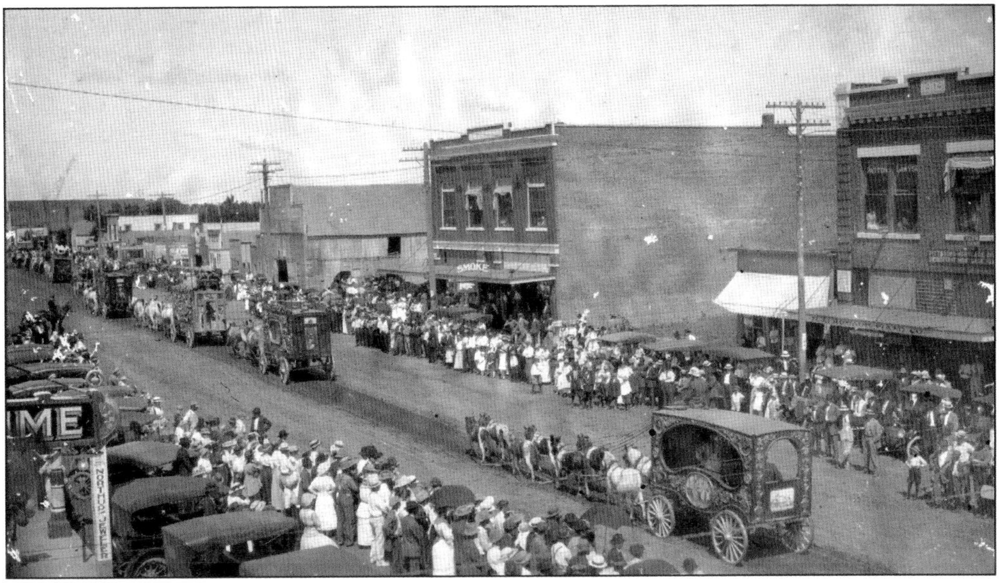

The Ringling Brothers Circus came to the county in 1914. Advertising their arrival with this grand spectacle, they came through the county seat in this parade on Main Avenue. The brick building in the center of the photograph was then the post office. It is now the home of Jerry Rizley's law office and Figley-Salz Insurance.

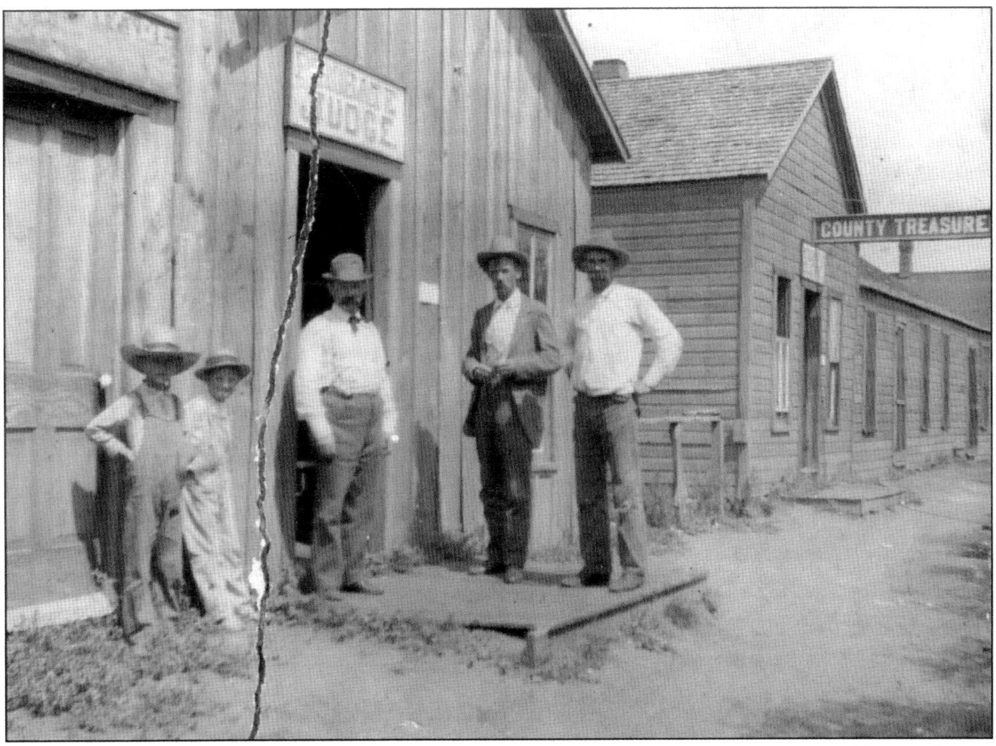

Bert E. Roll stands in the doorway of the Woodward County Probate Judge's office with two unidentified men. The wood-frame office stood on the corner of Tenth Street and Texas Avenue until a modern courthouse was built on the location in 1901.

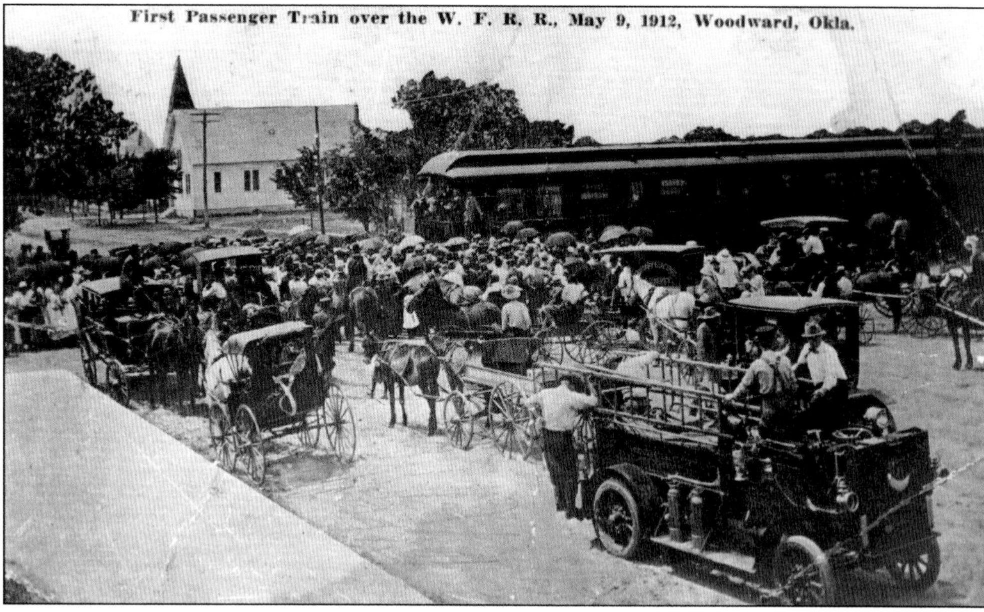

Excitement filled the air as the first train rolled into the county seat on the Wichita Falls and Northwestern Railway on May 9, 1912. This photograph captured the moment the engine crossed Main Avenue headed for the depot a block south. The United Brethren Church, which sat on the corner of Thirteenth Street until 1947, is visible in the background. Woodward Fire Station's pride and joy, the 1909 fire engine, is in the foreground.

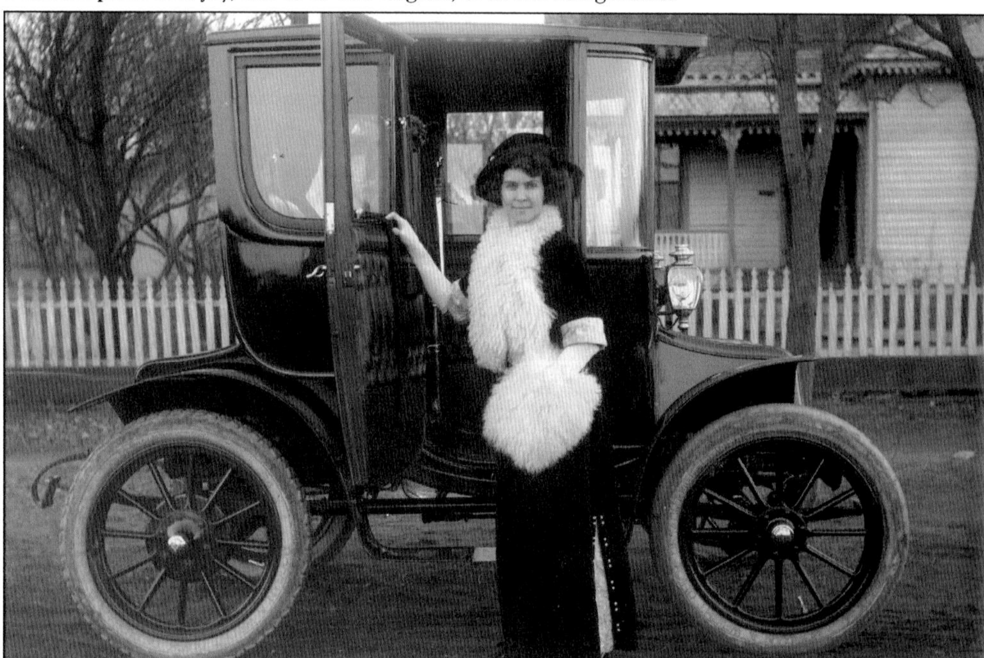

Bertha Stine, wife of Woodward banker Len L. Stine, posed for Frank Saunders with her Ohio Electric car on December 17, 1911. It was the first automobile in Woodward. When a new engine arrived for the fire department in 1909, Stine was the only man in town that could drive it. He drove it from the Santa Fe depot to the firehouse and soon taught Pop Snow to operate it.

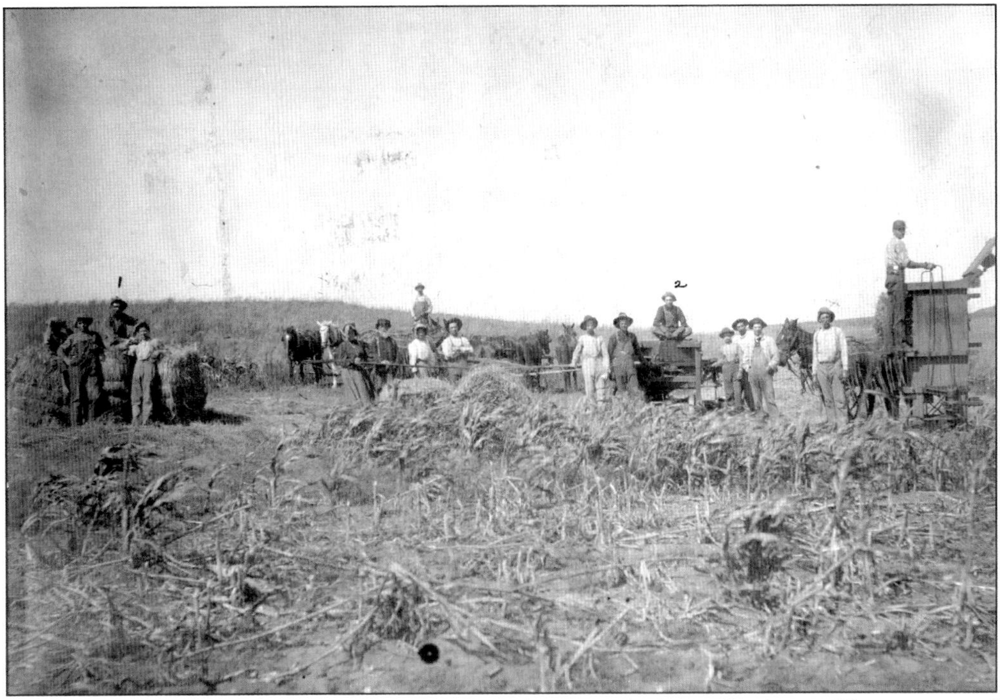

This photograph is of a broomcorn harvest around 1910 in the Mooreland area. The man seated on the bale at left is Andrew Williams. The man seated on the equipment at right is Garrett Williams. The other 14 individuals in the photograph are not identified.

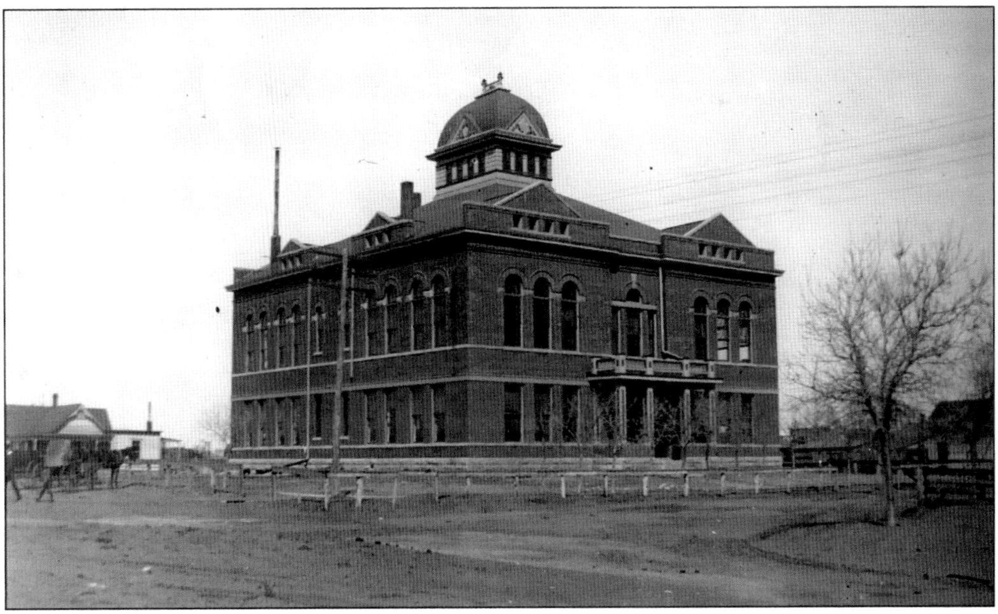

The original Woodward County Courthouse, in this 1902 photograph, was constructed on the northwest corner of Tenth Street and Texas Avenue in 1901. It served as the primary building for county offices until the current courthouse was constructed in 1936. The original courthouse was badly damaged in the April 9, 1947, tornado and was torn down. The Stock Exchange Bank main office is located here now.

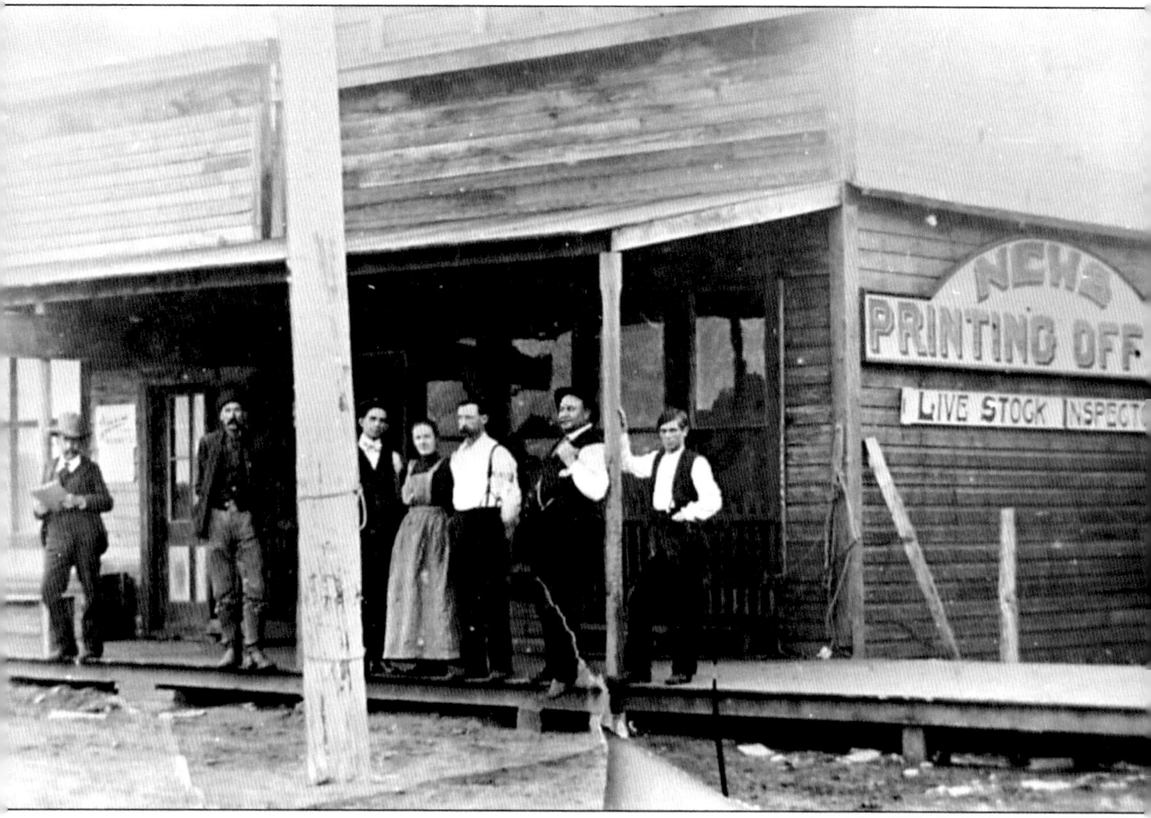

The first issue of the *Woodward News* was published on June 1, 1894, with borrowed ink from a rival newspaper. Editor William (Billy) Bolton was still waiting for the bulk of his supplies to arrive in his new home. He moved to Woodward from Greensburg, Kansas, where he continued to publish the *Kiowa County Signal*. The office in this photograph sat on the west side of Tenth Street between Main and Texas Avenues. Bolton stands with a large cigar in his mouth. He was on the first board of directors of the Oklahoma Historical Society, a member of the Oklahoma A&M College (now Oklahoma State University) Board of Regents and served as president of the Oklahoma Press Association in the 1890s. He died on December 13, 1909, with no heirs and a widow of three weeks, leaving an estate of $25,000. His home on Texas Avenue still stands.

Three

The Land We Belong to Is Grand
1915–1918

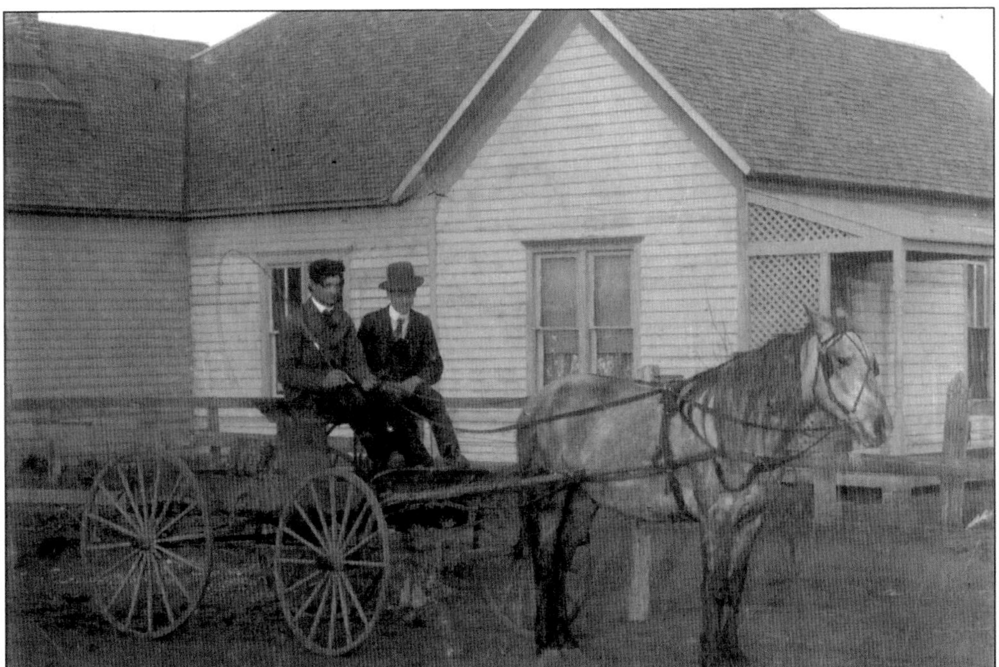

This wagon was used to deliver purchases to customers of Peter Martinson's general store. Henry McAfee and Javon Butcher worked for Martinson and are seated on the wagon. Martinson's daughter Esther Martinson Eoff was born in the house behind.

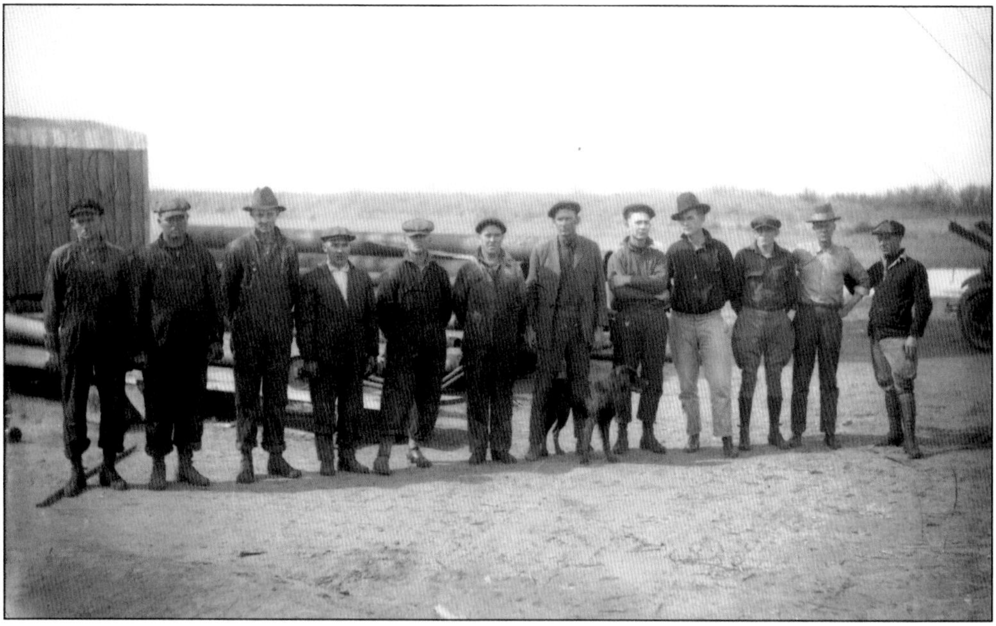

Woodward County lies in an oil and natural gas area on the shelf of Oklahoma's Anadarko Basin. Although shallow wells were drilled during the second decade of the 20th century, no substantial amount of oil was discovered. Oil and natural gas was discovered in abundance in the county during the late 1950s.

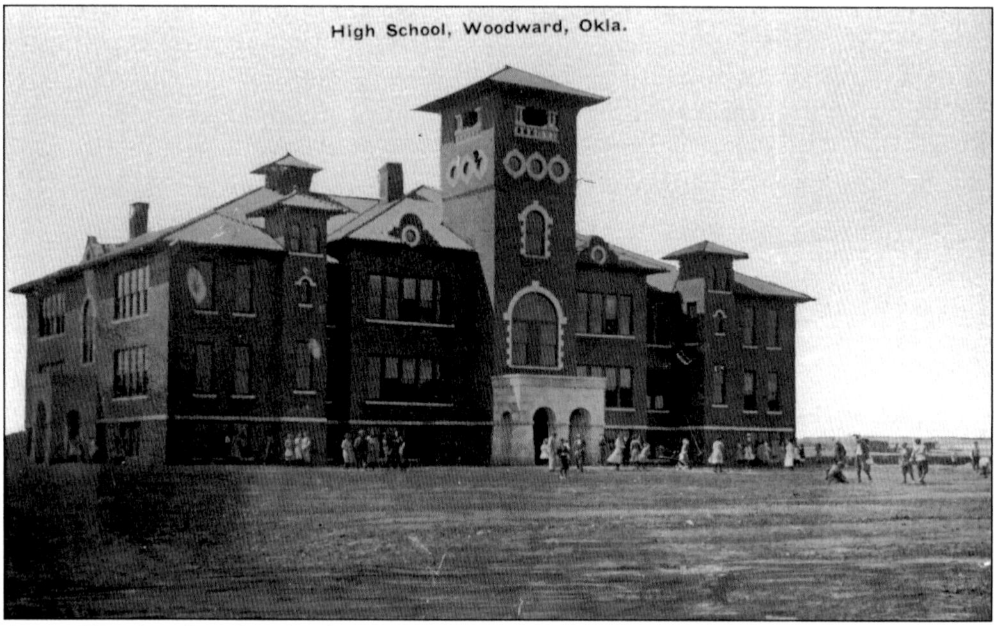

A new Woodward High School was constructed in 1910. A grand structure of brick, complete with a cupola, it was called "Old Central." At one time, it housed Woodward's business college. By the time it was badly damaged by the 1947 tornado, it had not been in use for a number of years. It was razed shortly thereafter, and the bricks were used to construct a memorial to the children killed by the monster storm.

Dr. John L. Day was a doctor at the Fort Supply Hospital. He was a major in World War I, serving on the battlefields of Chateau Thierry and the Argonne while in the medical corps. During the war, Day rode a horse while mules pulled the medical wagons. He was a reserve officer until he retired as lieutenant colonel. He was awarded the Silver Star for his service. Day helped to organize the Plains Indians and Pioneers Historical Foundation in 1956.

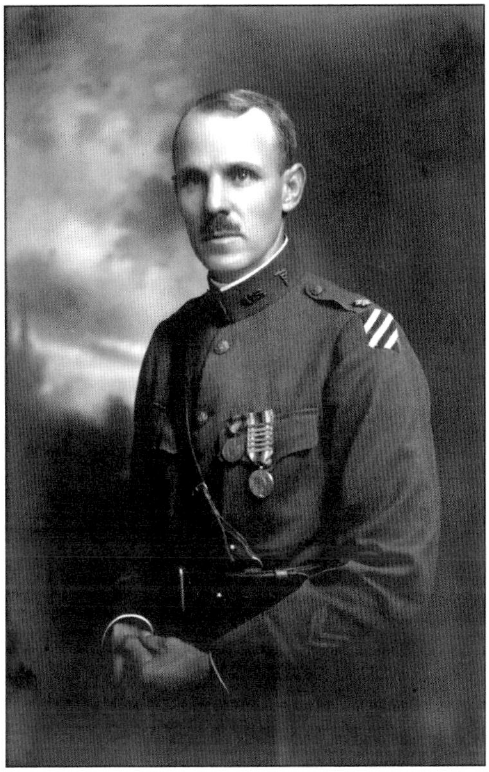

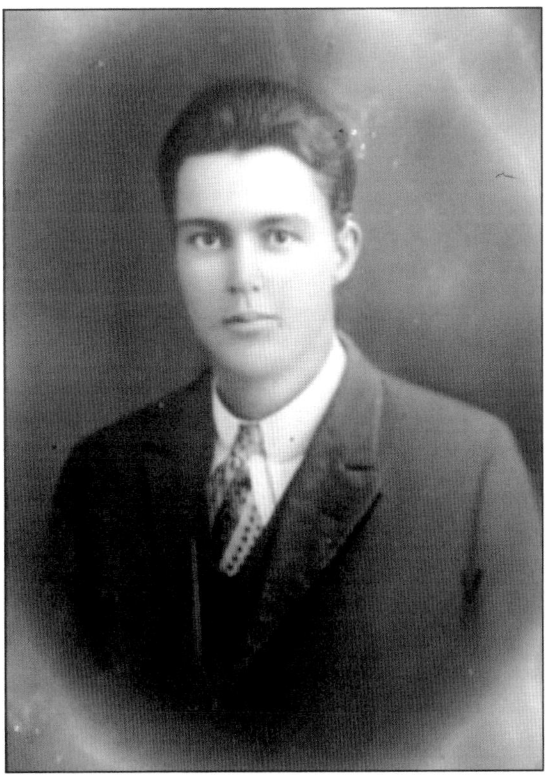

Clarence Victor Moore was the first Woodward County boy to die in World War I. Woodward County suffered 25 casualties during the conflict.

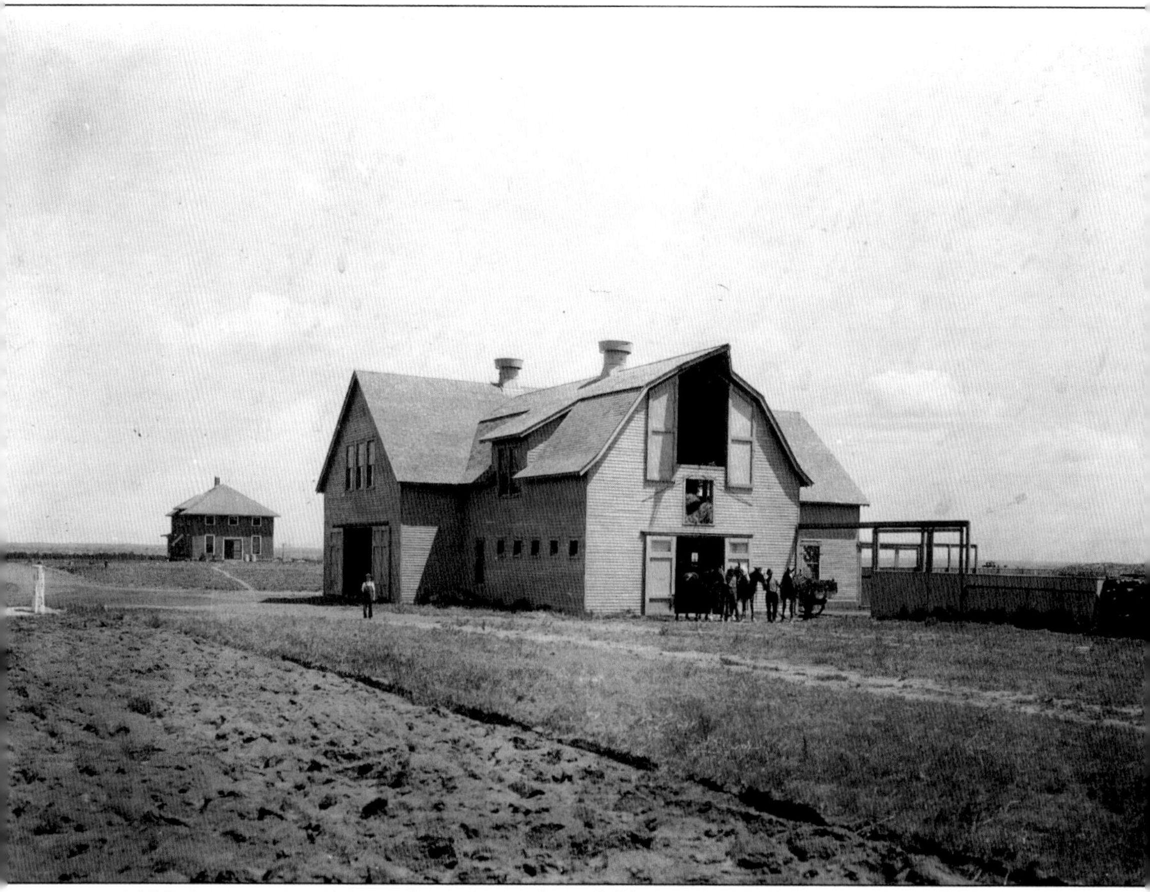

A U.S. Department of Agriculture Great Plains field station was placed southwest of Woodward in 1913. This large barn, which is still standing, was constructed in 1915. It was a 33-foot-by-40-foot structure with stalls for nine horses, harness and feed rooms, and a hayloft. County commissioners arranged to purchase a 160-acre piece of land for $9,000. It was described as a "wind-swept country without trees except a few knotty bushes," It was leased to the government for 99 years for $1, with the idea that if crops could be grown here, they would grow anywhere. Now known as the Southern Plains Range Research Station, over 10,000 varieties of trees and shrubs have been tested here. The research station was placed on what was Woodward's first cemetery. An undertaker from Mooreland, C. E. Lambert submitted the low bid for disinterring and reburying bodies in Elmwood Cemetery at the price of $6.75 each. The undertaker finished the job in March 1914, and construction on the station's first buildings began.

Drillers of the first test well for oil in Woodward County posed for this photograph in 1917. From left to right, they are (first row) M. D. Roark, operator J. H. Warden, and geologist C. F. Hensley; (second row) George F. White, J. D. White, J. S. White, and F. C. White.

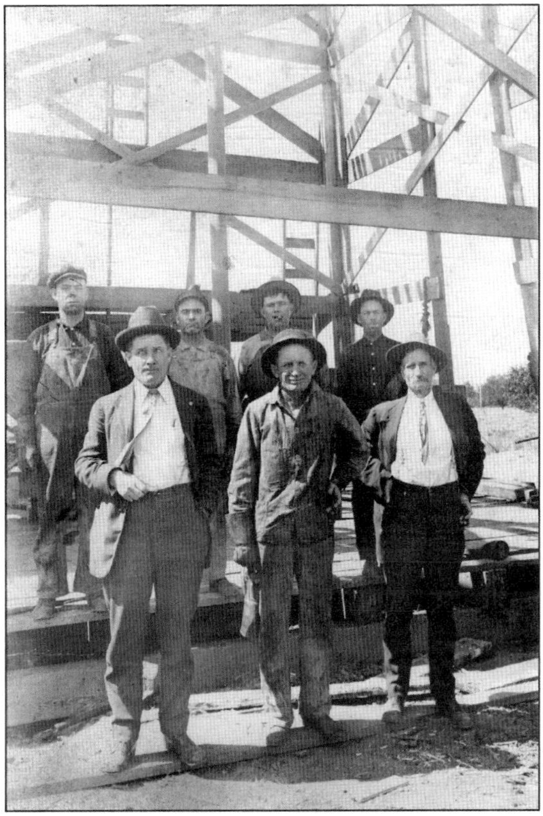

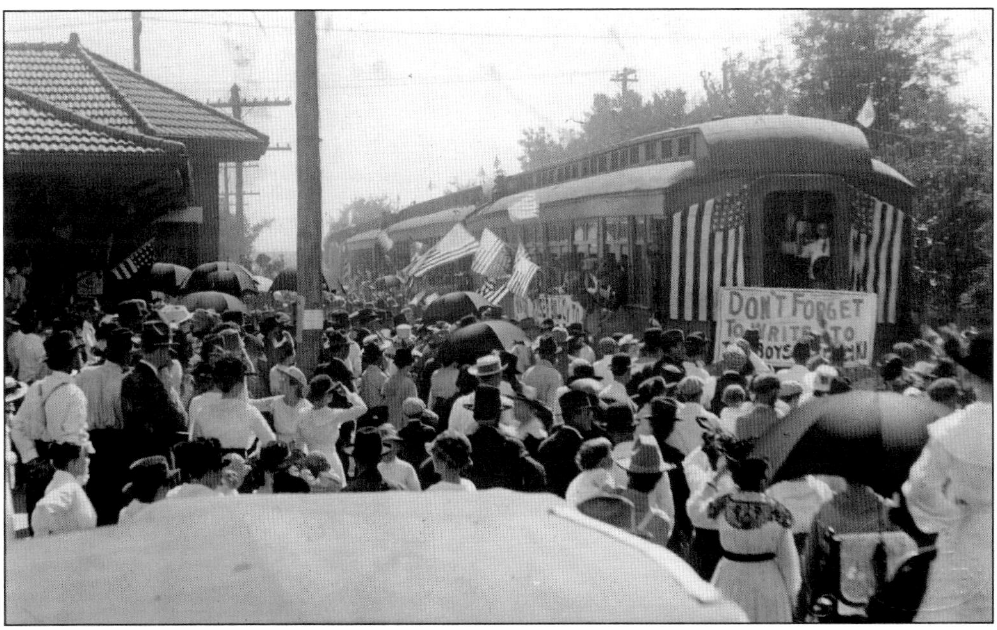

A large crowd gathered at the Missouri-Kansas-Texas Railway (Katy) depot on Main Avenue in Woodward to see their young sons leave for World War I. Many of these men never saw Woodward County again.

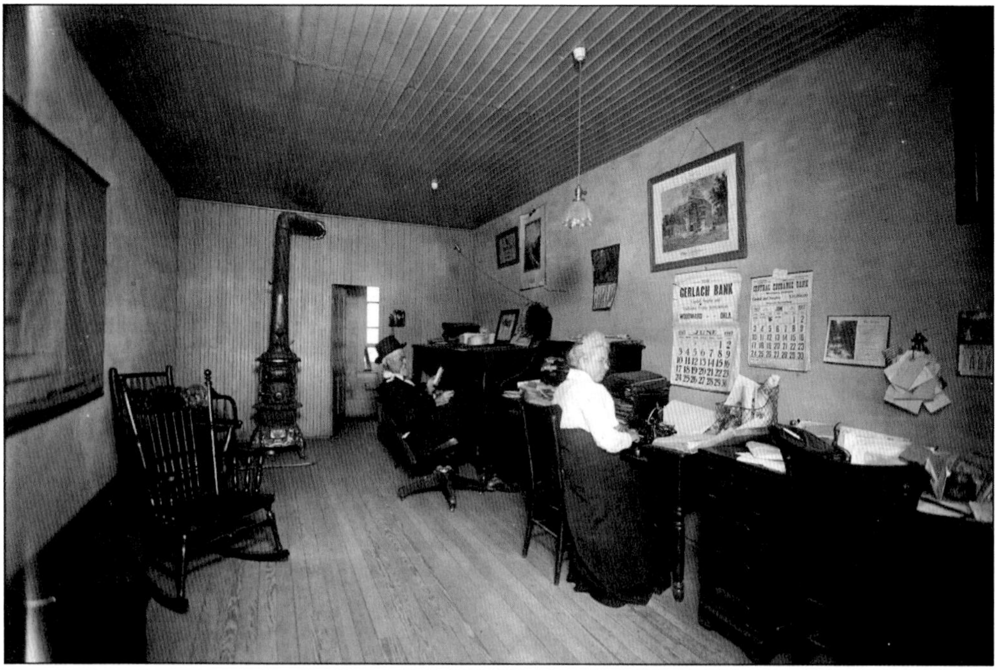

Isaac Dillon Haning and his daughter Alpha work diligently in their real estate office at 916 Main Avenue in Woodward around 1917. Calendars for the Gerlach Bank, Central Exchange Bank, and others are located on the wall.

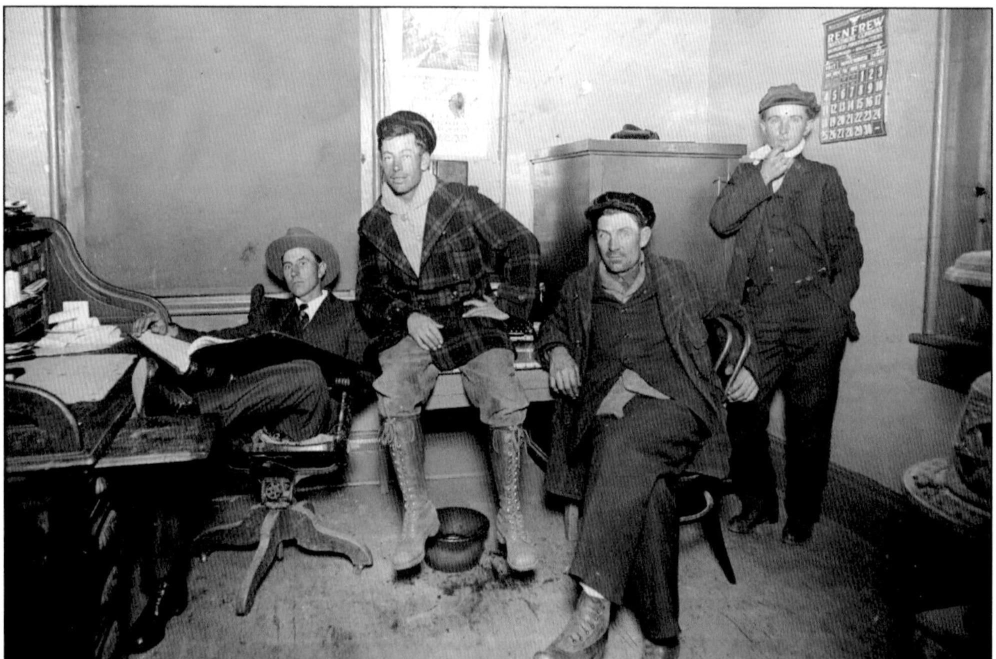

This photograph shows the Woodward County Sheriff's office in Woodward in 1917. Sheriff Ed Durant, who served from 1915 through 1921, is at his desk. The other men, from Cestos in Dewey County, include Will Balleel, Allen Terrel, and a Mr. Hinkston.

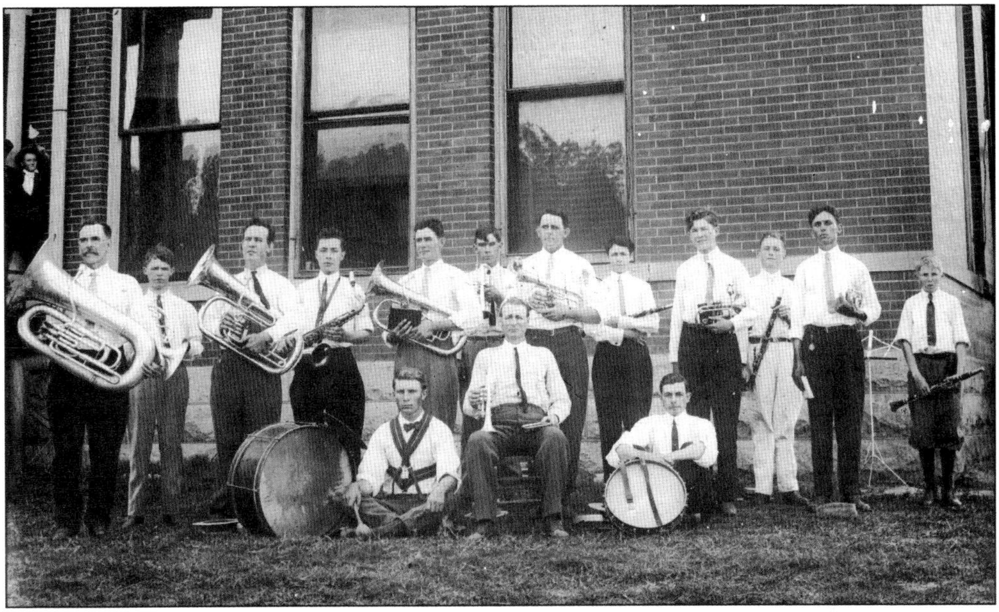

Members of the Woodward Commercial Club Band pose for this photograph in front of the 1901 Woodward County Courthouse. The commercial club was founded in 1916 and later became the chamber of commerce. From left to right are (first row) Dyas Kenney, Alex Carlisle, and Fred Beatte; (second row) Pop Grissis, George Corbitt, Tad Appelget, Ear Grissis, ? Lahr, Claude Bell, Joe Thomas, Allen Appelget, Irvin Walker, Louis Malone, Jim Young, and ? Saunders.

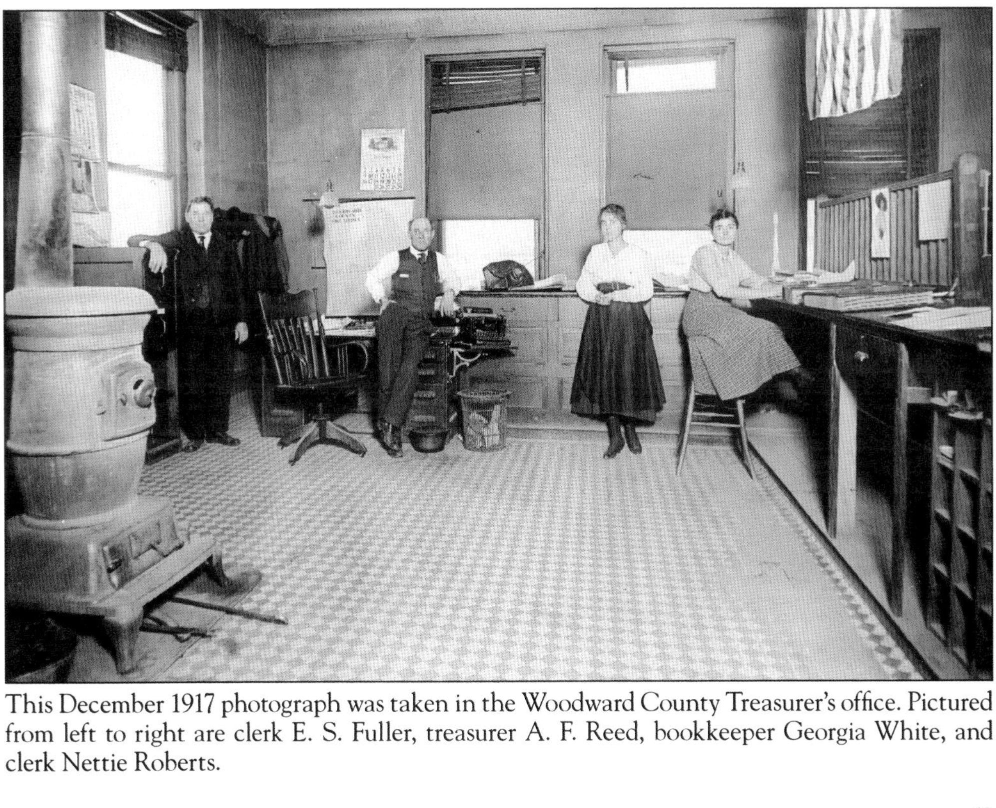

This December 1917 photograph was taken in the Woodward County Treasurer's office. Pictured from left to right are clerk E. S. Fuller, treasurer A. F. Reed, bookkeeper Georgia White, and clerk Nettie Roberts.

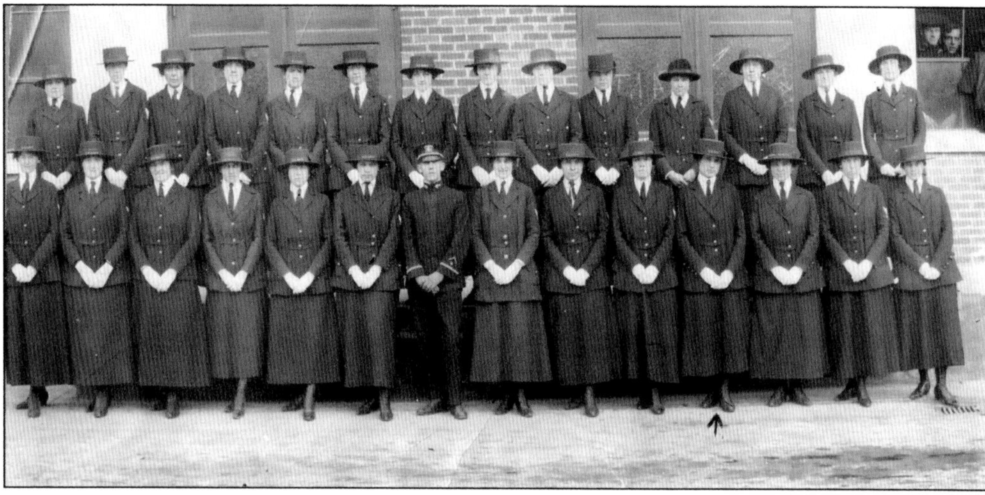

This photograph of the Yeomanettes includes Esther Laubach and fellow navy personnel in 1919. An arrow points to Laubach. During World War I, Congress created the U.S. Naval Reserve, which included women, called the Yeomanettes, to work alongside men in shore jobs. About 11,275 women served as Yeomanettes in the navy. Since women did not have the opportunity to make a career in the navy, they were all discharged from active duty by the summer of 1919.

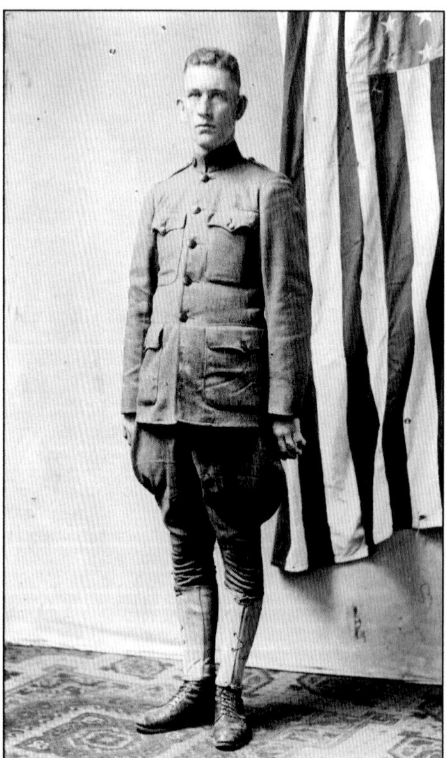

Pictured is Pvt. Jack A. Gradert of Woodward County during World War I. He was 21 years old when he signed up for the draft in 1917. He was described as a tall man with a medium build, blue-gray eyes, and light brown hair.

Rosa Anna Randall Gradert Herbert, mother of Jack A. Gradert, was a nurse with the Red Cross. In this photograph, she holds a blue star flag, which was also known as a war mother's flag. They were flown to signify that an immediate family member was serving in the military. If the man the blue star represented died, mothers would often sew a gold star over the blue one.

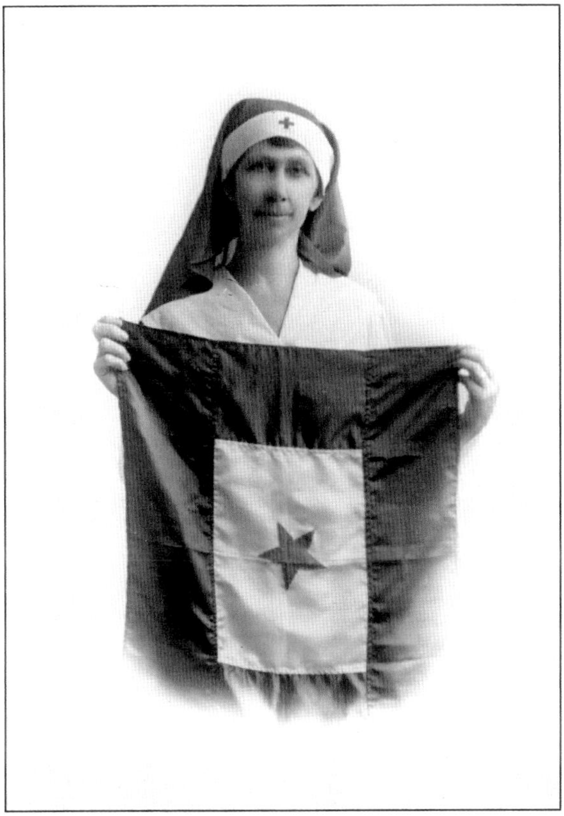

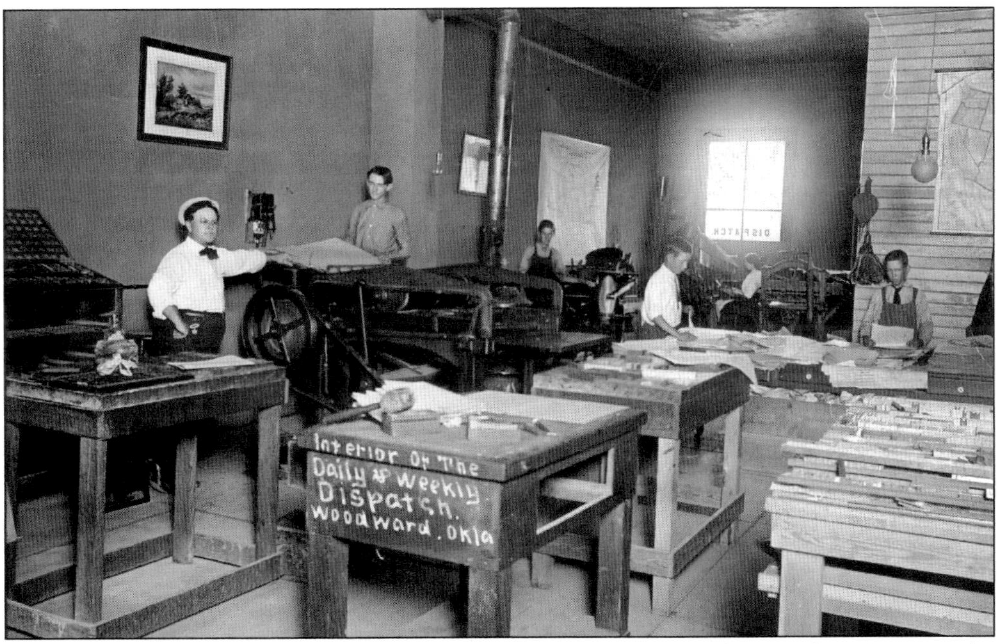

Employees of the *Woodward Dispatch* pause to take a quick photograph around 1915. Notice the printing press and other machinery utilized to create the newspaper. The typesetting machine can be seen on the left. By 1915, at least 12 newspapers had been created in Woodward.

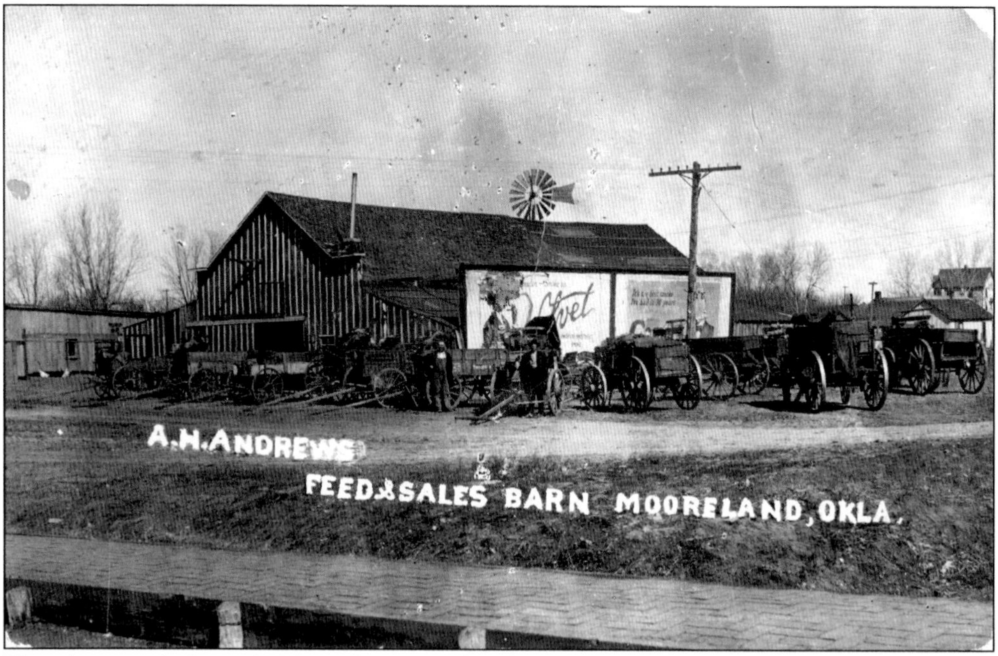

This photograph shows A. H. Andrews's Feed and Sales Barn, which was located in Mooreland.

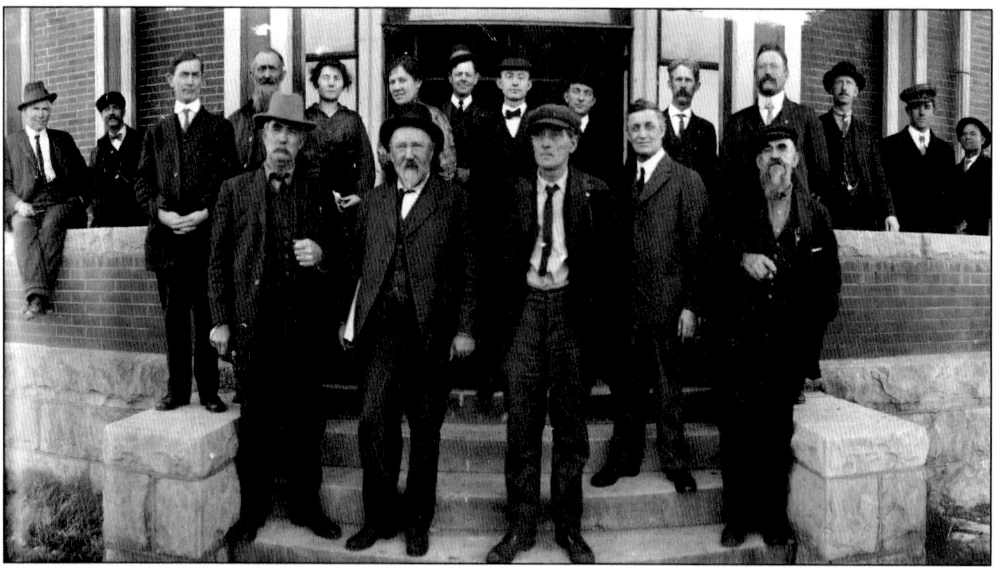

The officers of Woodward County stand on the front steps of the courthouse in 1915. From left to right are (first row) J. H. Stevens, commissioner; David P. Marum, editor of the *Woodward Democrat*; Fred Wegner, commissioner; S. P. Johnson, assessor; and J. C. Triplett, commissioner; (second row) Joe Innis, surveyor; E. J. Richard; C. H. Wyand, county judge; T. C. Hayes, janitor; Leah M. Sparks, register of deeds clerk; Pearl Blood, treasurer clerk; Frank Brown, register of deeds; Vince Shy; R. D. Dockerty, county clerk; L. A. Foster, county judge; W. L. Pittman, superintendent; George Crosno, court clerk; Floyd Richard; and A. F. Reed, deputy treasurer.

Four

THE GOLDEN 1920S
1919–1931

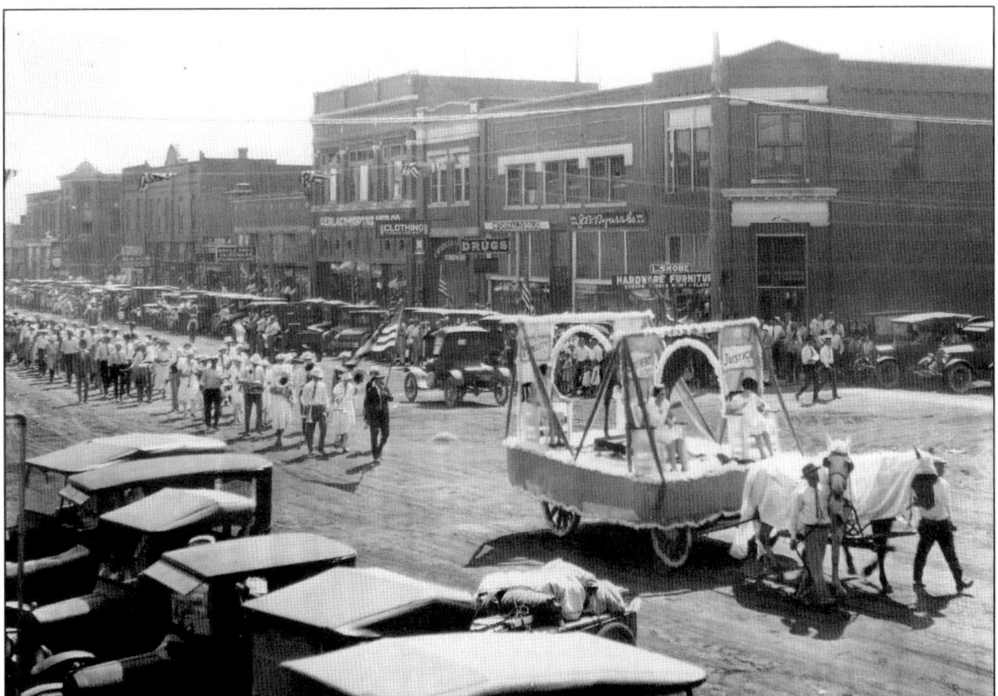

This 1920s parade photograph looks east down Main Avenue in Woodward. The horse-drawn float is likely for the Woodward Elks. Note the elk horns on top of the float with the words *justice*, *fidelity*, *brotherly love*, and *charity* appearing on the four corners.

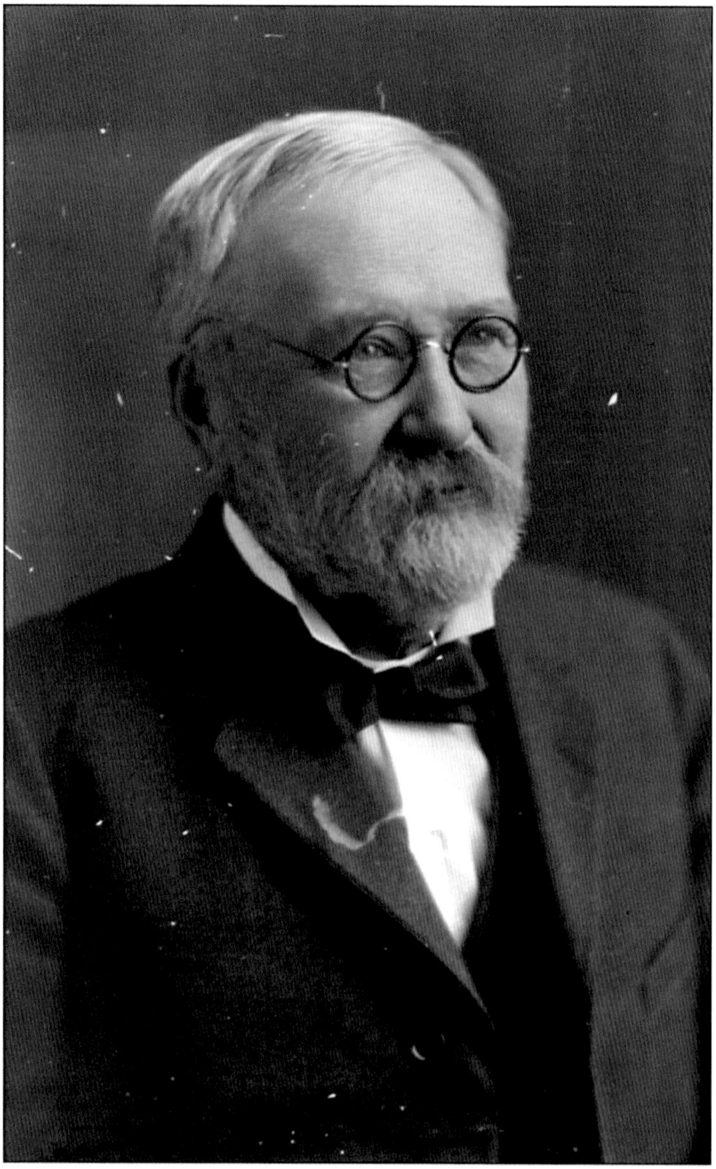

David P. Marum, often called "Judge Marum," came to Oklahoma from New York in November 1889, accepting a position as commissary clerk at Fort Supply. He was admitted to the bar in 1891 and practiced law in Woodward. Marum was a law partner of Temple Houston for a time. In 1897, he was elected to the Oklahoma Territorial Legislature, representing eight western counties. He was a member of the board of regents for territorial colleges from 1897 to 1902. In his later years, he published a weekly newspaper, the *Woodward Democrat*, in which he pushed his political thoughts. He was present in Washington City when Pres. Theodore Roosevelt signed the act enabling Oklahoma to become a state with a quill Marum had furnished from a golden eagle in captivity in Woodward. Marum brought the quill back to Woodward to show his friends, and it is now in the possession of the Oklahoma Historical Society. He was instrumental in securing the U.S. field station and a federal courthouse in Woodward. Both stand as a testament to his political influence and his devotion to Woodward County. He died at the Main Avenue Hotel on April 13, 1929, after a brief illness and is buried in Woodward.

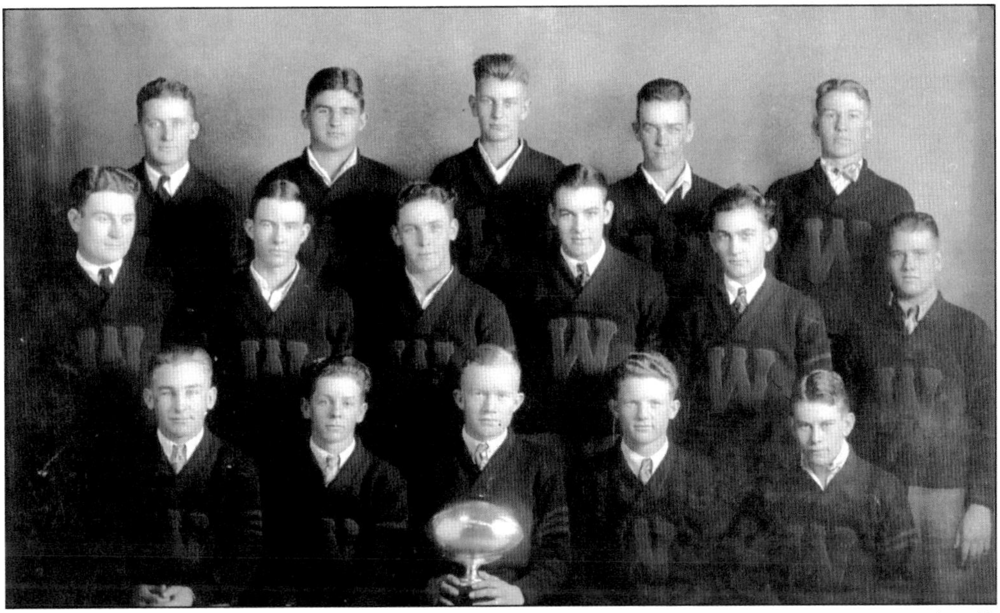

The 1928 Woodward basketball team included Mr. Crosswy, Veldon Gaston, Raymond Bell, coach Henry Warren, Glen Weese, Eugene Rawdon, Melvin Jones, Mr. Reid, Kenneth Lafon, Fred Hudson, Cecil Scovel, and Bob Hudson.

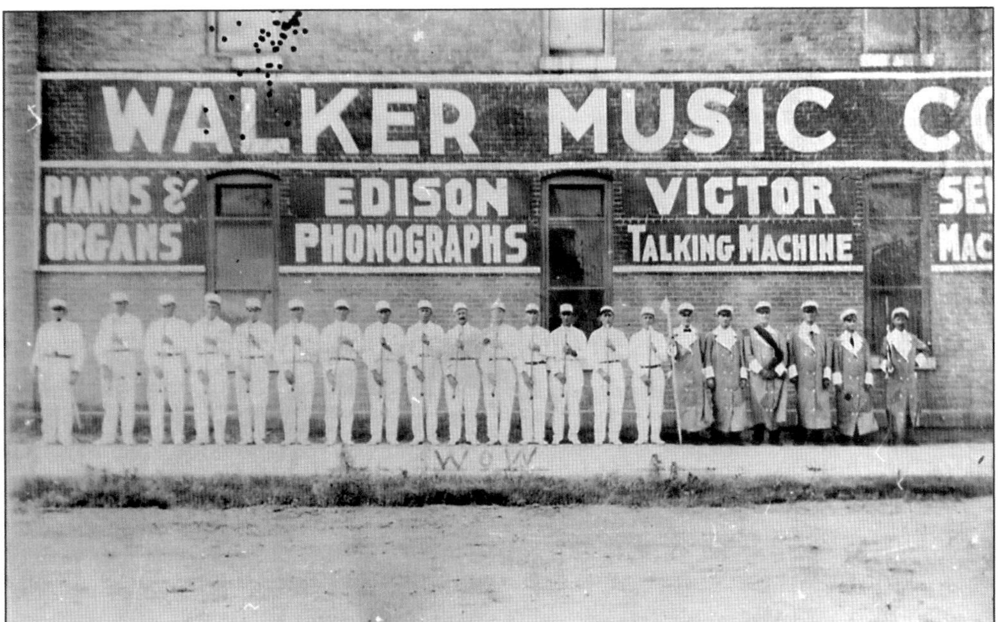

The Woodmen of the World, the largest fraternal benefit society with open membership in the United States, was founded in Omaha, Nebraska, by Joseph Cullen Root on June 6, 1890. The local chapter of the Woodmen stand on the corner of Eighth Street and Main Avenue in Woodward next to the Knights of Pythias hall.

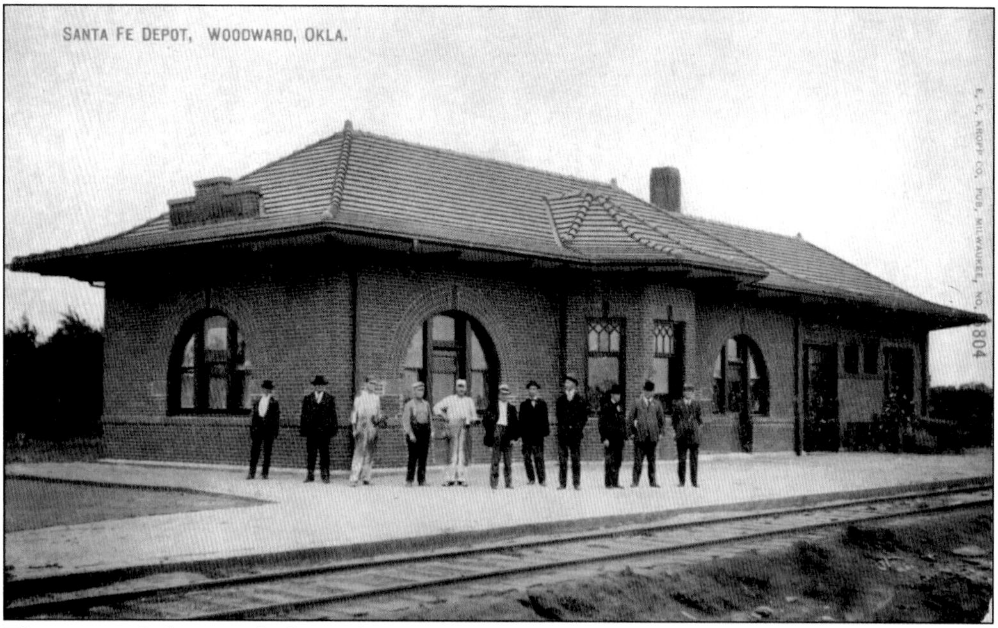

This postcard photograph shows the Santa Fe depot in Woodward. The depot was utilized for the loading and unloading of passengers and freight. Notice the elaborate brickwork around the windows and the rails in the foreground. Standing in front of the brick structure are 11 unidentified men. This postcard, numbered 6804, was published by the E. C. Kropp Company of Milwaukee, Wisconsin.

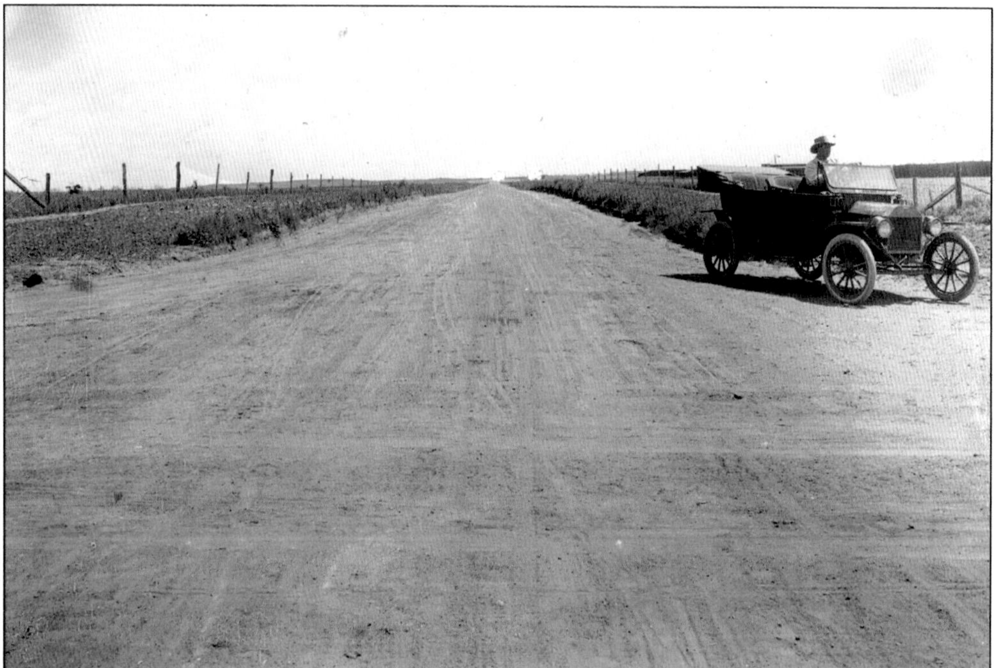

Many county roads, such as the one seen here, were improved in the 1920s. A unique feature in western Oklahoma is that most county roads are laid out on a grid due to the nature of the area's settlement.

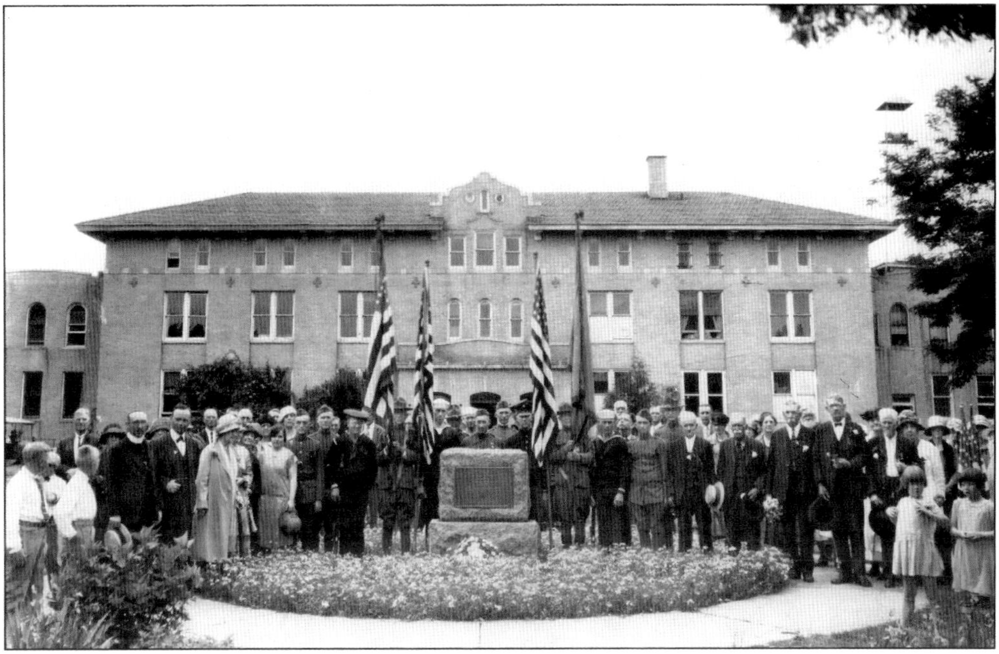

A large crowd posed in 1926 during the dedication of a monument to Woodward County veterans of World War I. The monument stands on the north side of Woodward Convention Hall, which is now the location of the city offices. The monument reads, "In honor of the boys from Woodward County who served in The Great World War 1914–1918. Erected by the Woodward Chapter, Daughters of the American Revolution, 1926."

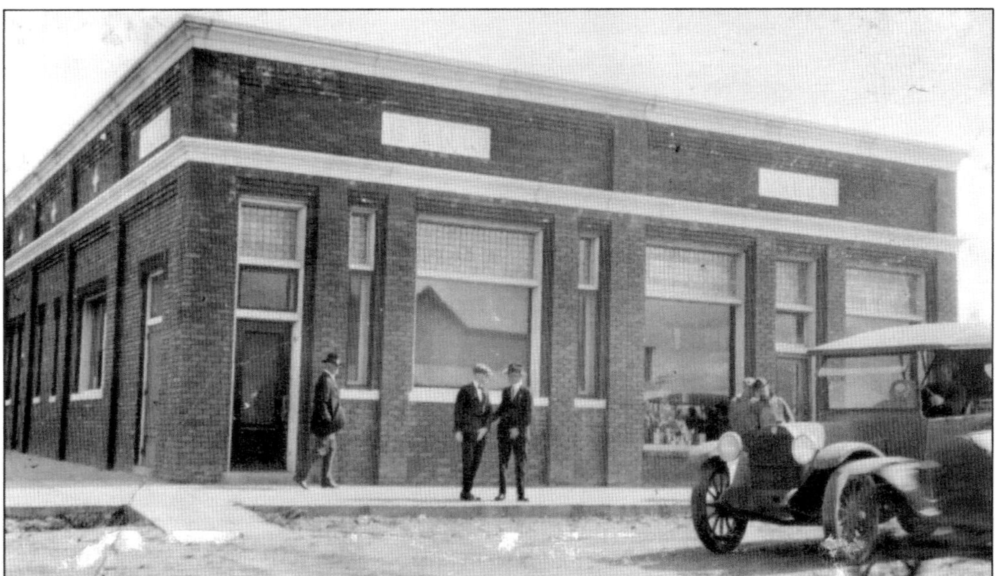

This brick building, located at Fort Supply, housed the new bank and the Davis Drug Store. The previous frame building was destroyed by fire in 1917. The image reveals that the road was unpaved and that a ramp allowed for easy access onto the sidewalk.

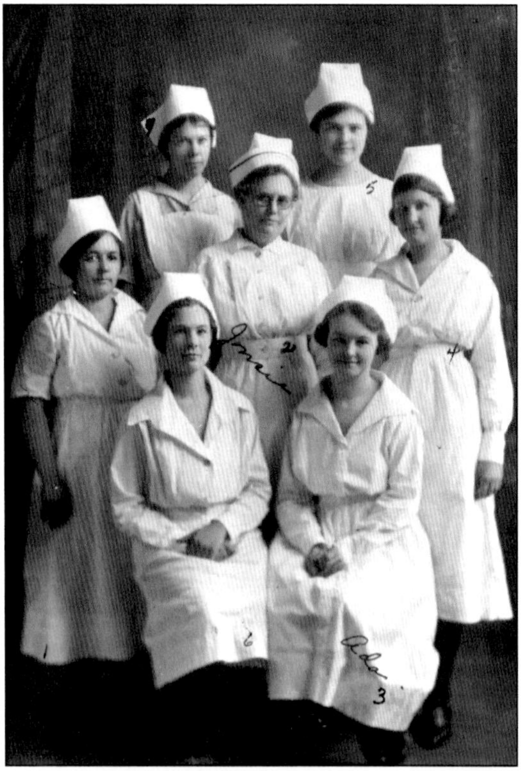

The nursing staff of the Woodward Memorial Hospital posed for this photograph in 1922. The women are numbered as follows: Flora Gillenwater (1), nurse Alma Jones (2), Ada Watkins (3), Faye Patrick Stuart (4), Mable Rogers Eckert (5), Vivian Scott Gilbert (6), and Gladys Smallwood (7).

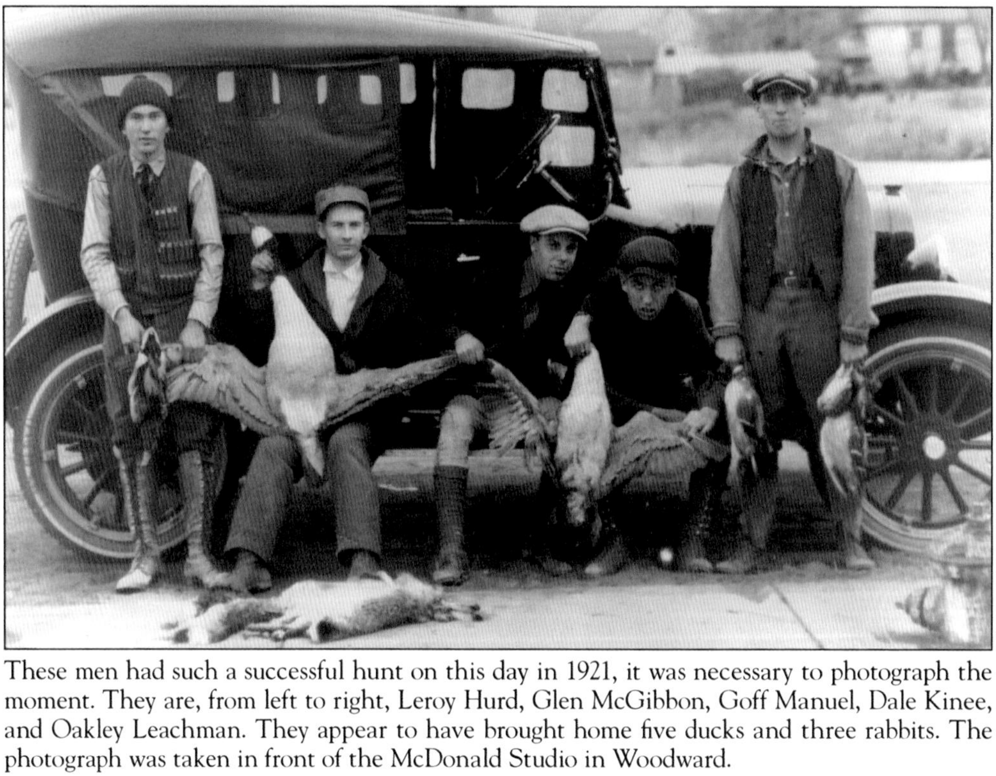

These men had such a successful hunt on this day in 1921, it was necessary to photograph the moment. They are, from left to right, Leroy Hurd, Glen McGibbon, Goff Manuel, Dale Kinee, and Oakley Leachman. They appear to have brought home five ducks and three rabbits. The photograph was taken in front of the McDonald Studio in Woodward.

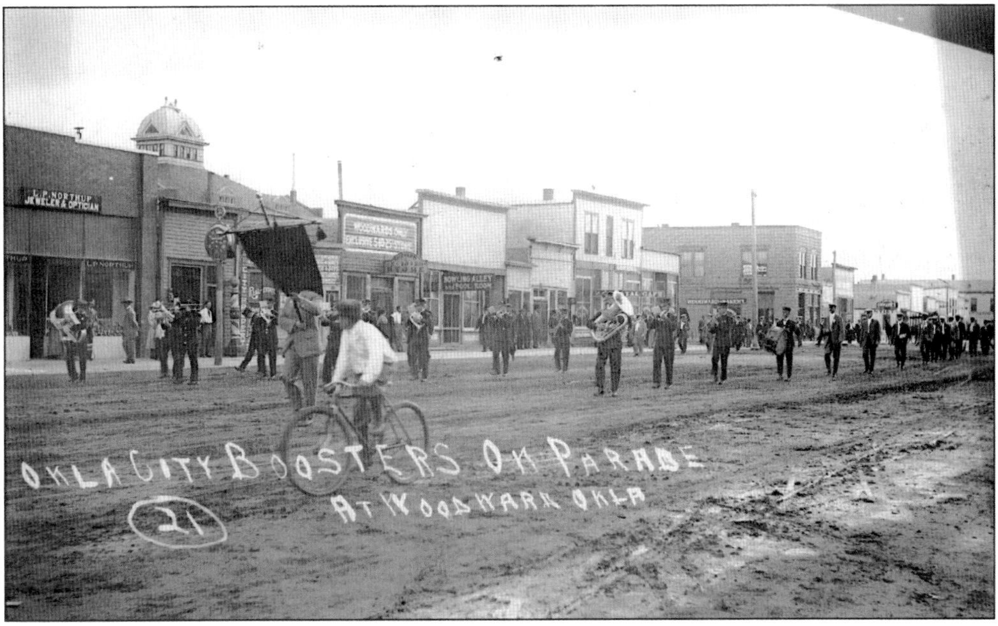

Oklahoma City Boosters march east down Main Avenue in Woodward in this 1921 parade. The cupola of the Woodward County Courthouse can be seen in the background.

A problem for the 1920 Woodward basketball squad was that they had no venue in which to play. The chamber of commerce raised funds to construct a community building that year, and it was "considered one of the best basketball courts in western Oklahoma." Men in this photograph are coach L. A. Ward, Jesse Steele, Russell Enlow, Crusen Updyke, Webster Sharp, Arthur Morey, Kenneth Pettyjohn, and Dallas Enlow.

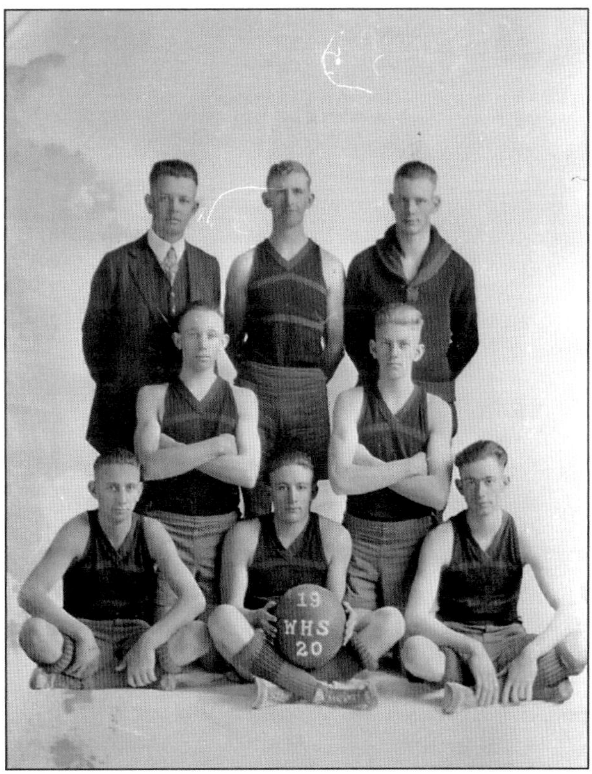

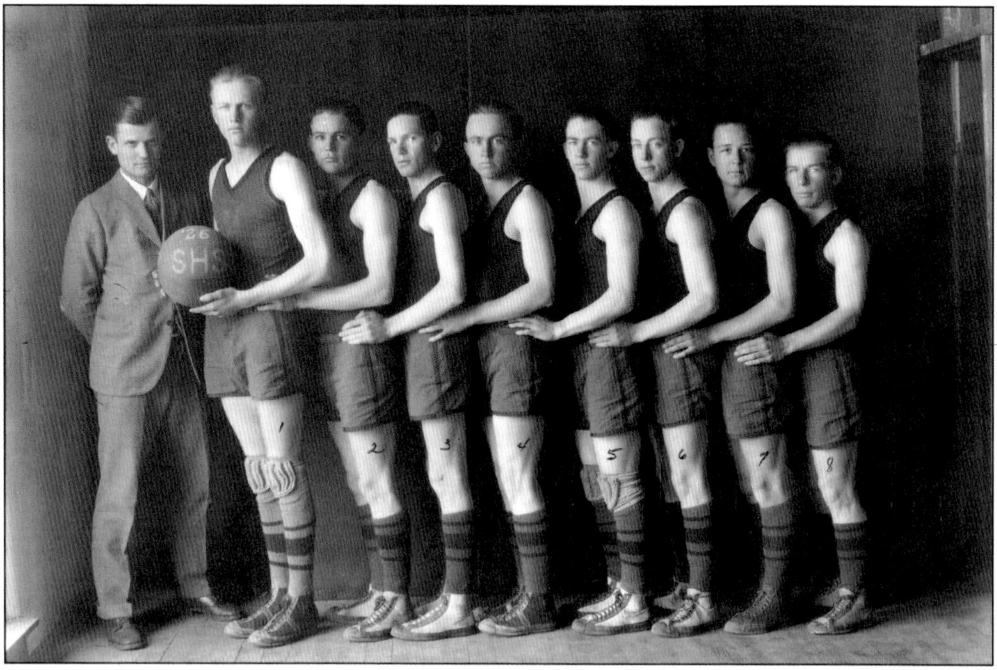

The 1926 Fort Supply boys' basketball team was coached by Mark Alden. From left to right, the players are Ed Hughes, Wayne Shuey, Homer Rouse, Robert Root, Donald Perry, Everett Gatrell, Lester Miller, and Chester Hurst.

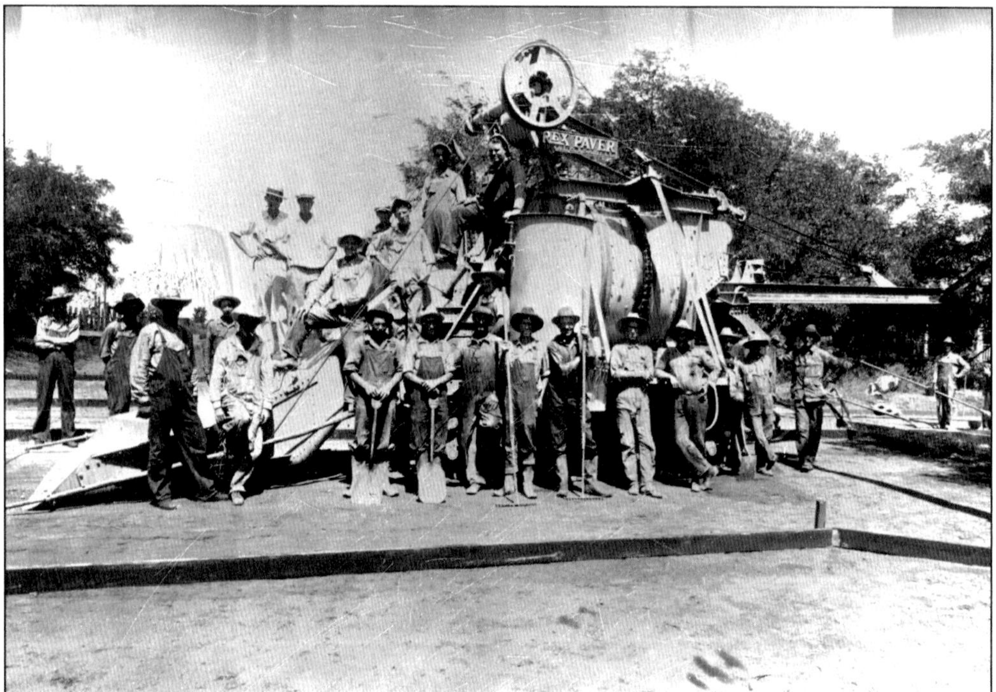

Peter Martinson was mayor when it was decided that Woodward's thoroughfare should be paved. The crew of L. S. Fisher took a break from their work for this photograph in 1927.

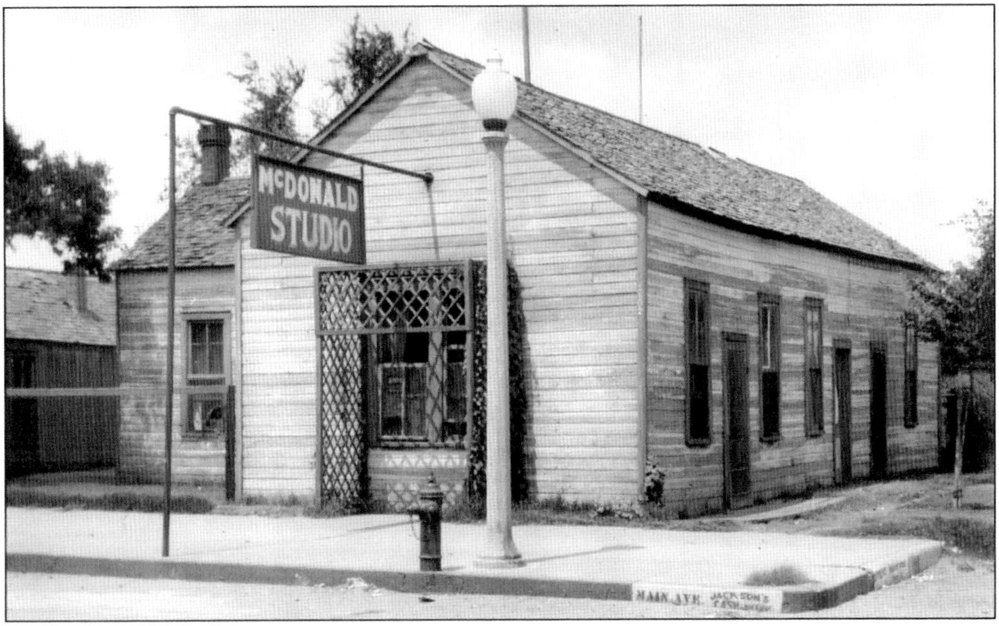

This is one of two known photographs of the original land office at Woodward. It was built prior to the land run and later became Everett McDonald's photography studio. It sat on the northwest corner of Eleventh Street and Main Avenue. Two men killed each other during the construction of the building when a fight occurred. The workmen paused long enough to build two crude coffins and bury the dead.

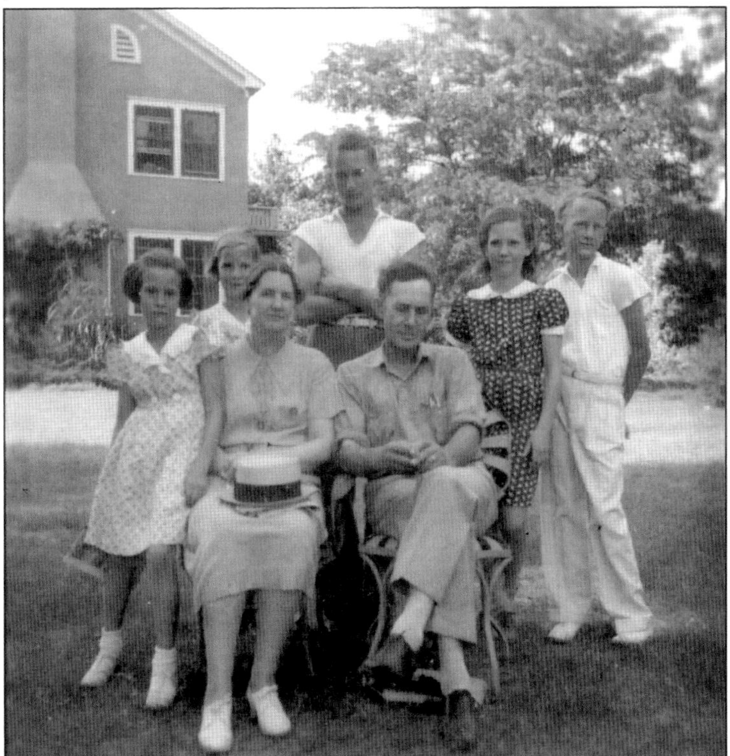

The Ellery Franklin and Winona Hunter Chilcott family posed for this photograph in 1930. Ellery Franklin Chilcott was the U.S. field station's first superintendent. He served in that capacity until his tragic death in a 1939 car accident.

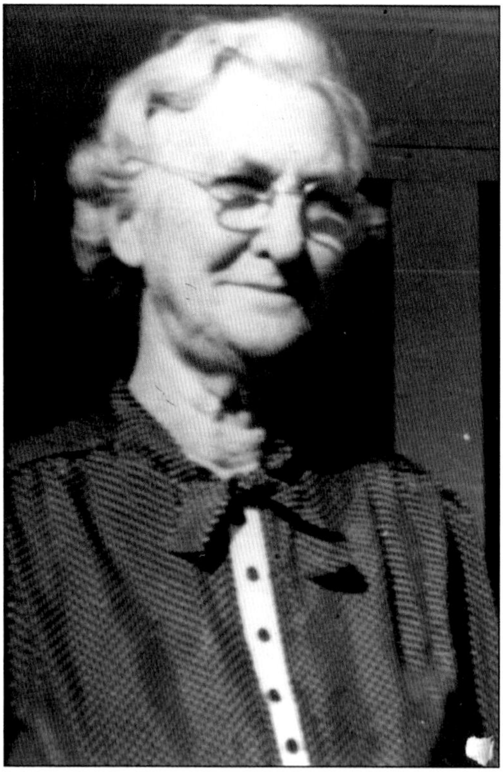

Anna Josephine Knittel Bouquot, wife of John J. Bouquot, was the first and only female sheriff of Woodward County. Her husband became the first sheriff of Woodward County after statehood in 1907. Serving one term, he lost reelection in 1911. In 1924, he ran again and was elected to the post. When he suddenly died on June 2, 1927, returning a stolen car to Des Moines, Iowa, she stepped into the role and completed his unfinished term. She served as such from 1927 until 1929. A daughter recalled that her mother was not just a figurehead; she had once pulled a gun on a suspect.

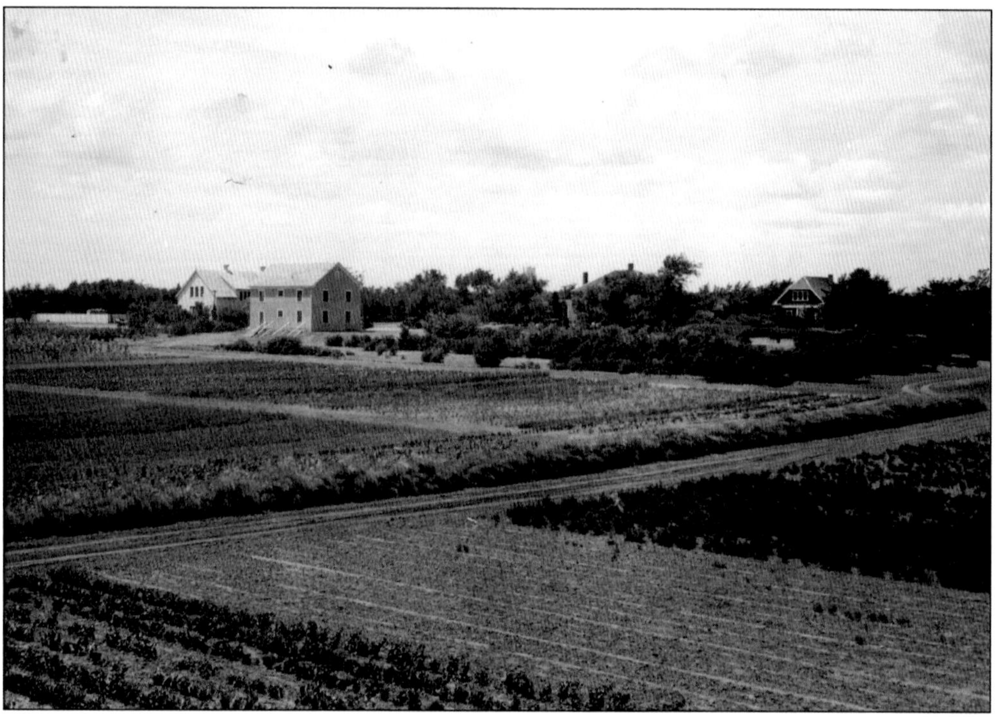

This photograph was taken at the U.S. Department of Agriculture Great Plains field station outside Woodward on July 31, 1931. The camera is pointed to the southwest.

Five

HARD TIMES AND DIRT 1932–1939

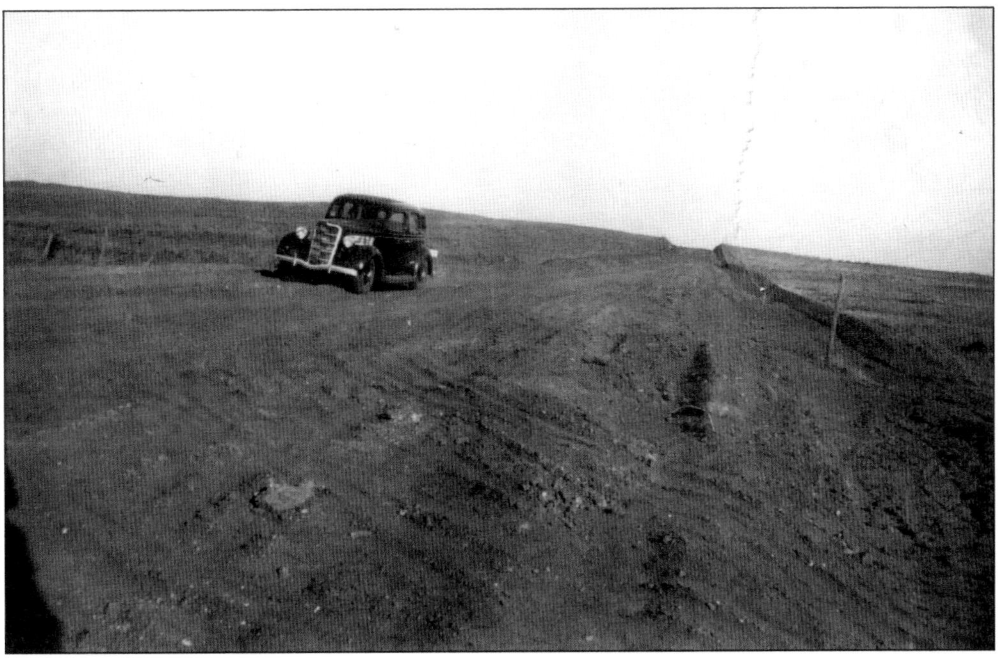

A road under construction four miles east of Sharon is the subject of this photograph. The project was part of the federal Works Progress Administration (WPA) created by Pres. Franklin D. Roosevelt. The WPA provided employment to many out-of-work Americans during the Great Depression of the 1930s.

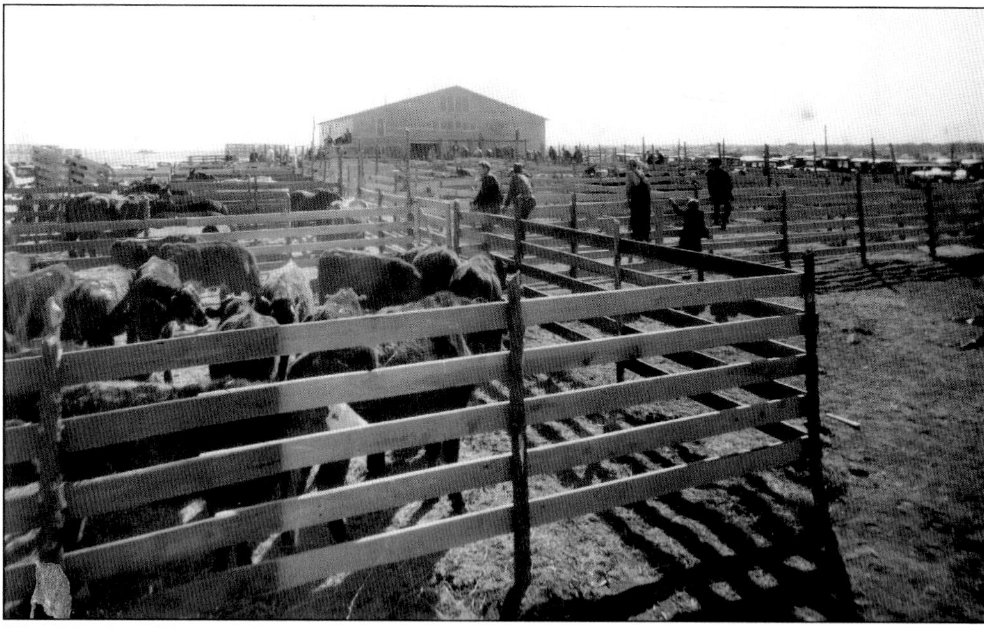

The Woodward Livestock Commission Company opened on East Main Avenue on February 23, 1933, the date of this photograph. The business, started by Fred Kibby and J. C. Curtis, quickly flourished. Within four years, over $1 million of stock had been auctioned in Woodward.

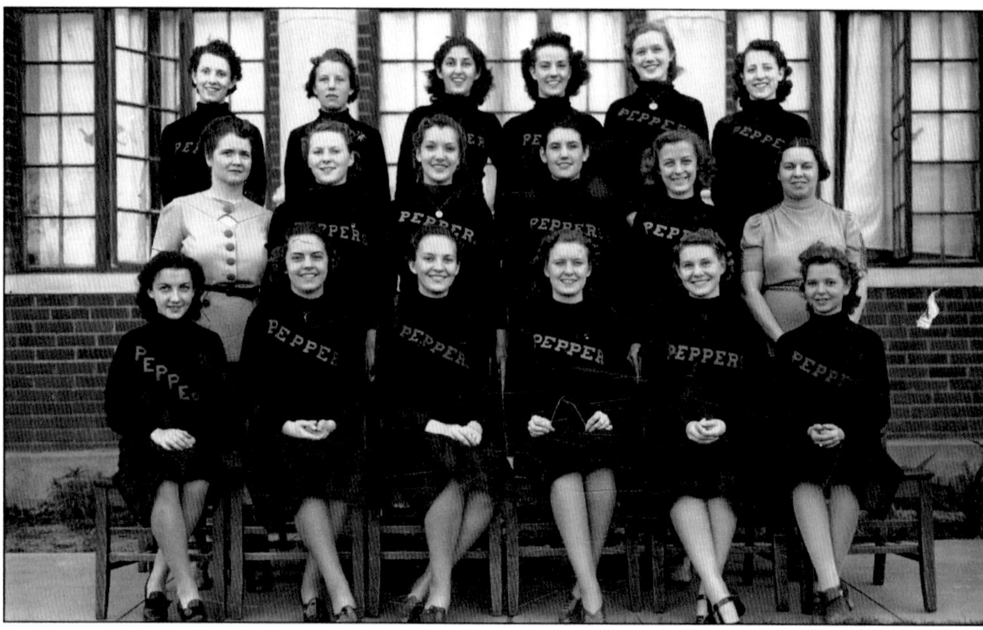

The Woodward High School Peppers was founded in 1923 as the only pep organization for girls. Grace Hayes Foster was the club's first sponsor. The club was noted for its pep at athletic events. This photograph was taken on May 11, 1938. From left to right are (first row) Betty Norma Wells, Dorothea Pierson, Maxine Cullen, Charlene Blackburn, Marry Ellen Edwards, and Ada Mae Gardner; (second row) Miss McClung, Helen Street, Marcella Fuller, Azalea Miller, Edwinia Coffland, and Miss Ernst; (third row) Beth Hadley, Betty Lou Costello, Willa Lee Van Devander, Ricky Adams, Virginia Martin, and Betty Lou Philips.

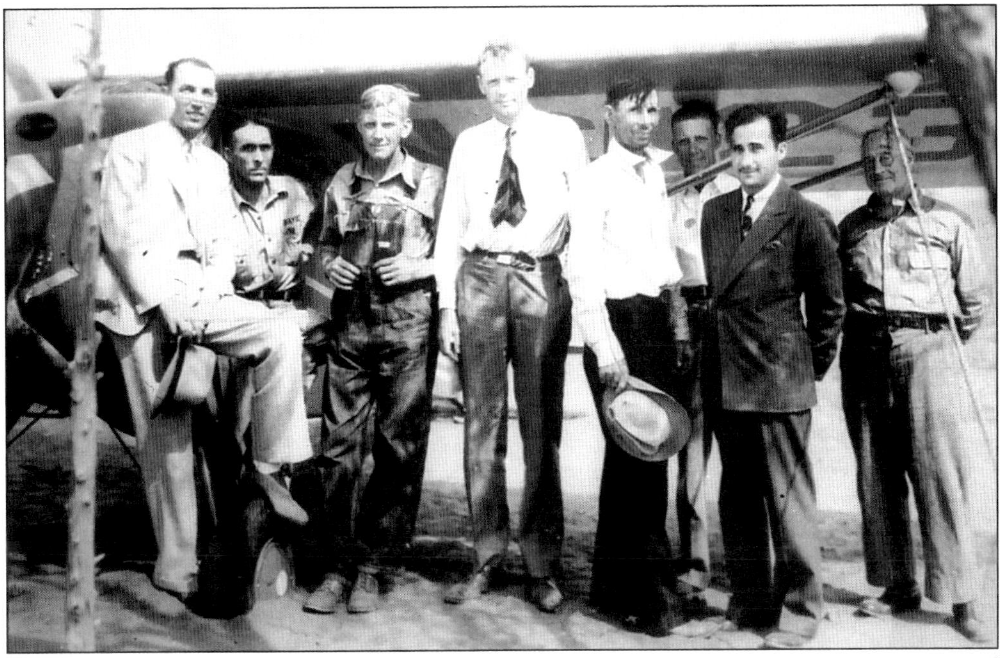

In 1934, pilot Charles Lindbergh and his wife, Anne Morrow Lindbergh, made an unexpected landing in northern Woodward County. Men in the area posed for this photograph on the Aitkens farm. In the photograph are Ralph Hunt, Mr. Aitkens, Charles Lindbergh (center), Harrison Parsons, Garland Aitkens, and Meno Scoenback. The Lindberghs stayed long enough for a relief plane to arrive.

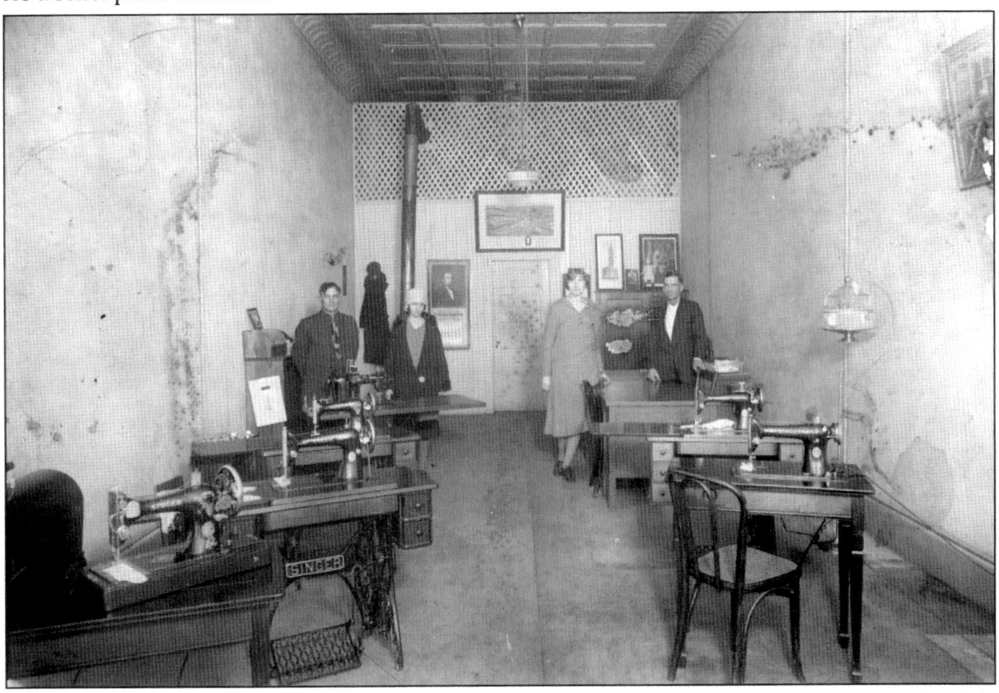

The Singer Sewing Machine Shop was located on Main Avenue in Woodward. John W. Fuller, left, stands next to his daughter Lowayne. The other two individuals in the photograph are unidentified.

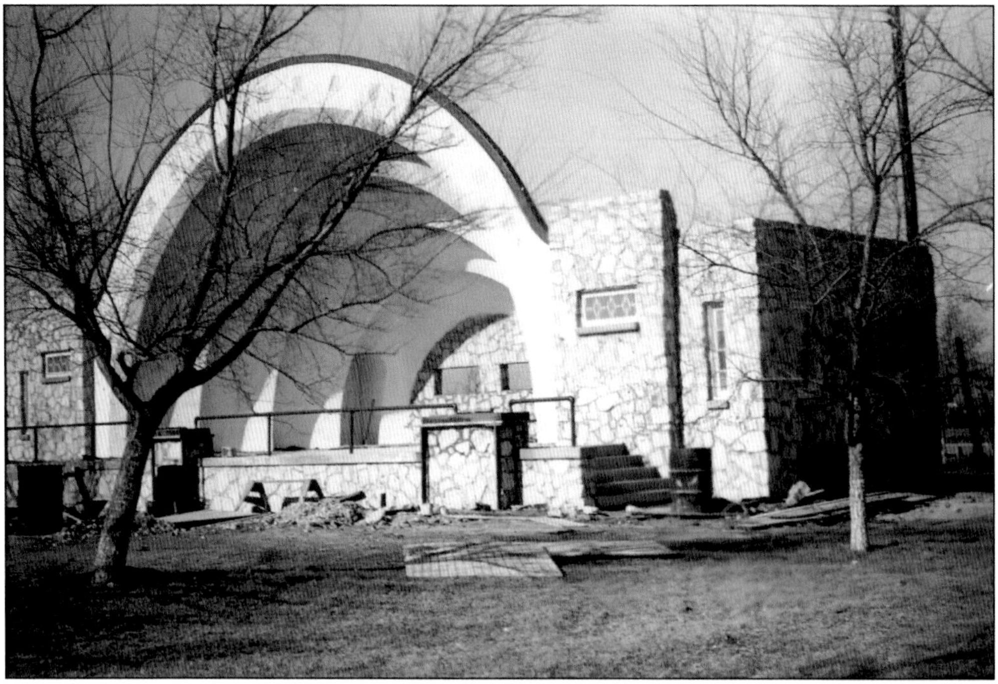

The Band Shell at Crystal Beach in Woodward was constructed in 1937 by the WPA. The WPA created employment for out-of-work citizens during the Great Depression of the 1930s. It still stands at Crystal Beach Park.

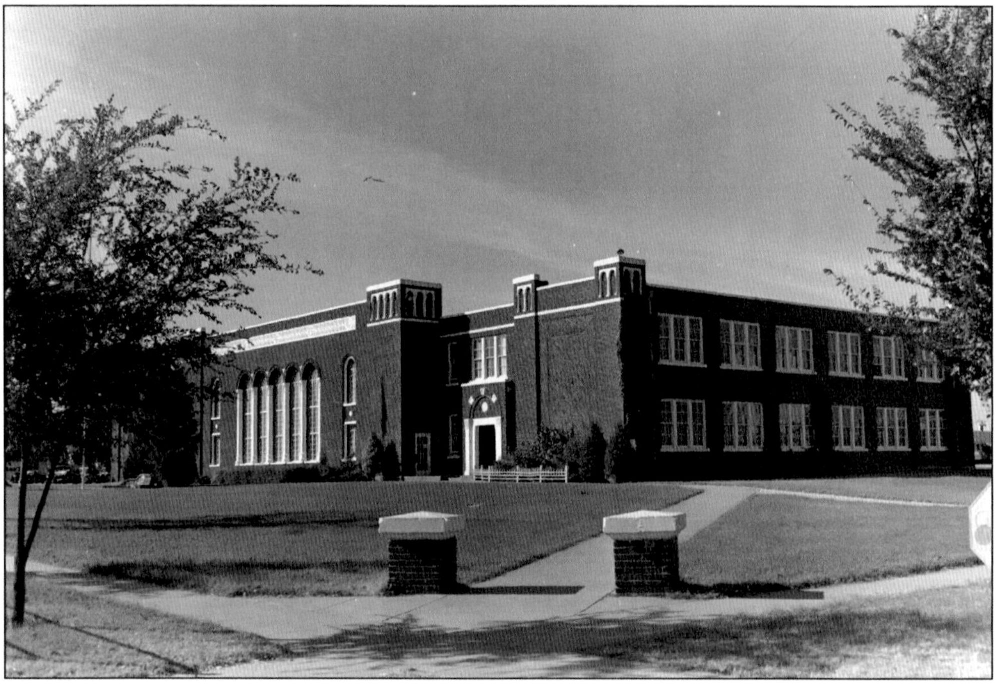

A new high school was built in the county seat in 1937 on the corner of Ninth Street and Locust Avenue. The structure became Woodward Middle School-South in 1978 after the current high school was constructed. It still serves in that capacity.

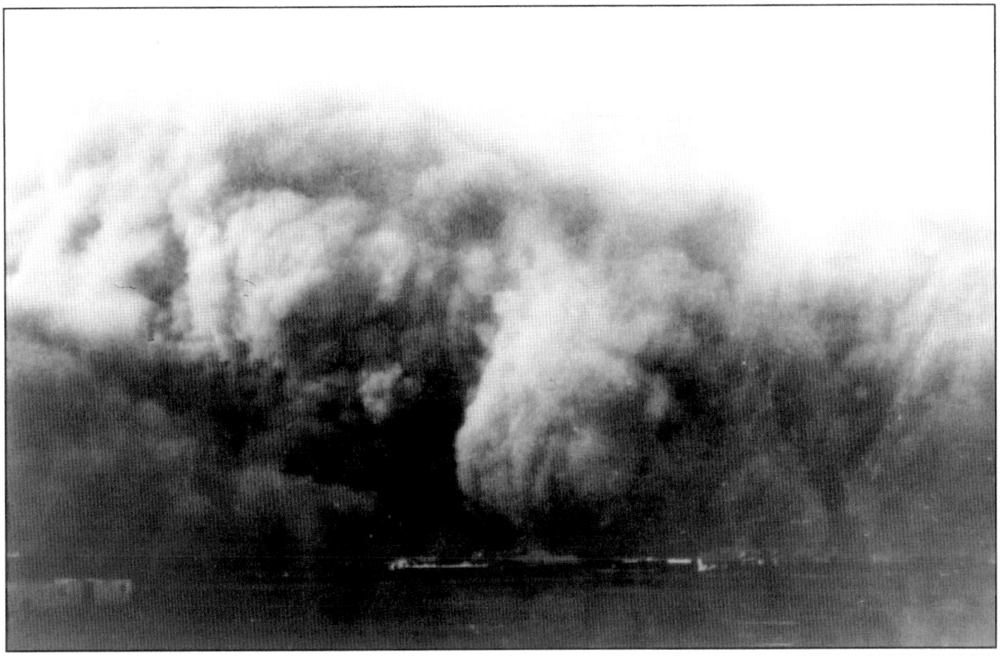

Dust storms such as this one plagued western Oklahoma during the dust bowl from 1934 to 1939. During the winter of 1934, red snow fell on the streets of New York City, and dust covered the decks of ships harbored in the Atlantic Ocean. This black blizzard was photographed in 1935 near Boiling Springs State Park.

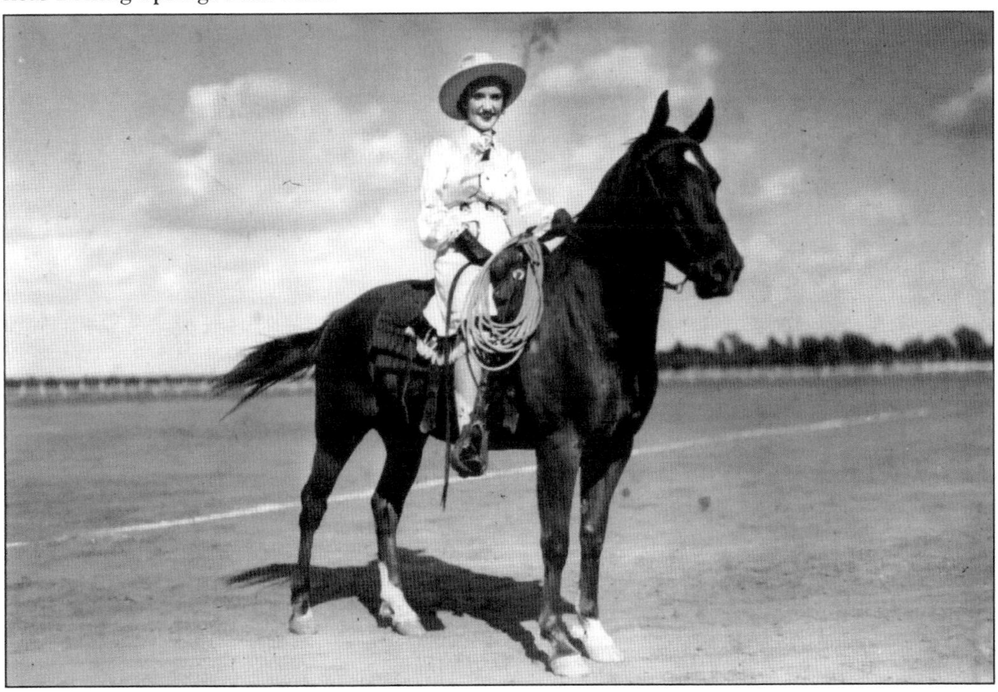

Marcella Fuller (Plank-Bynum), granddaughter of Peter Martinson, became the Woodward Elks Rodeo Queen in 1937. She was the first queen to wear a western costume, and in doing so, she set in motion a tradition that continues to this day.

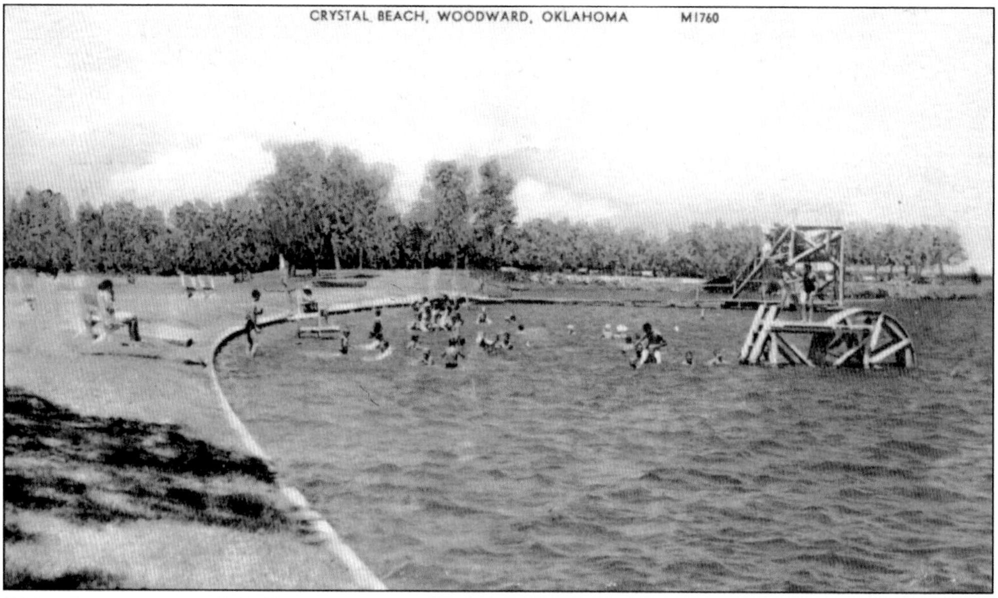

What began as an oil-drilling project in 1929 turned into a playground for Woodward County. While drilling, an artesian well was opened that quickly turned into a flowing river near the Woodward airport. The drilling project was abandoned, and a dam was constructed, which created Crystal Beach Lake. In order to consolidate attractions at the newly created city park, the baseball field was moved in 1932. A few years later, the WPA constructed a bathhouse and band shell.

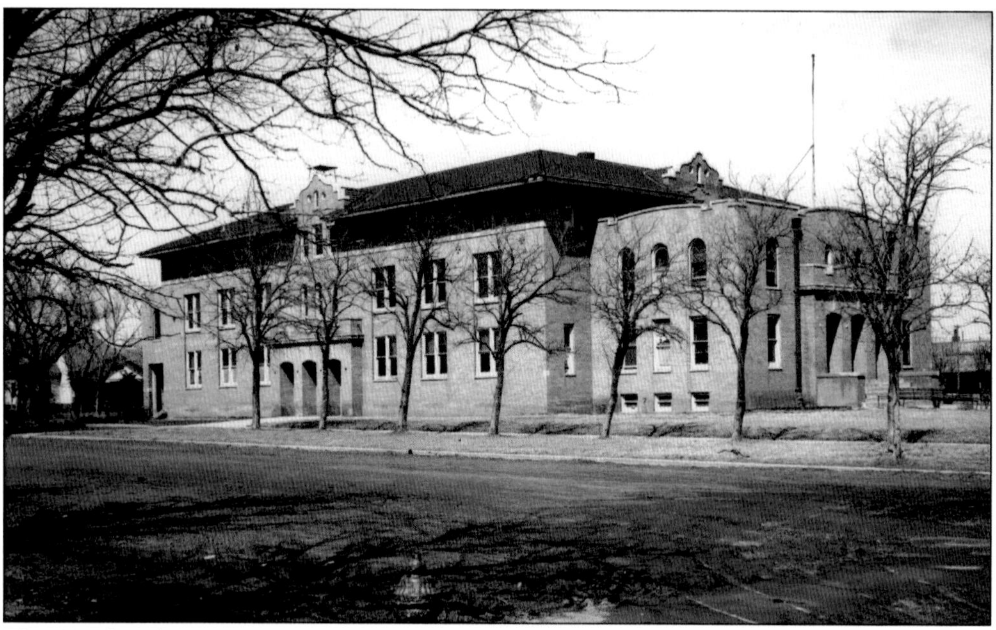

The Woodward Convention Hall was built in 1917 on the south side of the block donated to the city by Ben Key, an early day merchant. It was a disappointment for Key to see it built because many trees he planted were removed to allow for the construction of the building. The building was reputed to have had the best dance floor in northwest Oklahoma. It was saved from the wrecking ball and turned into city offices in about 1984.

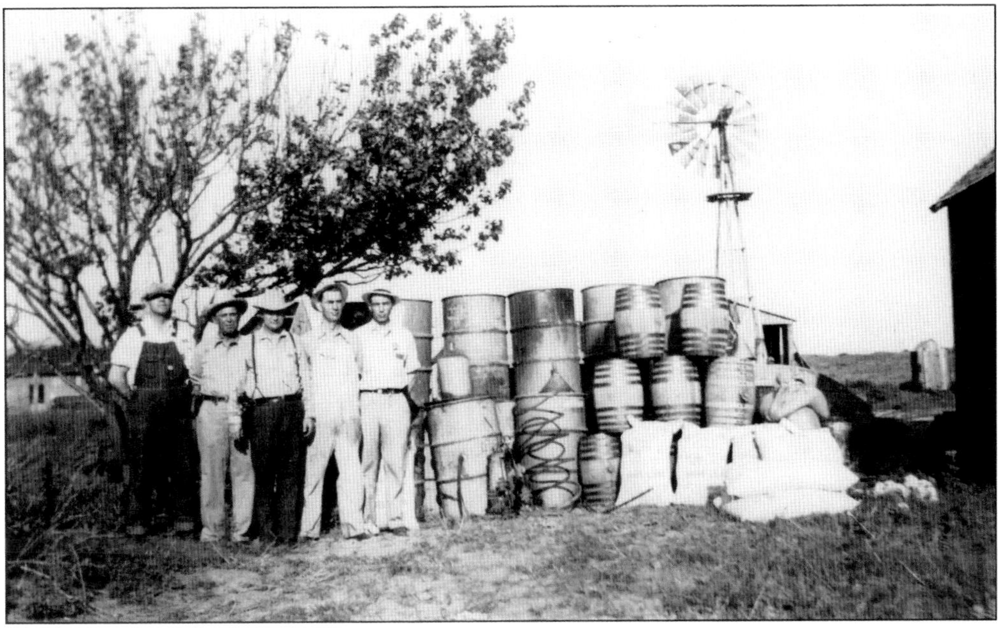

In 1937, the Woodward County Sheriff's Department raided an illegal moonshine still near Fort Supply. In this photograph, deputies stand near the materials used in the production of the whiskey.

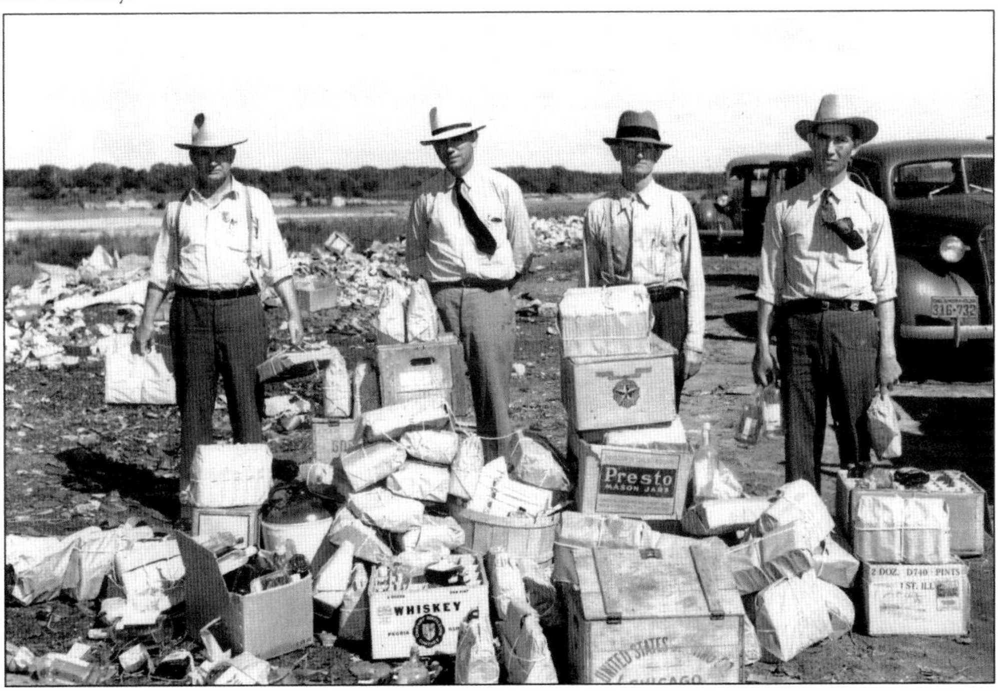

Woodward County sheriff Elmer A. Nelson stands with his deputies and some 2,000 pints of whiskey confiscated in 1937 after raiding a moonshine still in the county. The illegal booze was taken to the Woodward city dump and destroyed. "We shot 'em, threw 'em, anything to break the bottles," one of the officials said. The men in the photograph are, from left to right, undersheriff Bud Gregory, county attorney Jim Young, jailor Cliff Hayes, and Nelson.

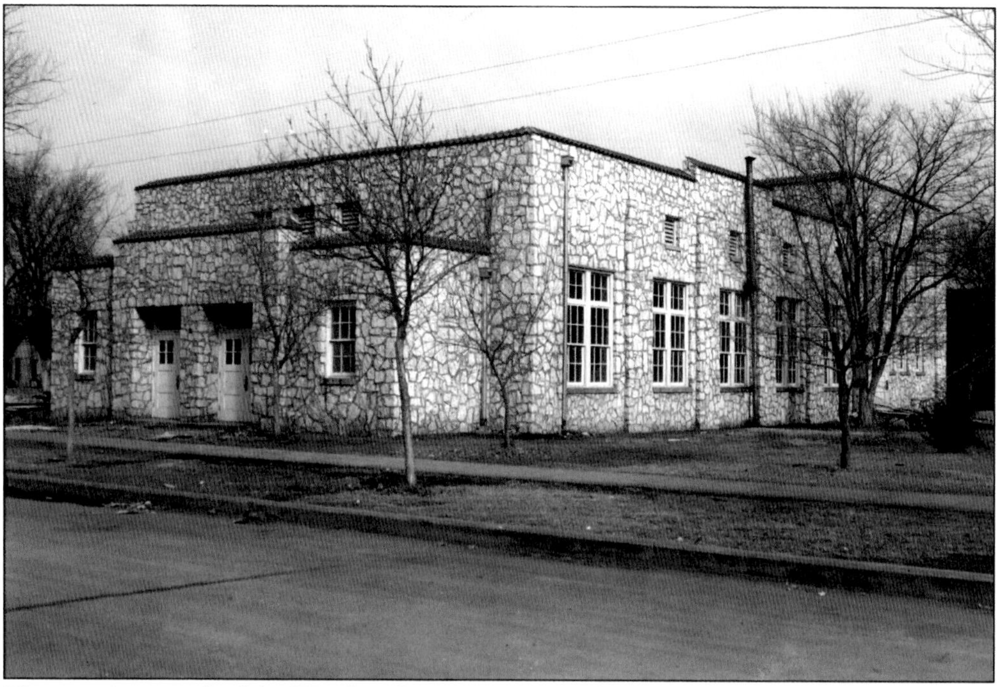

This is a photograph of the Woodward Community Building, located on Ninth Street between Texas and Oklahoma Avenues. It was built as a WPA project and was completed in 1937. It is now known as the Pioneer Room and continues to serve as a community building hosting a number of programs and receptions.

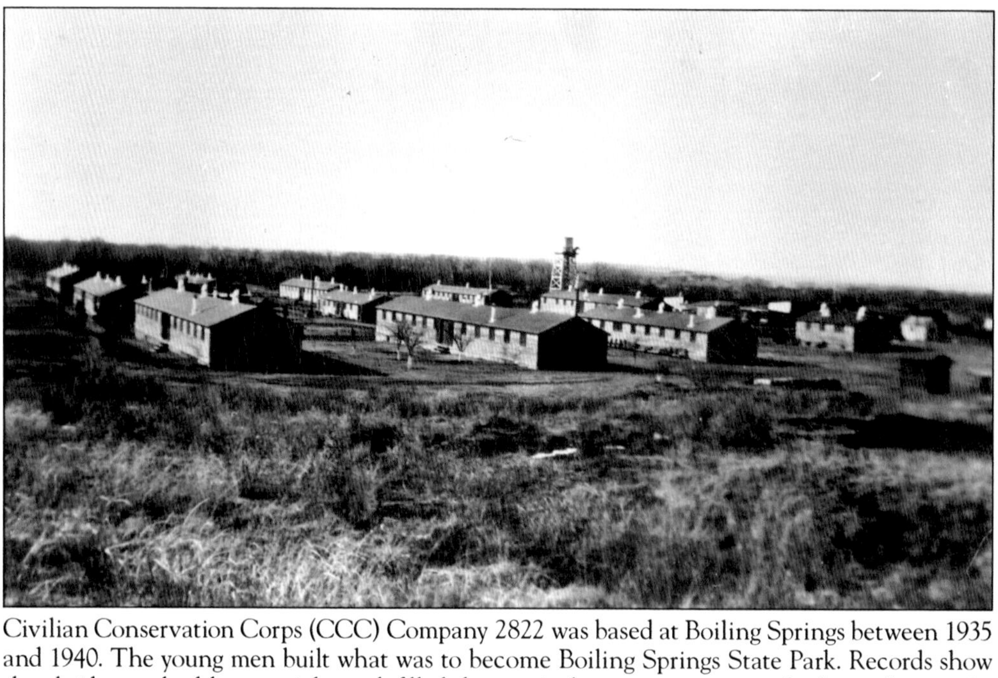

Civilian Conservation Corps (CCC) Company 2822 was based at Boiling Springs between 1935 and 1940. The young men built what was to become Boiling Springs State Park. Records show that bridges, a bathhouse, eight rock-filled dams, pipelines, water storage facilities, foot trails, and a parking facility were all constructed.

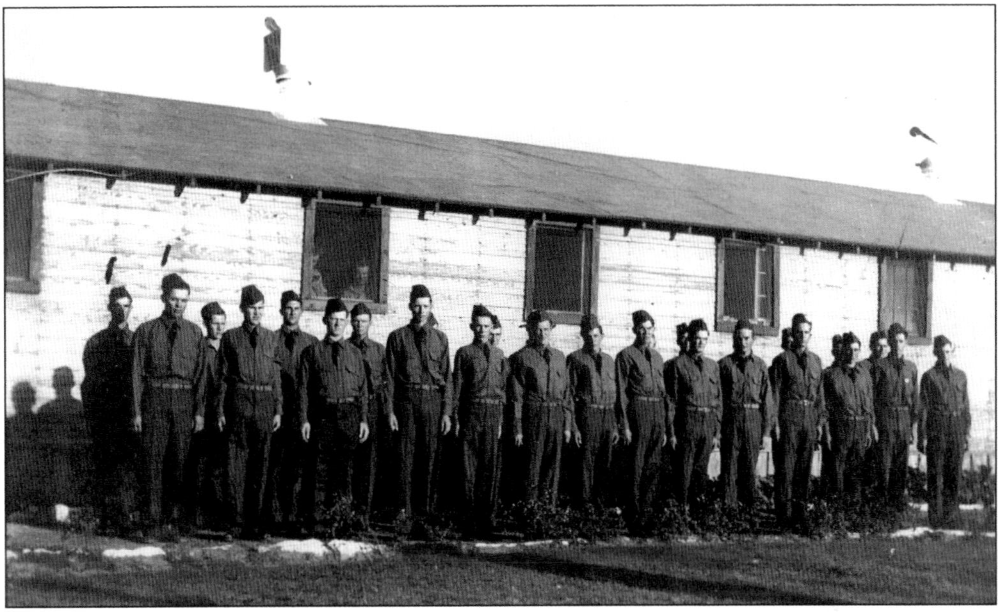

The CCC men stayed in barracks and were up at 6:00 a.m. every morning to build roads, construct a swimming pool, plant trees, crush rocks, make benches, and do everything else necessary to create a park.

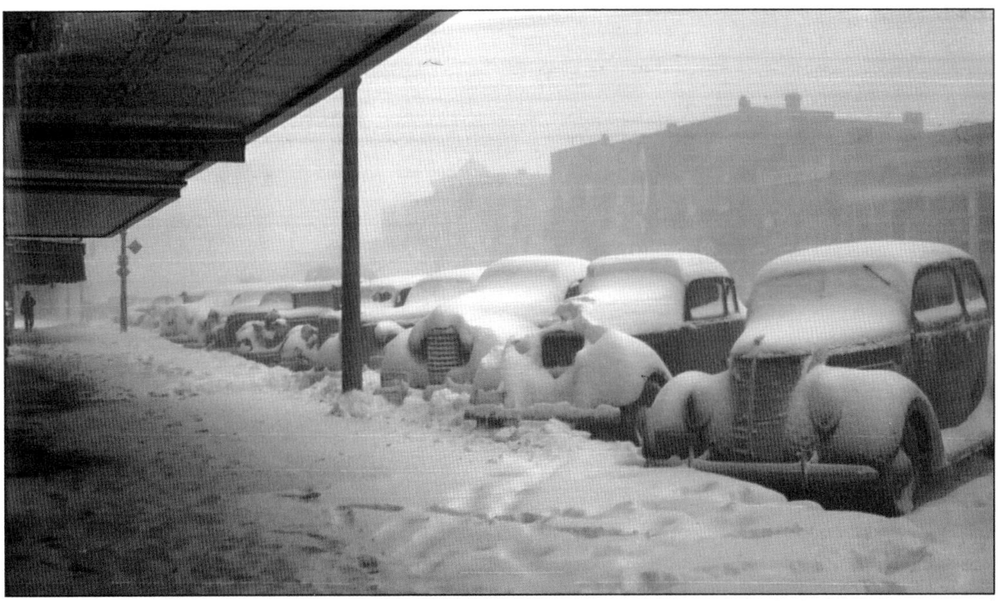

In April 1938, a rare spring blizzard hit Woodward County. This photograph shows snow-covered automobiles in downtown Woodward.

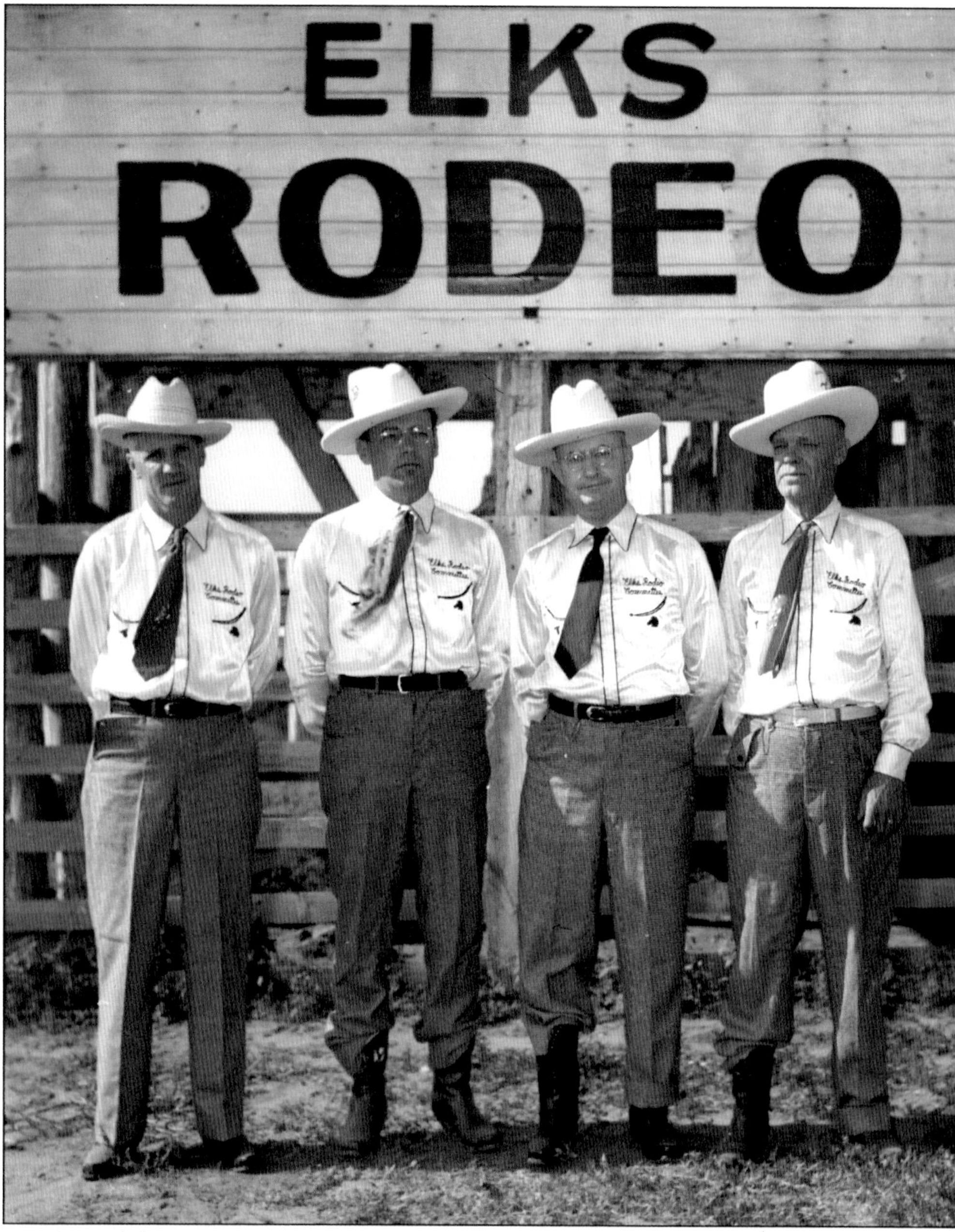

Members of the Committee for Elks Rodeo stand beneath the announcer's stand at Crystal Beach Park in 1939. From left to right are Frank Newell, Lewis Hawkins, Vince Shy, and Fred Perry. The rodeo grew in popularity during the 1930s and 1940s.

Six

THE WORLD AT WAR
1940–1946

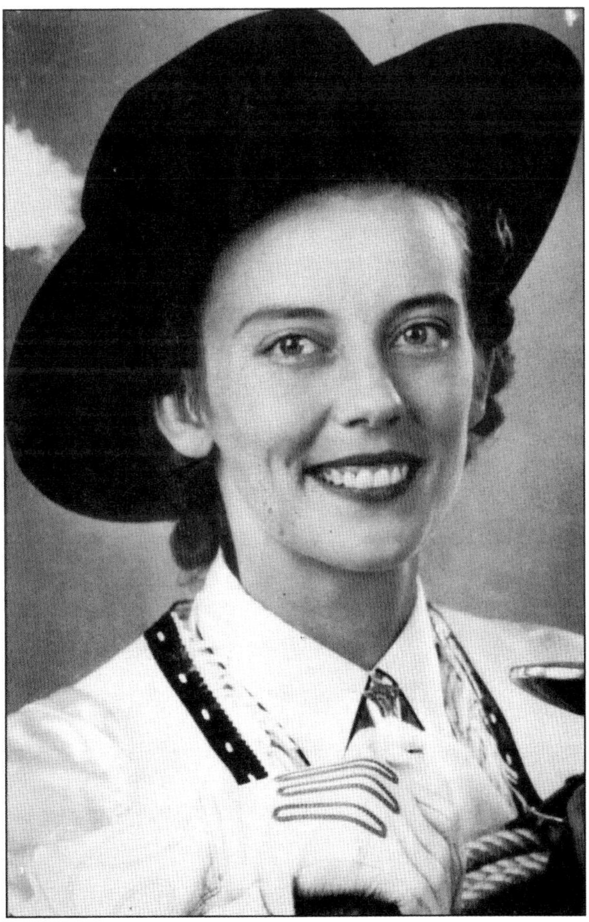

Wilma Selman, photographed here as the Woodward Elks Rodeo Queen in 1941, became queen again in 1943.

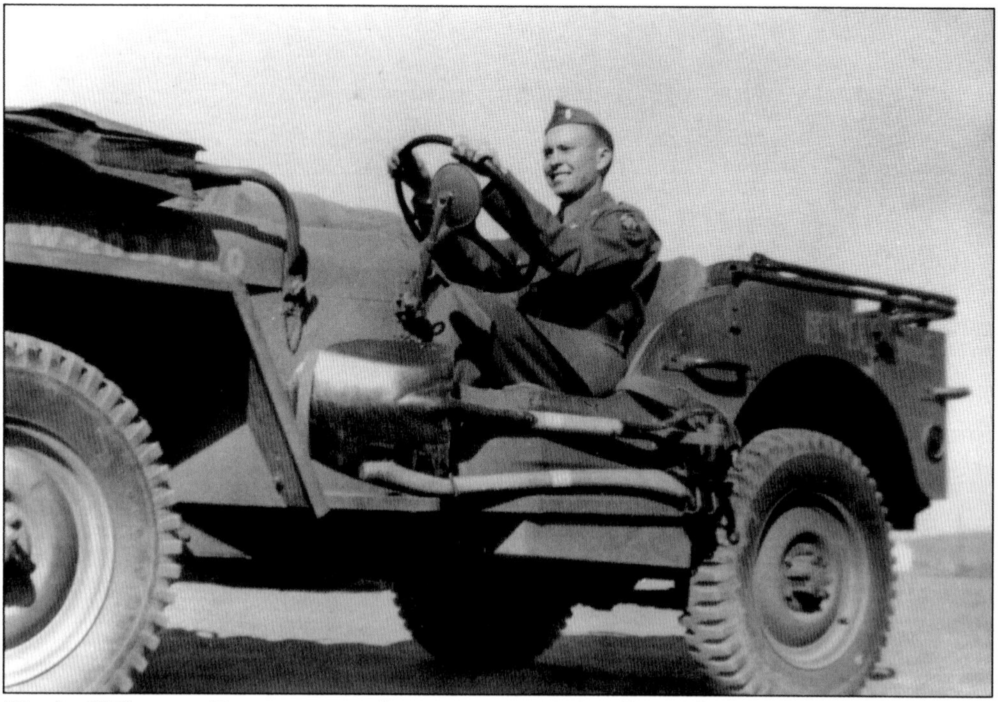

Charles Williams, a Tangier native, drives a jeep in 1942 at Fort Sill.

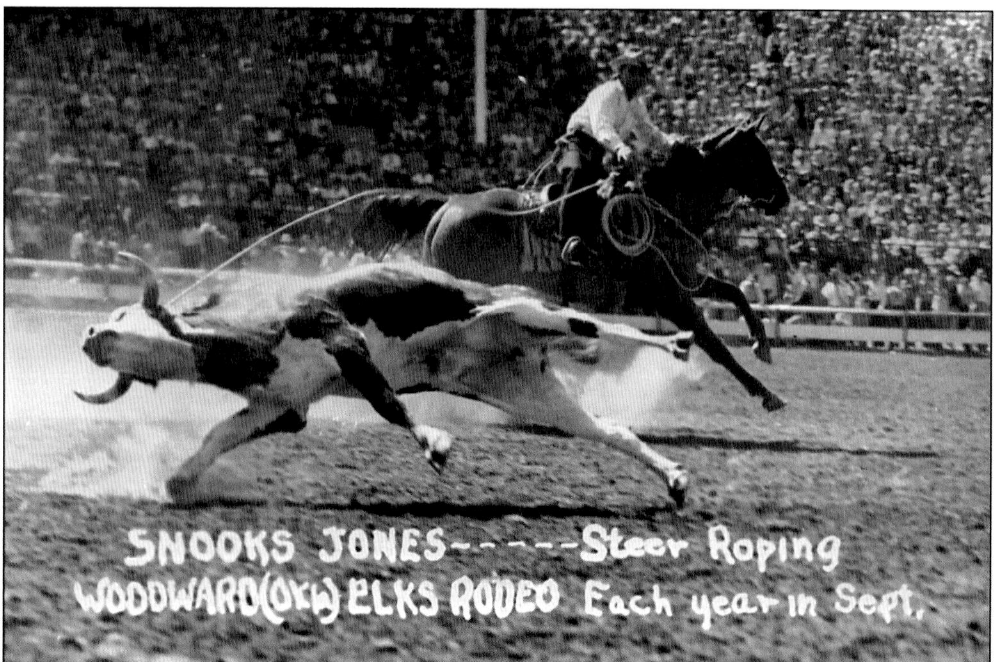

Snooks Jones takes part in the steer roping competition at the 1942 Woodward Elks Rodeo at Crystal Beach Park.

Judge James G. Young stands in military uniform with his two sons, Jim (left) and Bob.

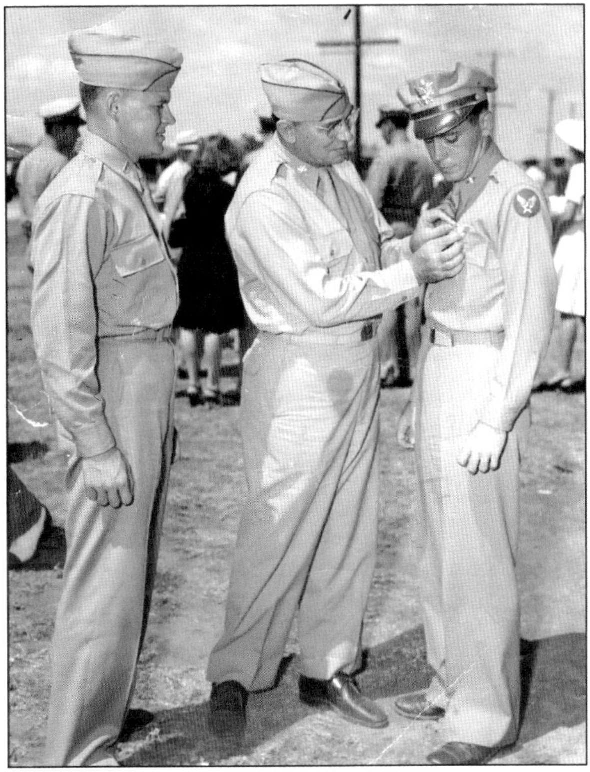

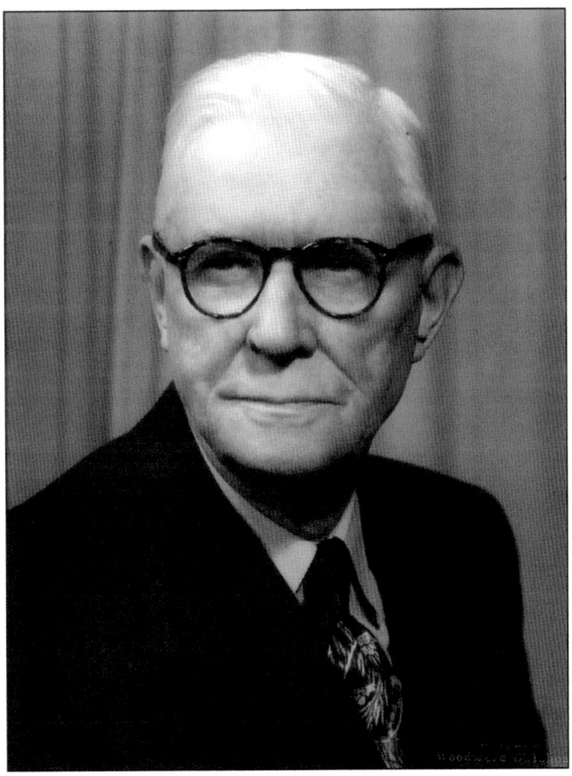

Dr. Charles W. Tedrowe, shown here in 1945, came to Woodward on November 1, 1916, and bought the small hospital. About a month after arriving in Woodward, he decided to marry his former nurse, Margaret Criswell, and sent for her by mail. She moved to Woodward to help him with the newly purchased facility. Tedrowe completed a tour of duty as an army surgeon in France during World War I. He died in Woodward in October 1967.

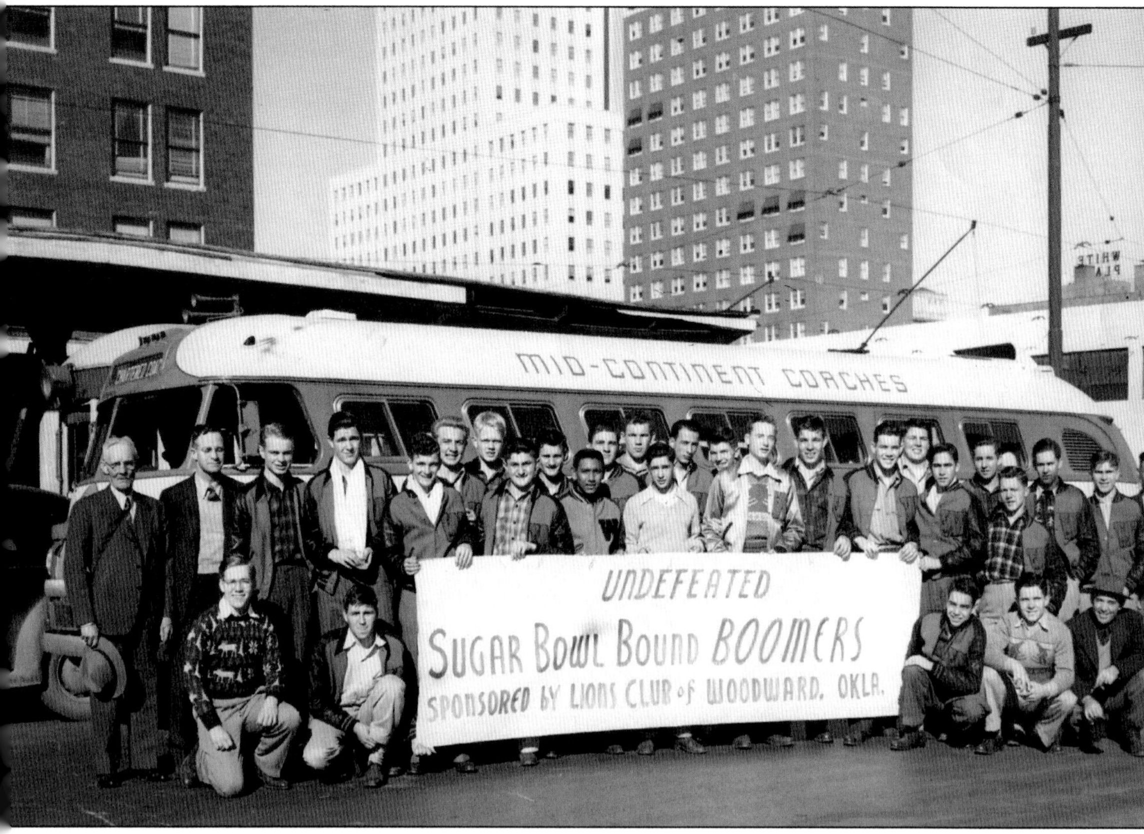

An undefeated Woodward football squad won the state title in 1945, and the Lions Club sponsored them on a trip to the Sugar Bowl. The championship was won by default after the opposing team, Wagoner, forfeited due to illness. At the Sugar Bowl, the Woodward boys watched Oklahoma A&M College beat St. Mary's College of California 33-3. Bob Fenimore, a Woodward boy, happened to be the star halfback for Oklahoma's Aggies. Fenimore, known as the "Blonde Bomber," finished third in the Heisman Trophy voting in 1945. He led the nation in rushing with 142 carries for 1,048 yards. In 1972, Fenimore was inducted into the College Football Hall of Fame. The Woodward team, from left to right, includes (first row) Mead Ferguson, Bob Barnett, Billy Joe Youngblood, Johnny Griffith, and principal Bill Russell; (second row) sponsor Bill Tullis, coach Joe Timken, Tom Duggin, Ed Terrill, Bob Mayes, Claude Beck, Bill Mancillas, Jimmy Hamlin, Mickey Brower, Jack Hyer, John Brandenburg, Raymond Coombs, and Bill Heaton; (third row) Donnie Duncan, John Hoffert, James Covalt, Evan Lucas, Donald Aurell, Leland Allen, Norman Terry, Bob Gill, Harold Lowrey, Evan Reynolds, Carl Baker, and superintendent R. R. Russell.

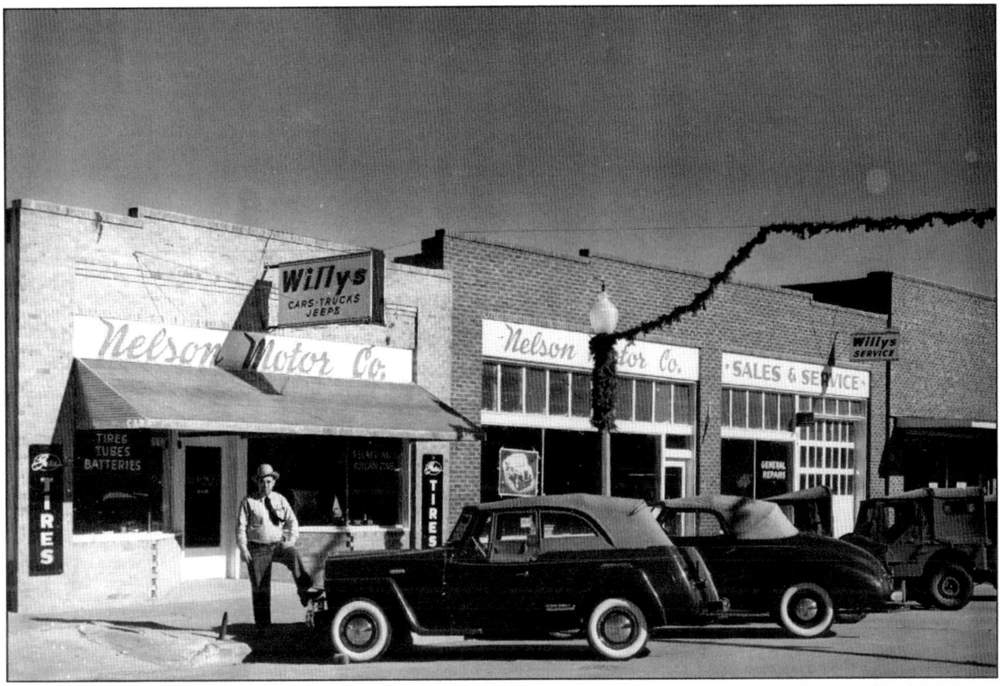

Nelson Motor Company in Woodward was located at 516 Main Avenue. Owner Earl Nelson stands in front of his business in this 1946 photograph.

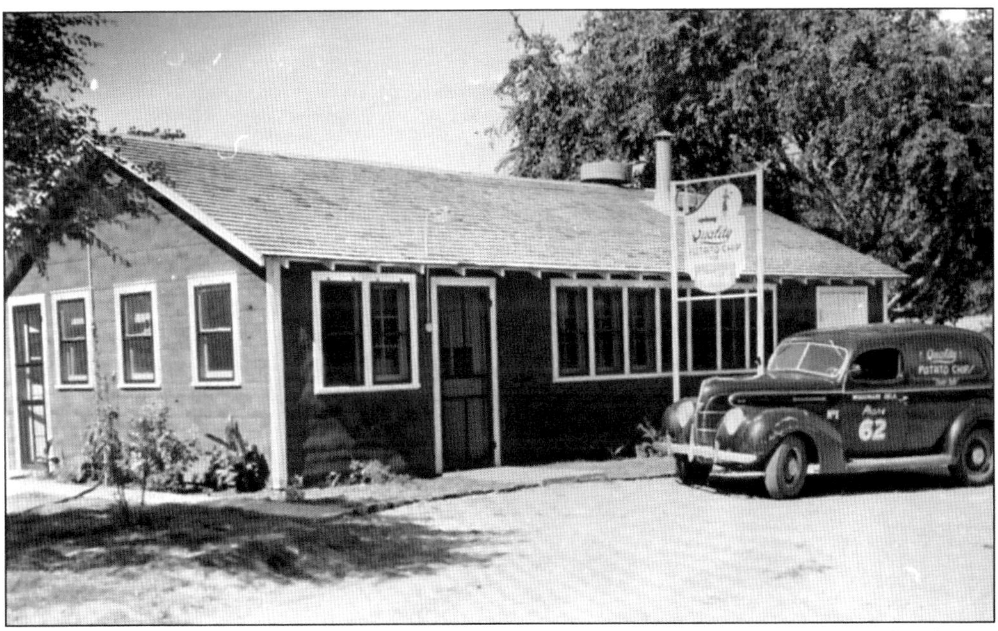

The Quality Potato Chip Company was located at 1322 Second Street in Woodward. It began production in the 1930s and closed its doors around 1960. During World War II, with potatoes, gasoline, and tires being rationed, Woodward-made potato chips were the only brand available in northwest Oklahoma. Erle Johnson worked for owners Oliver and Freda Eichman and drove a delivery route for 100 miles around Woodward.

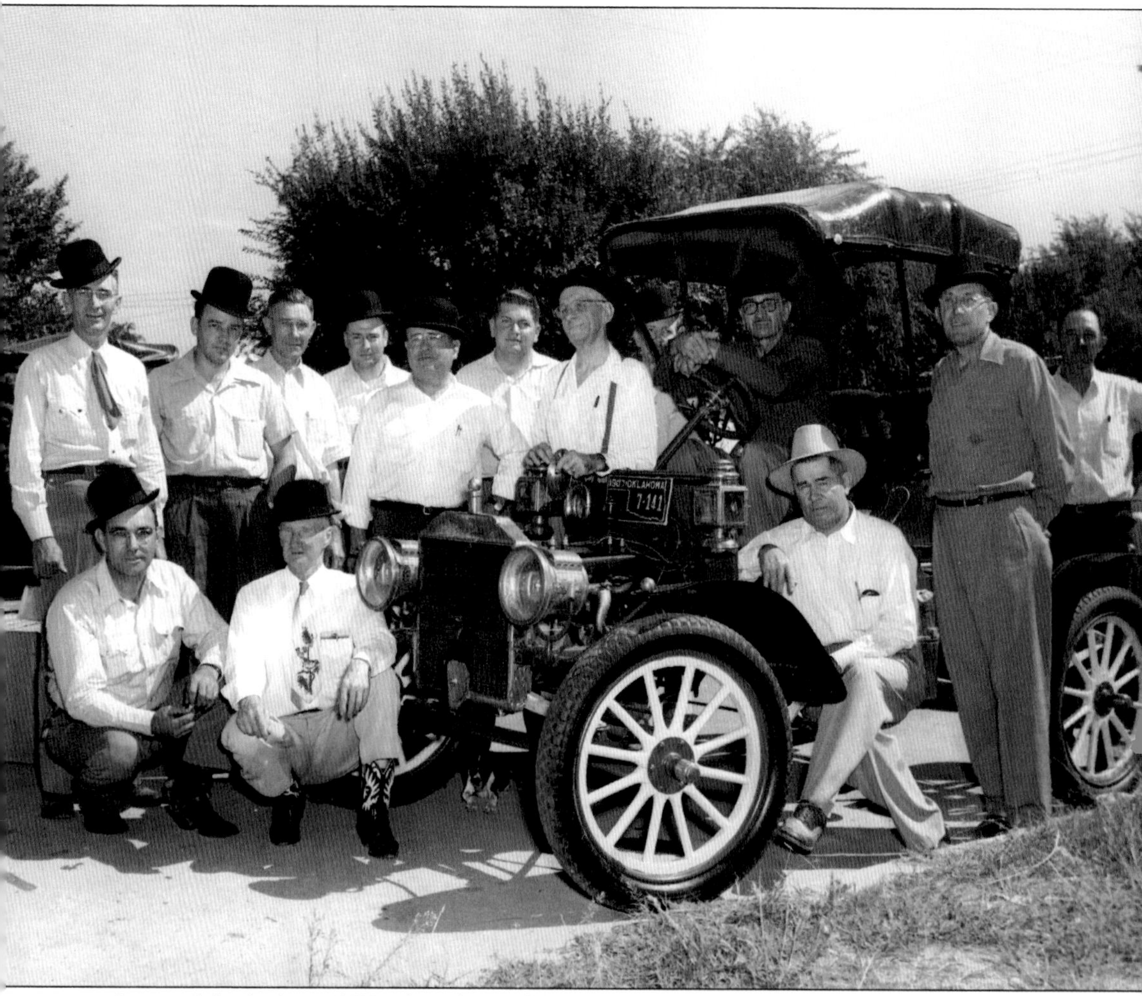

Automobile dealers of Woodward posed for this photograph in 1947. Leo "Barney" Bonifield sits in the antique automobile. From left to right are (first row) Earl Nelson, Red Anderson, Lee Wilson, and unidentified; (second row) Carl Ticer, Robert Laubhan, H. L. Belew, Pete Young, Roy French, Mr. Pierson, E. P. Williams, and unidentified.

Seven

RAGE IN HEAVEN
APRIL 1947

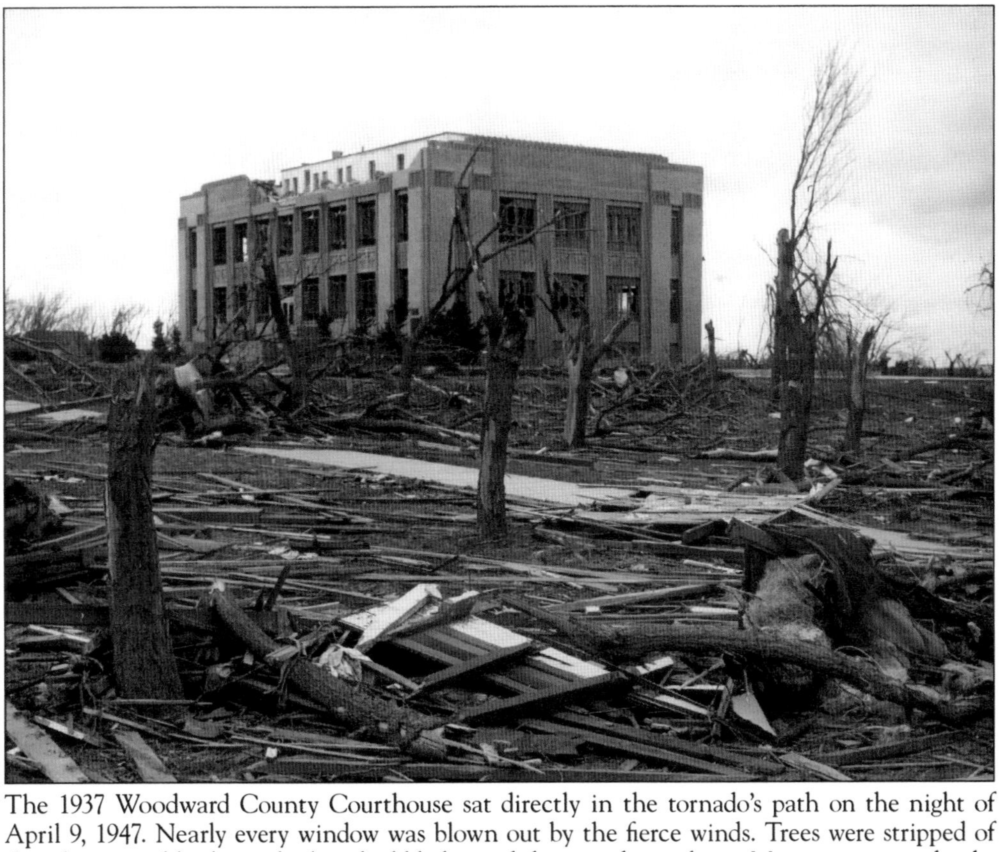

The 1937 Woodward County Courthouse sat directly in the tornado's path on the night of April 9, 1947. Nearly every window was blown out by the fierce winds. Trees were stripped of their leaves and limbs, and piles of rubble littered the courthouse lawn. Many county tax books were found on the northern bank of the North Canadian River. They were brought back and restored. Other mud-stained record books still show signs of that fateful night.

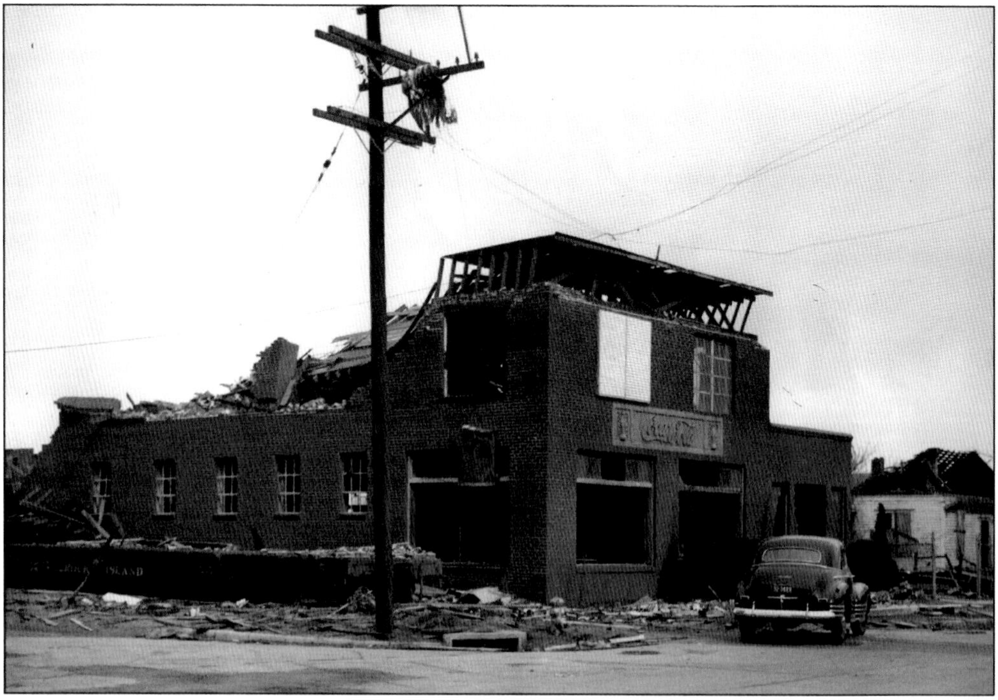

The Coca-Cola plant on Ninth Street suffered heavily from the tornado. The building was built during the first decade of the 20th century by Jeff Warren, who began his own bottle works. The front facade was salvaged, and the building continues to serve the Coca-Cola Company.

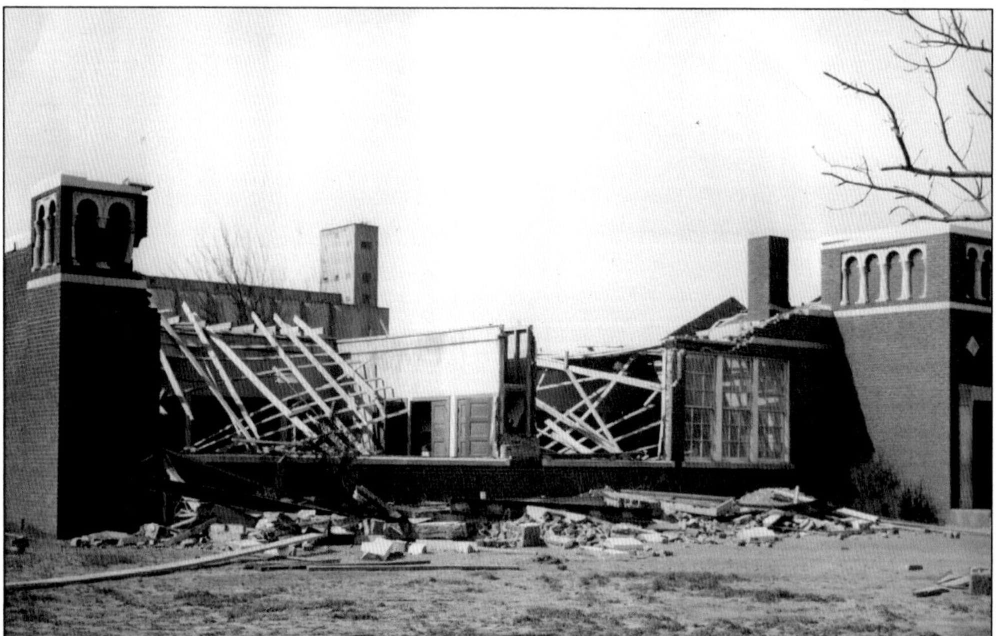

When the tornado ripped through Woodward, four schools served the city. Two were completely destroyed. Madison Park School, which lay north of the Santa Fe tracks, is shown here after the storm.

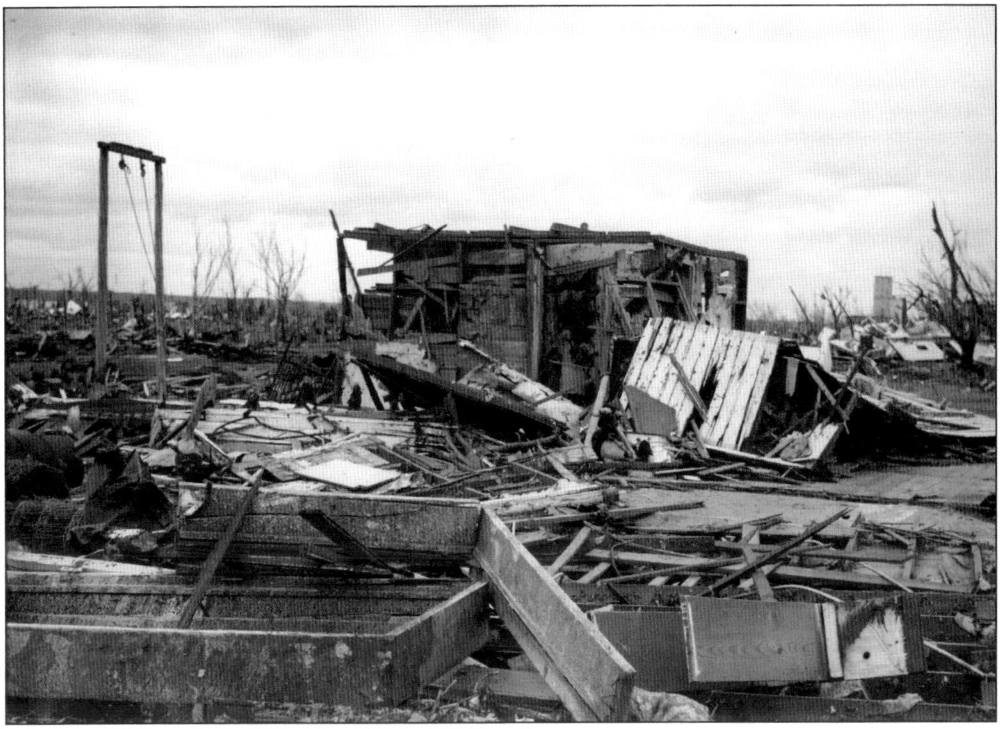

A block in the Highland Park Addition was reduced to this pile of rubble. The exact location of this photograph is unknown.

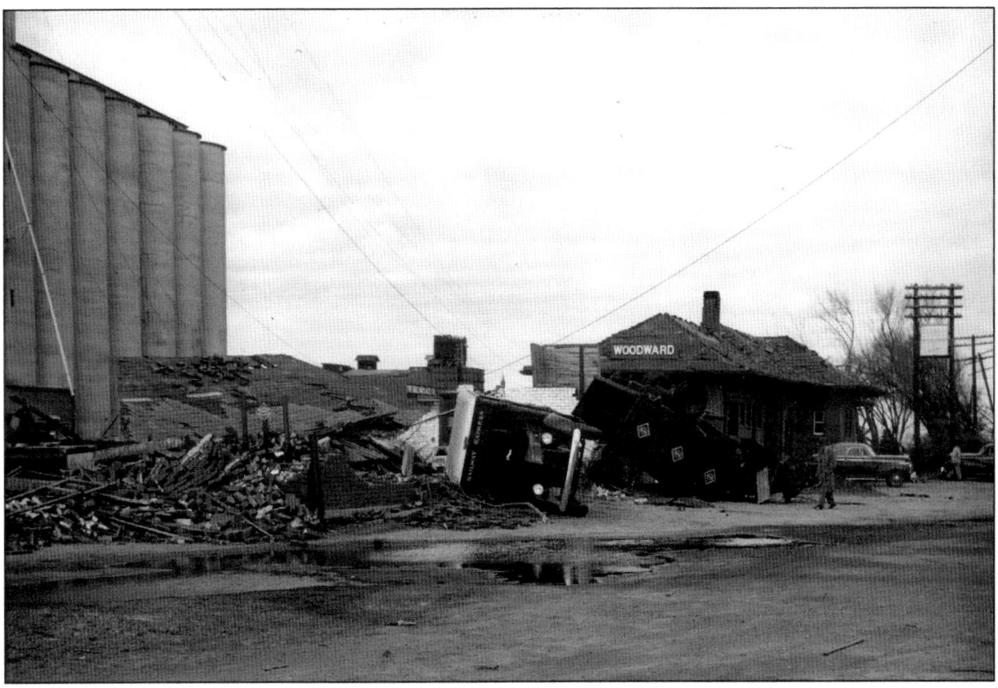

This is how the Santa Fe depot on Ninth Street appeared after the storm. The Fisher Grain elevators, however, withstood the fierce winds. The depot was torn down during cleanup efforts.

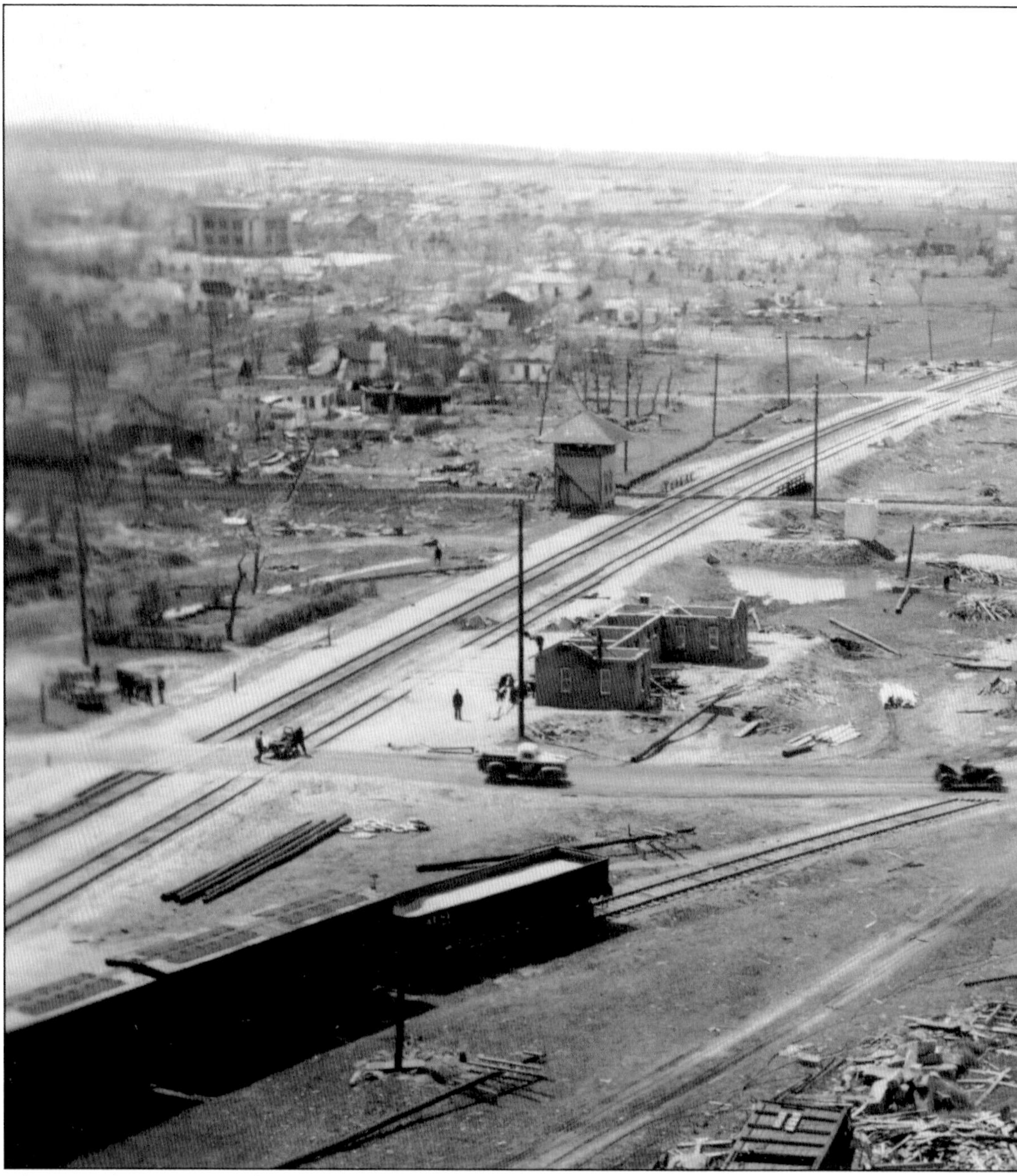

This aerial view was taken from the top of the Fisher Grain elevator looking to the west along the Santa Fe tracks. The Woodward County Courthouse is visible in the top left

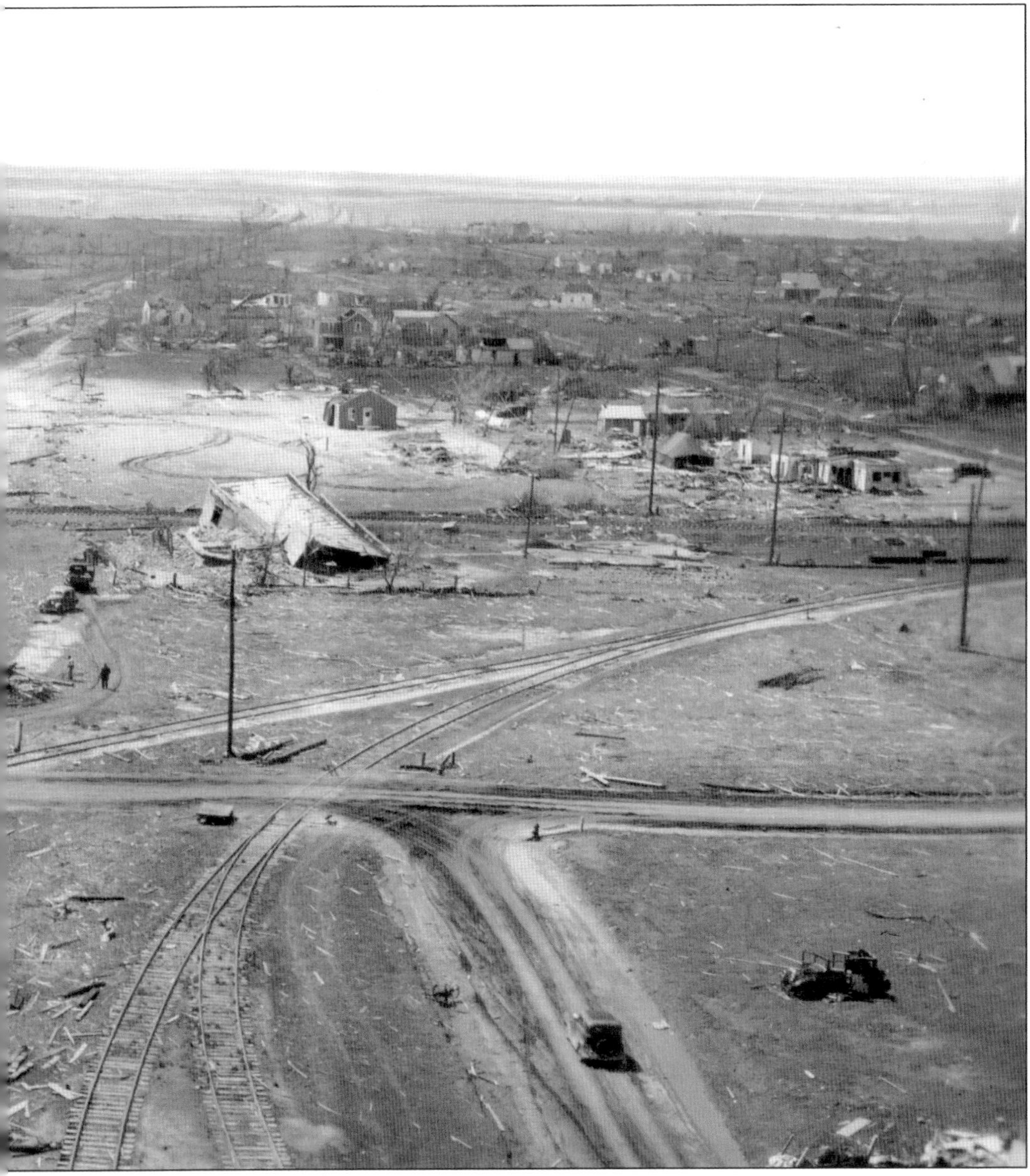

portion of the photograph.

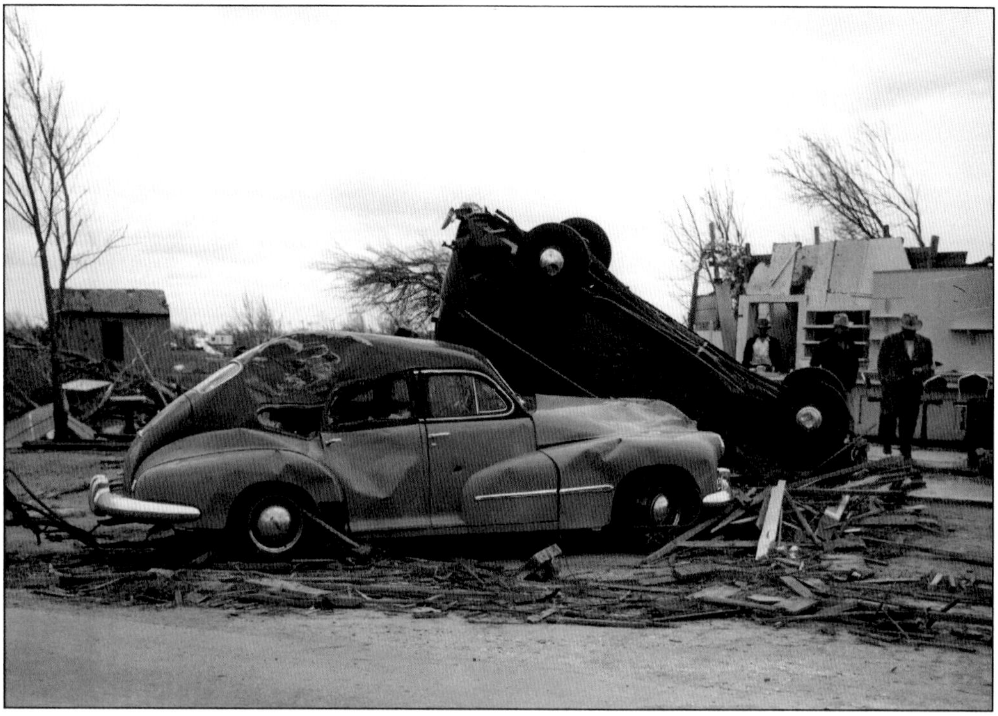

Automobiles were thrown around like tumbleweeds when the tornado hit Woodward. These two cars landed in a pile in the Highland Park Addition.

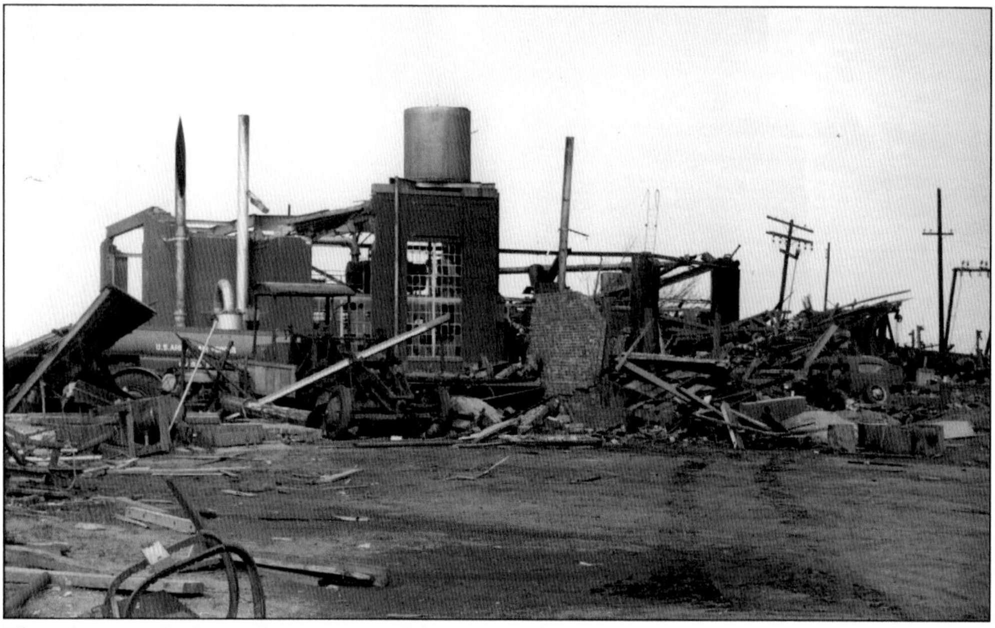

This photograph shows the remains of the power plant in Woodward. Erwin Vincent Walker, longtime manager of the plant, did not normally work nights, but as a favor to a Mr. Millard, he worked the night of April 9, 1947. He threw the master switch so downed power lines would be dead. Without his heroic efforts, severed electric lines most likely would have started fires across the already ruined city.

Walker is photographed here in about 1945. There were many heroes that night; however, Walker saved countless lives by shutting off power to the city. He sacrificed his own life for the lives of his fellow citizens.

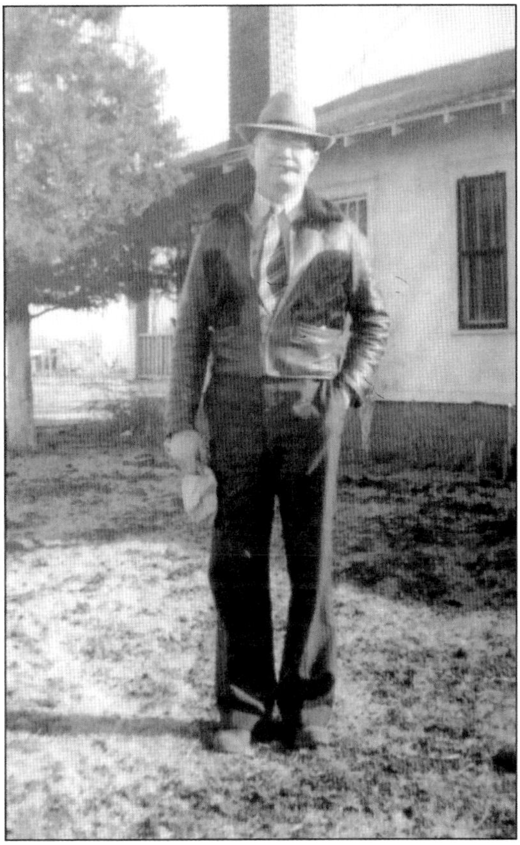

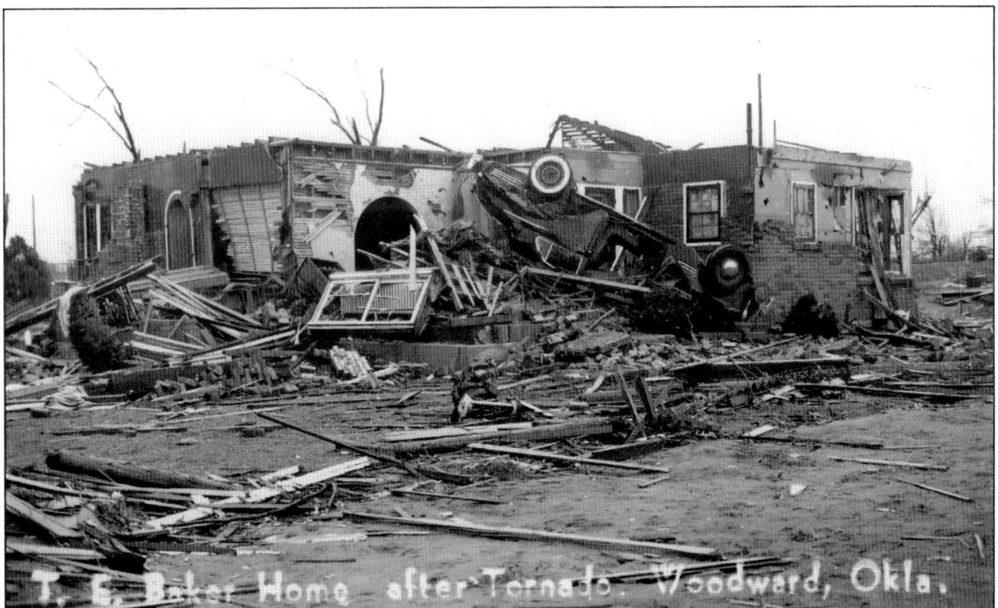

The home of T. E. Baker, proprietor of the Baker Hotel, sat on the corner of Seventeenth Street and Main Avenue. It was rebuilt after the storm and is now a law office.

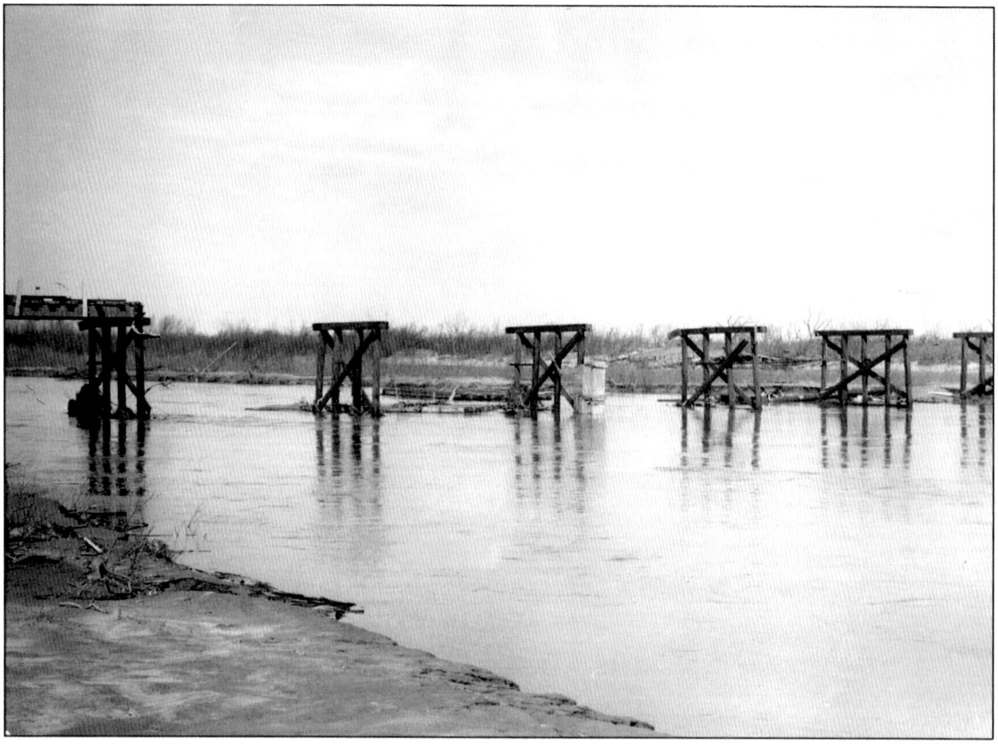

The tornado continued across Woodward heading northeast. When it crossed the North Canadian River on the edge of town, it took the bridge with it. With the bridge out, those wanting to travel in or out of Woodward had to go miles out of the way to get across the river.

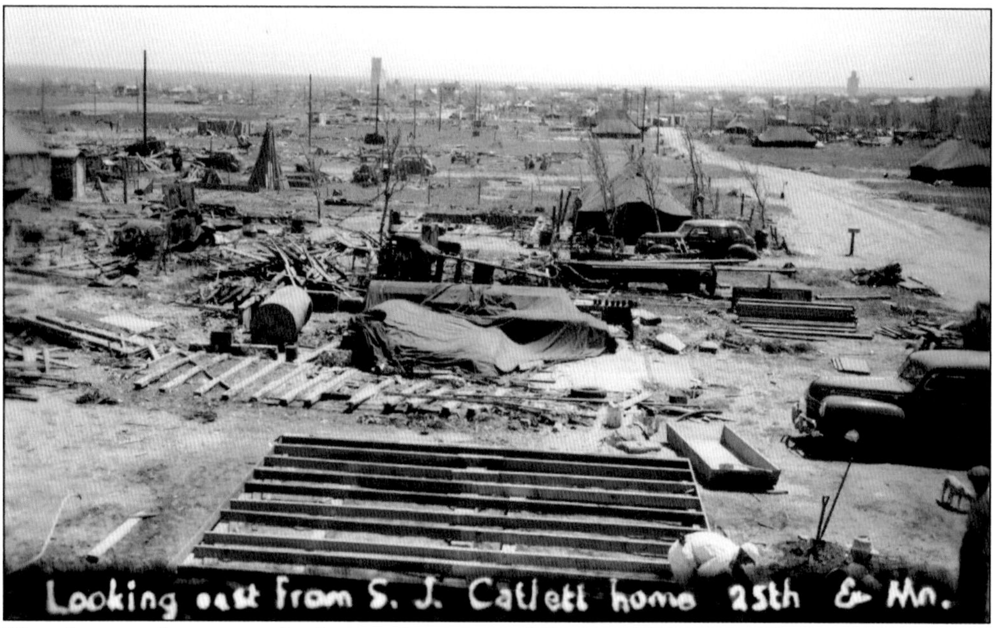

This photographic postcard, taken at the corner of Twenty-fifth Street and Main Avenue, looks to the east toward downtown. The large tents in the photograph were brought in by the Red Cross to serve as temporary homes.

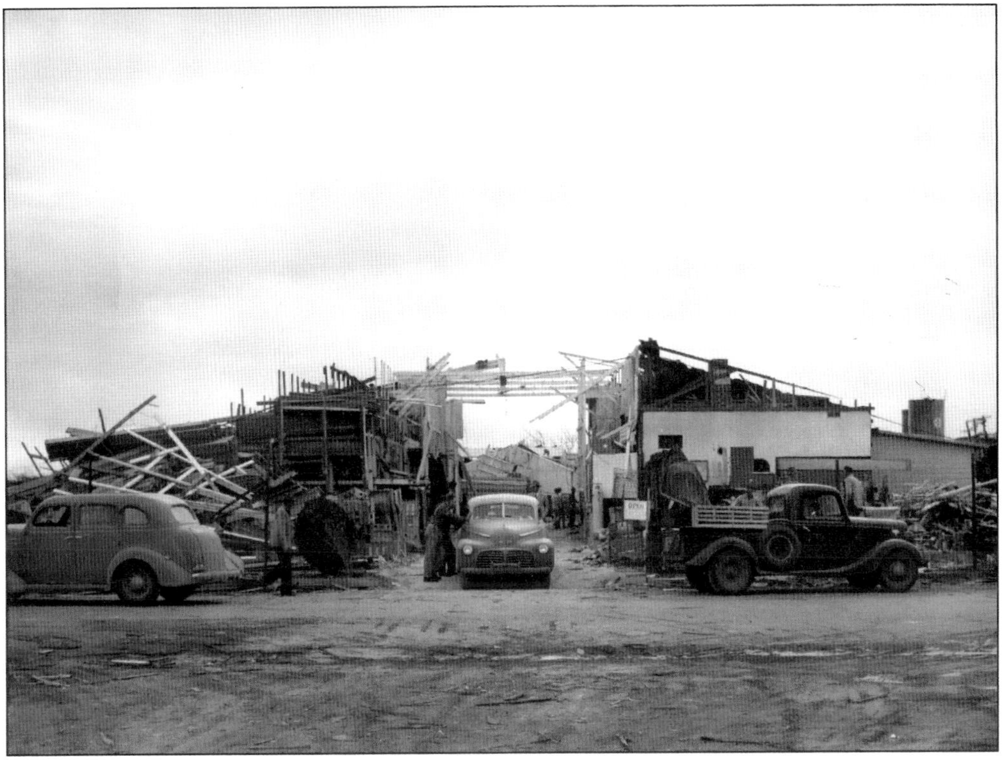

Woodward photographer Everett McDonald documented the destruction of the storm with his camera. This photograph shows what remained of the Osborne-Peebles Lumber Yard, which sat at 821 Eighth Street.

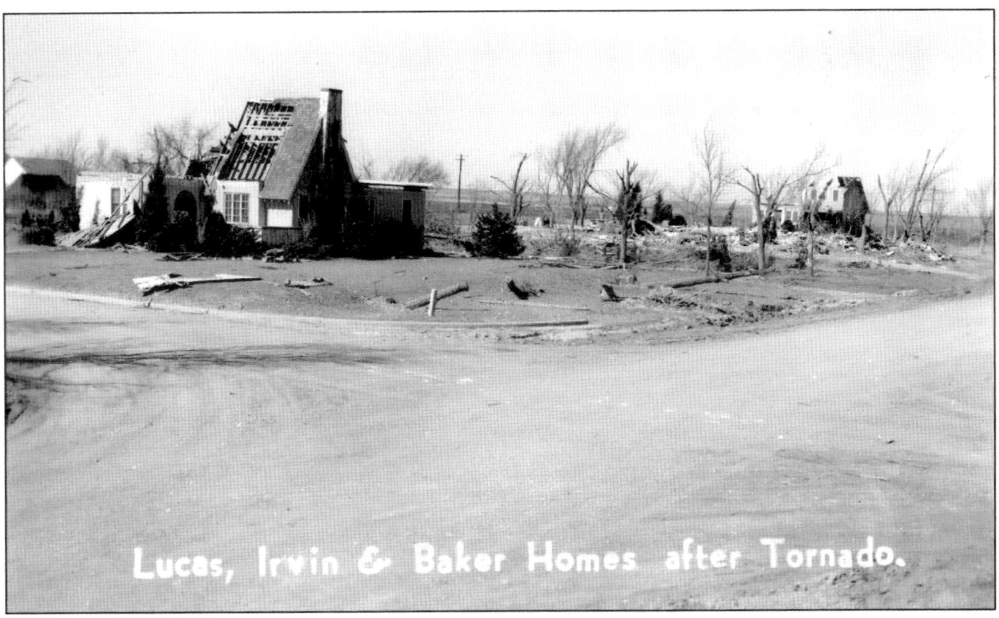

McDonald labeled this photograph, "Lucas, Irvin & Baker Homes after Tornado." This block has not been identified with addresses.

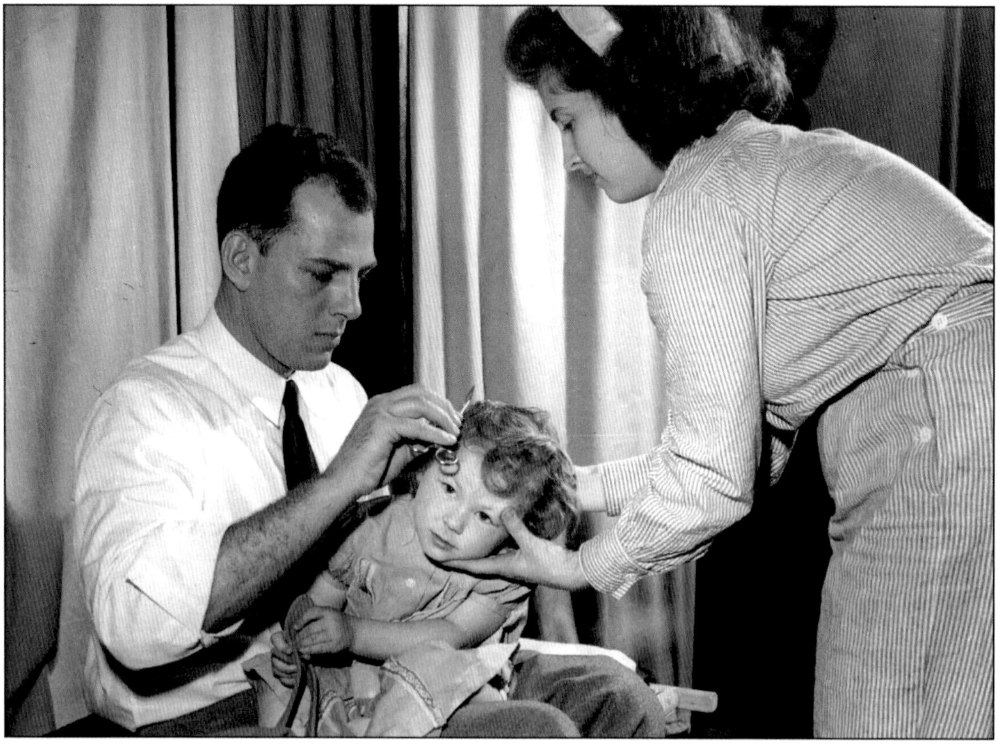

Dr. E. H. Arrendall of Ponca City is assisted by Mrs. A. C. Cuppy of Enid in this photograph. They treat scalp abrasions of Lucille Crouse, a young tornado victim.

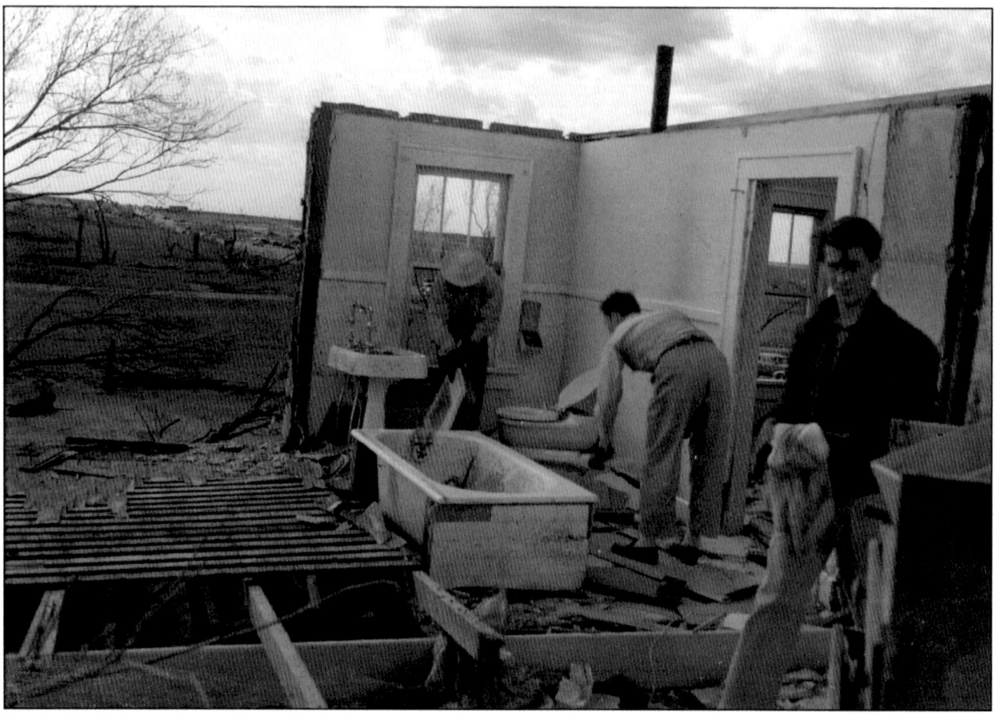

An unidentified family cleans up the rubble that once was a home.

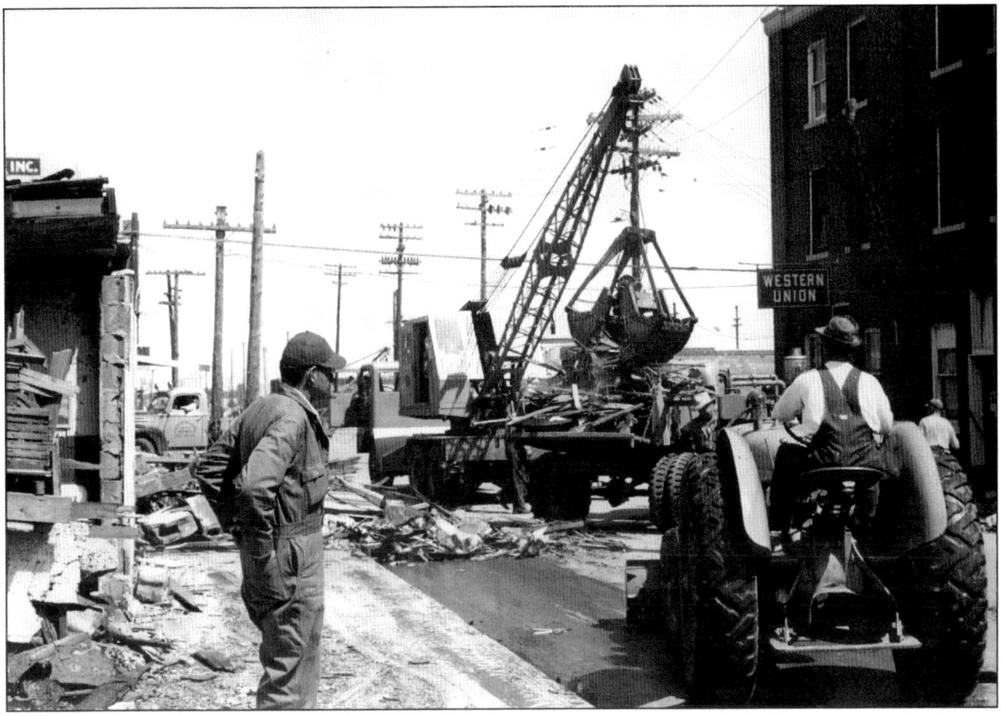

In this photograph, the Oklahoma Highway Department clears Eighth Street near the Baker Hotel in downtown Woodward.

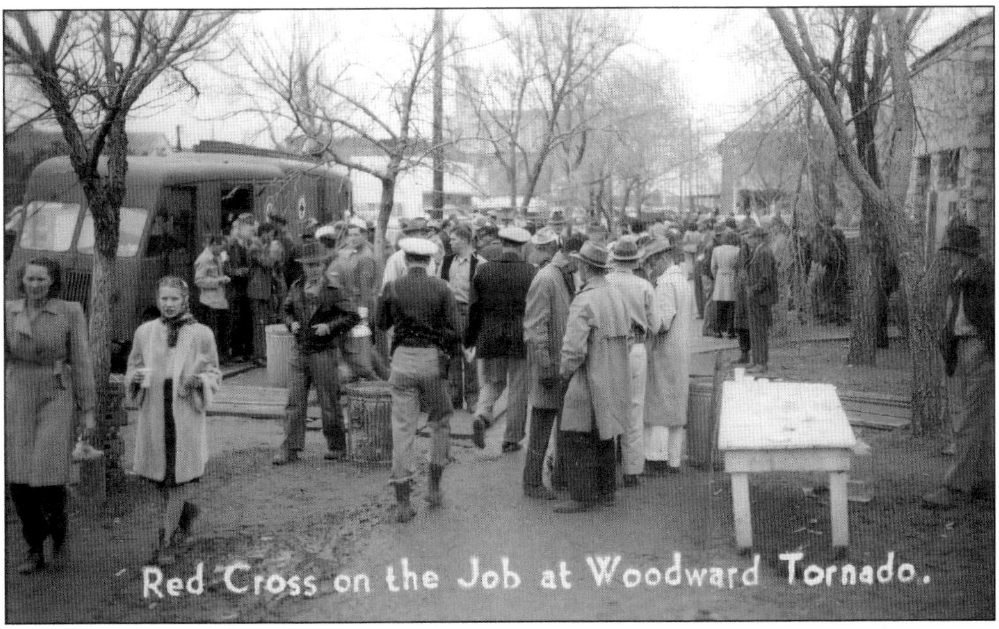

Woodward received much help from the Red Cross. Food lines were set up in what is now Centennial Park, where residents and volunteers could eat for free. Blankets, clothing, toiletries, and other necessities were given to those in need. The Red Cross also converted an old air base west of Woodward into a temporary village, where the homeless could have places to live until homes were rebuilt.

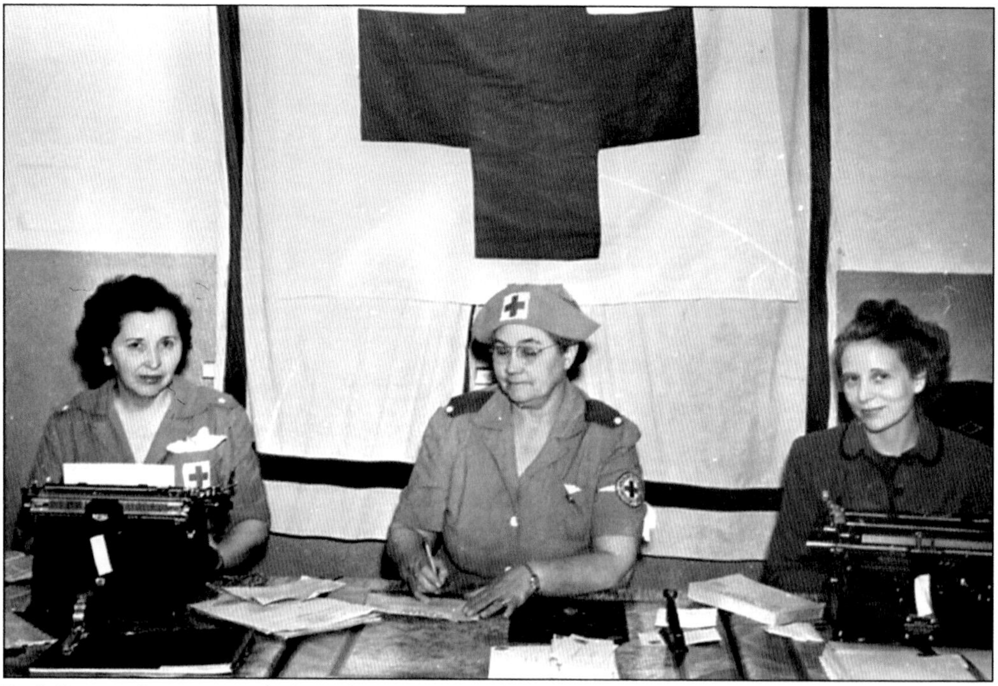

Red Cross volunteers, including Anna Lorry Williams (center), helped Woodward citizens after the tornado destroyed their homes.

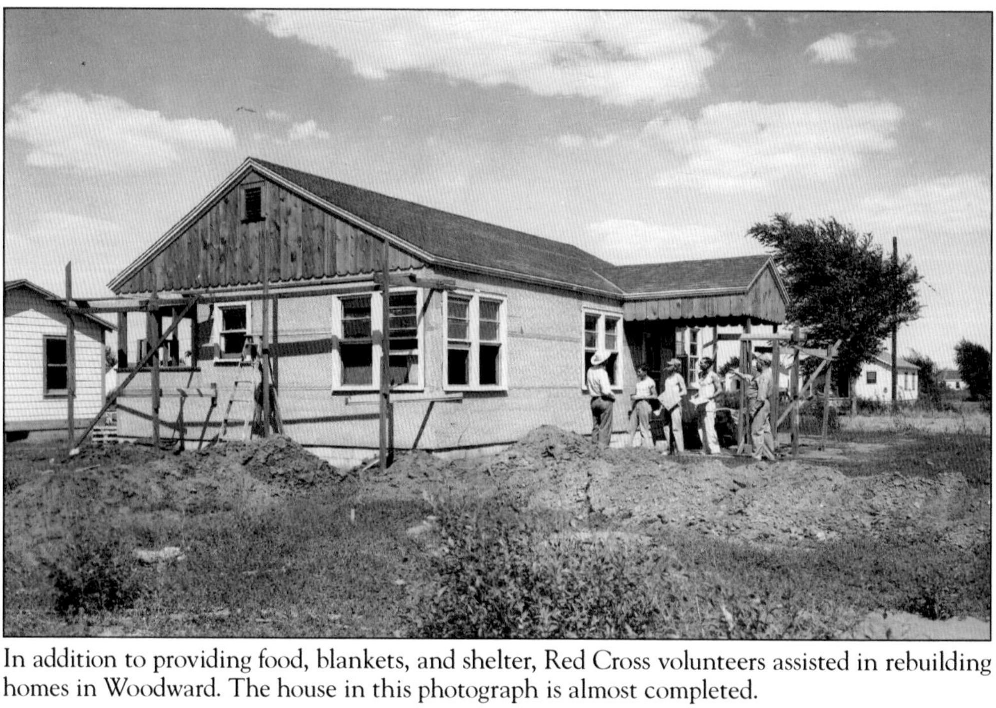

In addition to providing food, blankets, and shelter, Red Cross volunteers assisted in rebuilding homes in Woodward. The house in this photograph is almost completed.

Eight

Plenty of Heart, Plenty of Hope 1948–1960

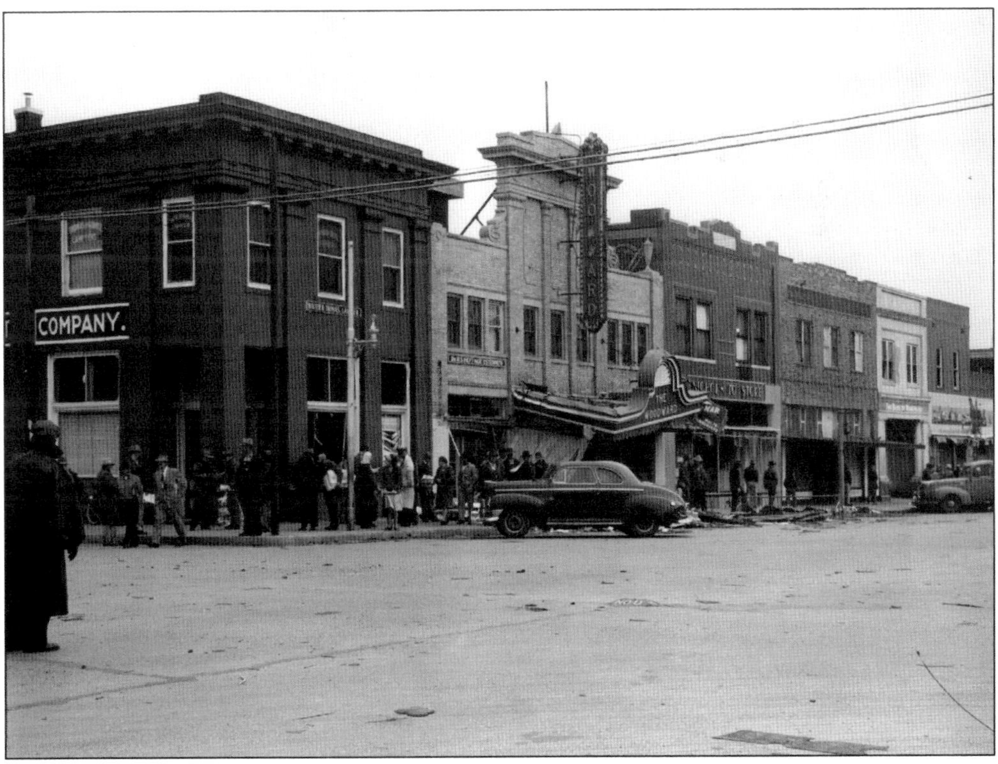

The 800 block of Main Avenue is shown here with the Woodward Theatre in the foreground. The theater's marquee was damaged and replaced.

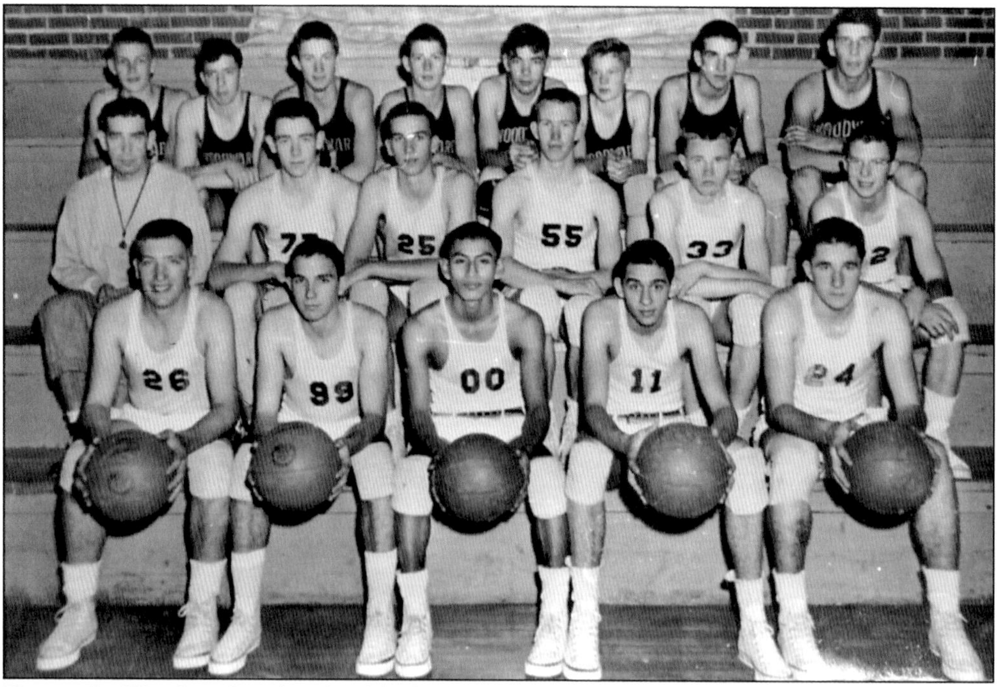

Here is the Woodward High School basketball team in 1949.

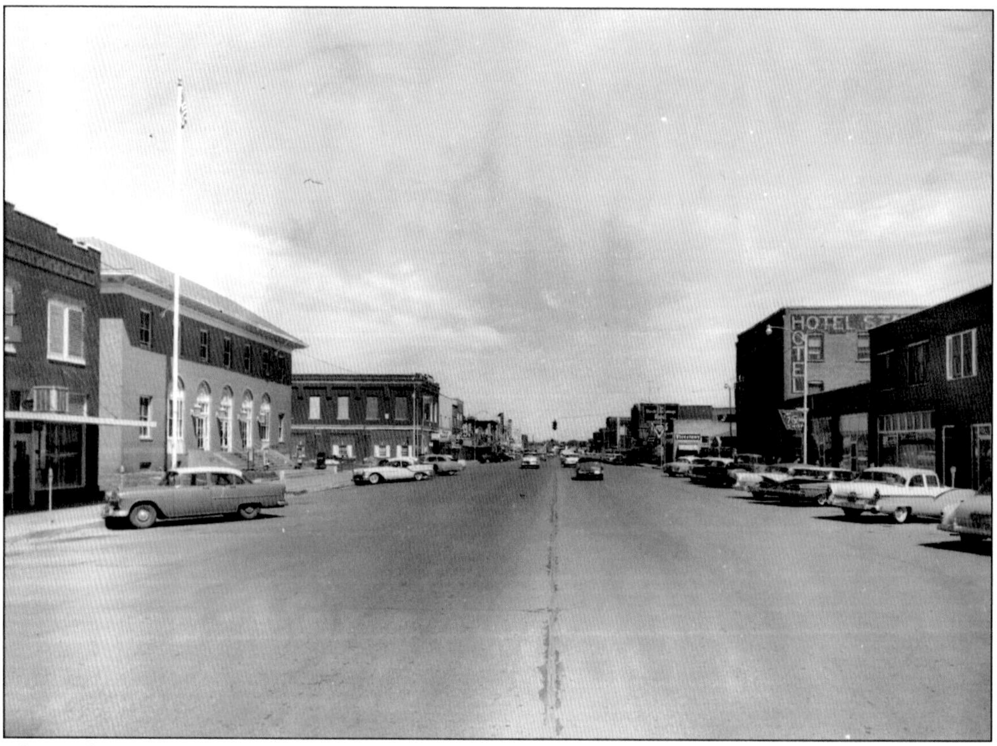

This is downtown Woodward around 1960. The photograph is looking east on Main Avenue.

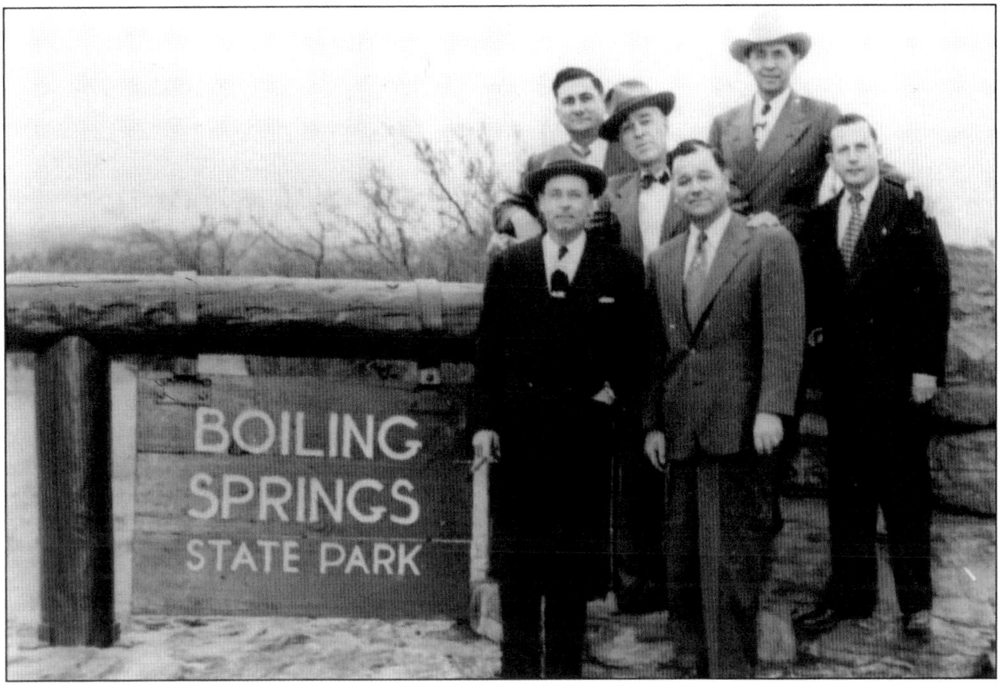

An appropriations subcommittee of the Oklahoma legislature visited Boiling Springs soon after it became a state park. From left to right are (first row) Ellis County representative A. R. Bert Larason, Sen. Ben Easterly, and Woodward Chamber of Commerce president Franklin Stecher; (second row) Jim Cook, Sen. Virgil Young, and Woodward County representative J. Don Williams.

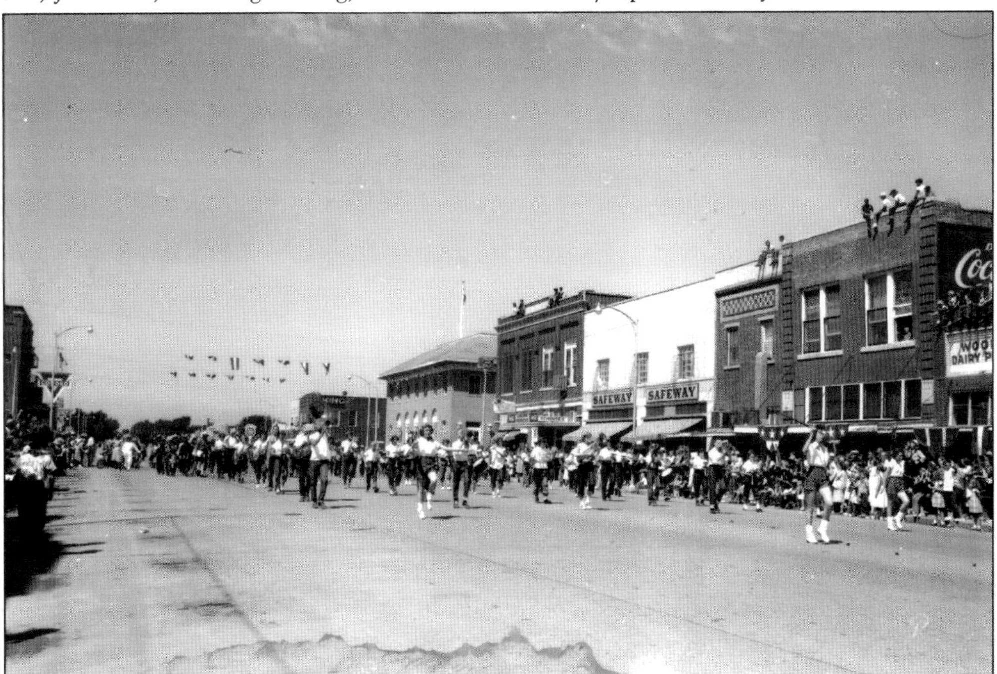

The Elks rodeo parade has been a tradition in the county seat for many years. This photograph of the 900 block of Main Avenue was taken during the 1950s by Everett McDonald.

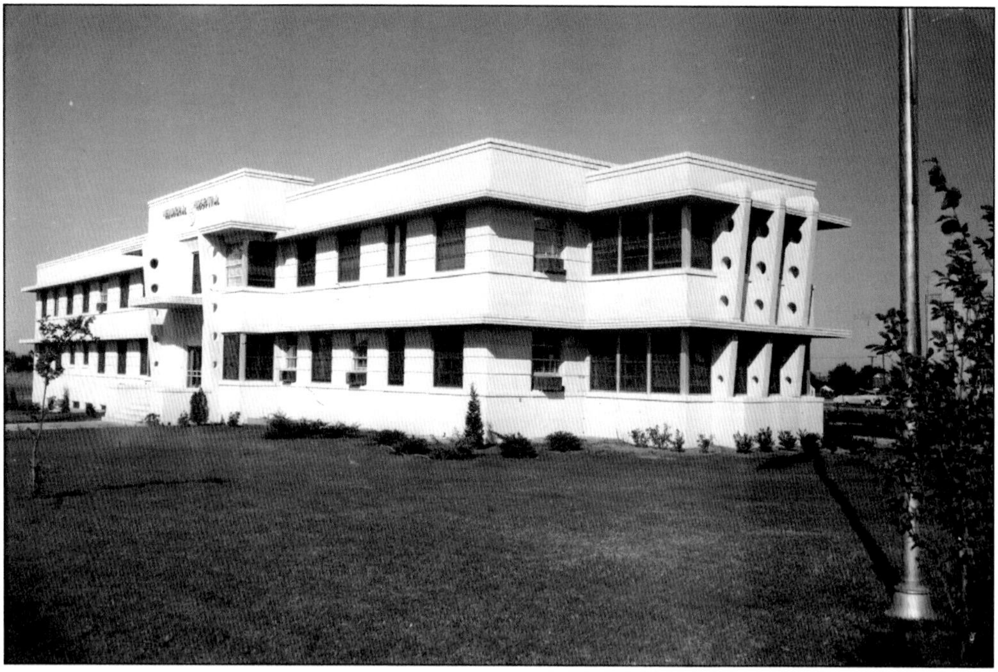

Woodward's Memorial Hospital was built in 1952. It is located on the Courthouse Square on the corner of Seventeenth Street and Main Avenue. Above the front door was a plaque reading "Dedicated to serve humanity with God's help." A modern addition was added to the north of the hospital in 1984.

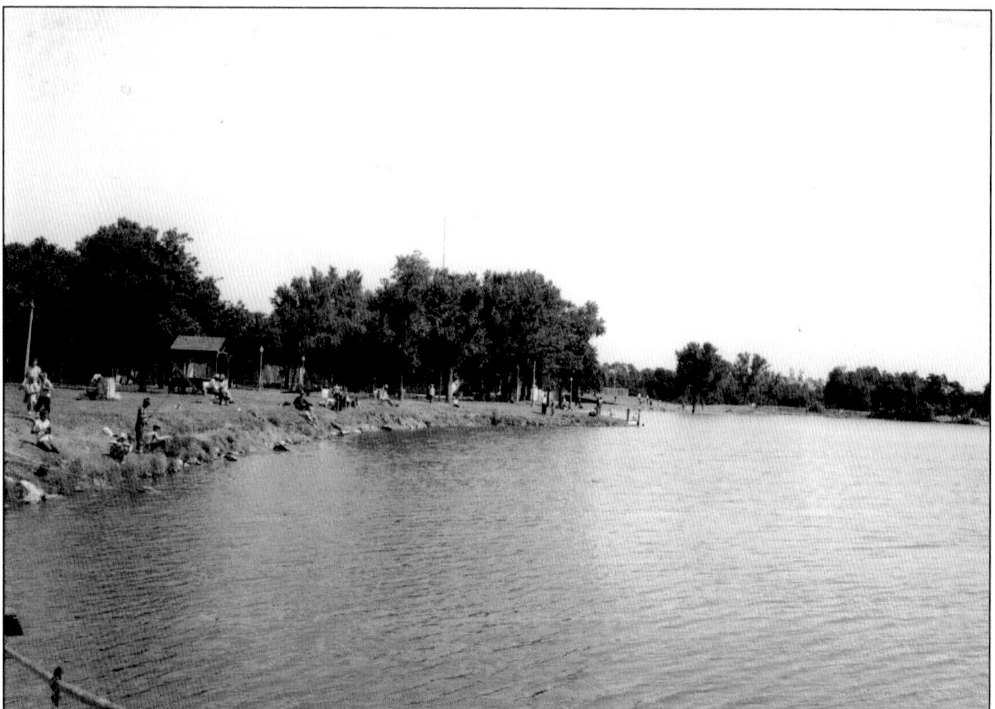

Along the western edge of Crystal Beach Lake, children of all ages go fishing.

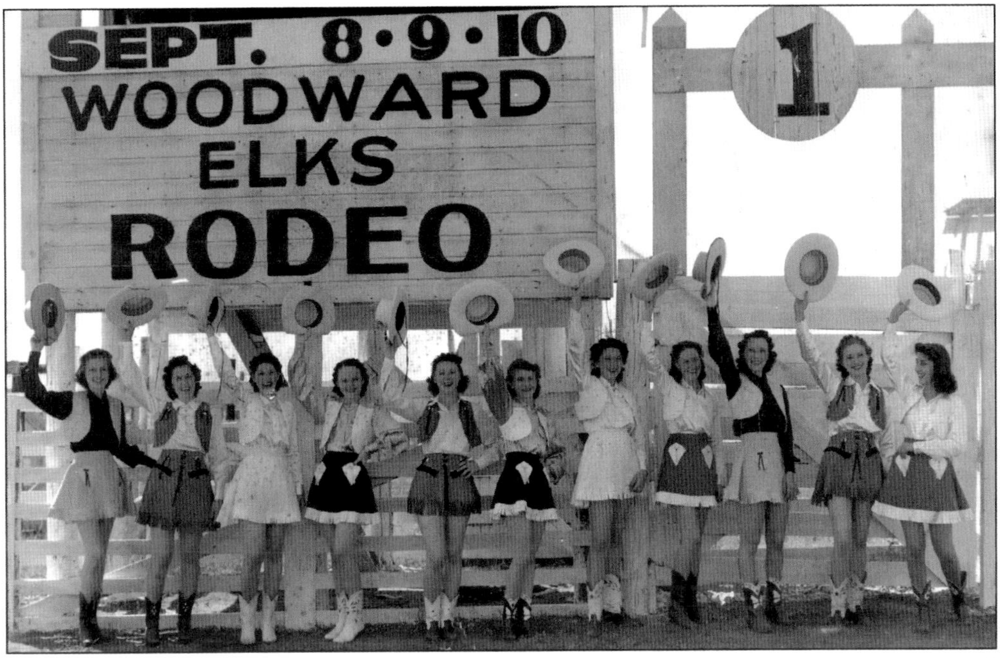

Woodward Elks Rodeo Queens, from left to right, are Alta Jane Williams Davis, Leora Russell Nichols, Delores ?, Mary Ellen Oats Trego, Helen Street Clark Berry, Jeanette Nashelshy, Patsy Blake Bogdhan, Lee Ann Lawrence, unidentified, Virginia Martin Mundell, and Willa Lee Van Devander Laubhan.

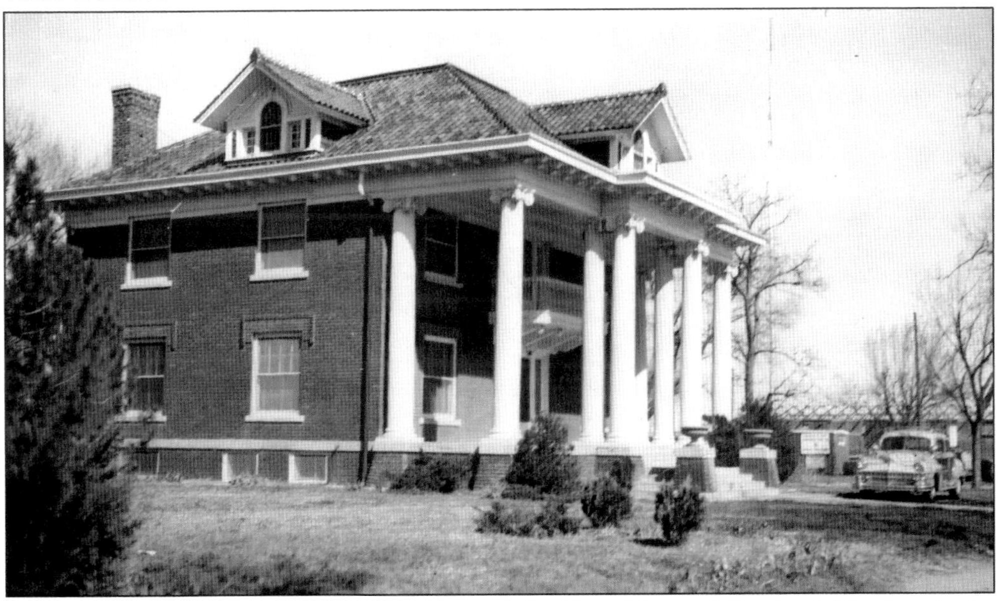
Built in 1916 by Len L. Stine, the owner of the First National Bank of Woodward, the Stine-Bradbury Mansion remains one of Woodward's finest dwellings. The home was bought by the Harold Bradbury family in the 1930s, and they owned it until 1994. It is now owned by the Great Plains Preservation and Development Foundation and is used as a venue for receptions, weddings, and other community events. It is Woodward's only home on the National Register of Historic Places.

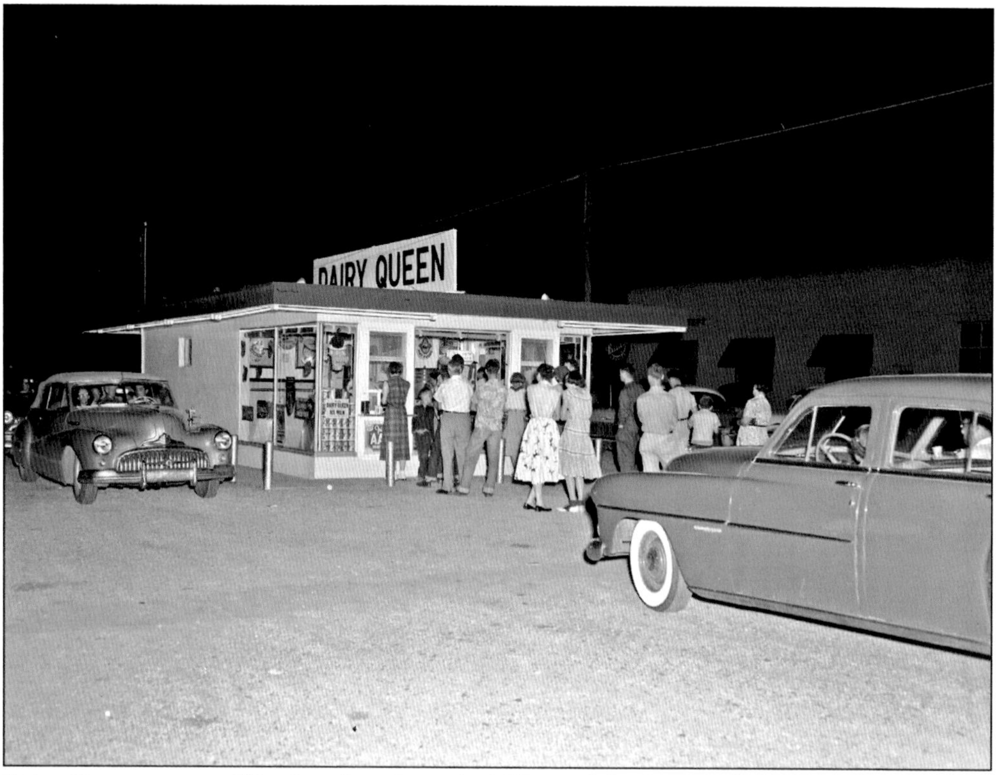

Dairy Queen came to Woodward in the early 1950s, as did other fast-food restaurants. It was a favorite spot for local teens, as is evident in this photograph. The business is still located in the same location at 1219 Main Avenue.

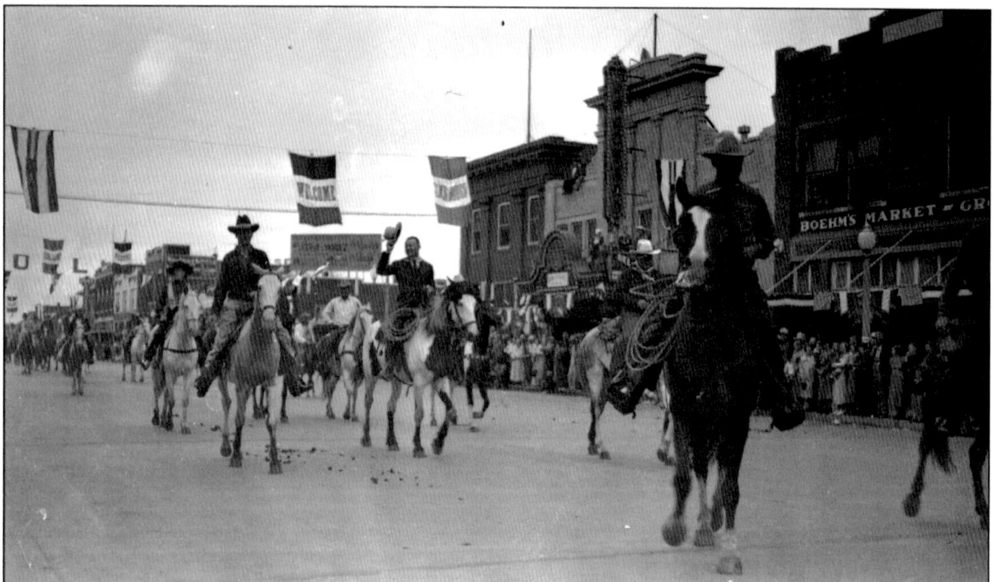

Members of the Woodward Elks lodge, including J. O. Selman and Phil Ferguson, participate in this parade on Main Avenue in Woodward. The Woodward Theatre and Boehm's Market and Grocery are visible.

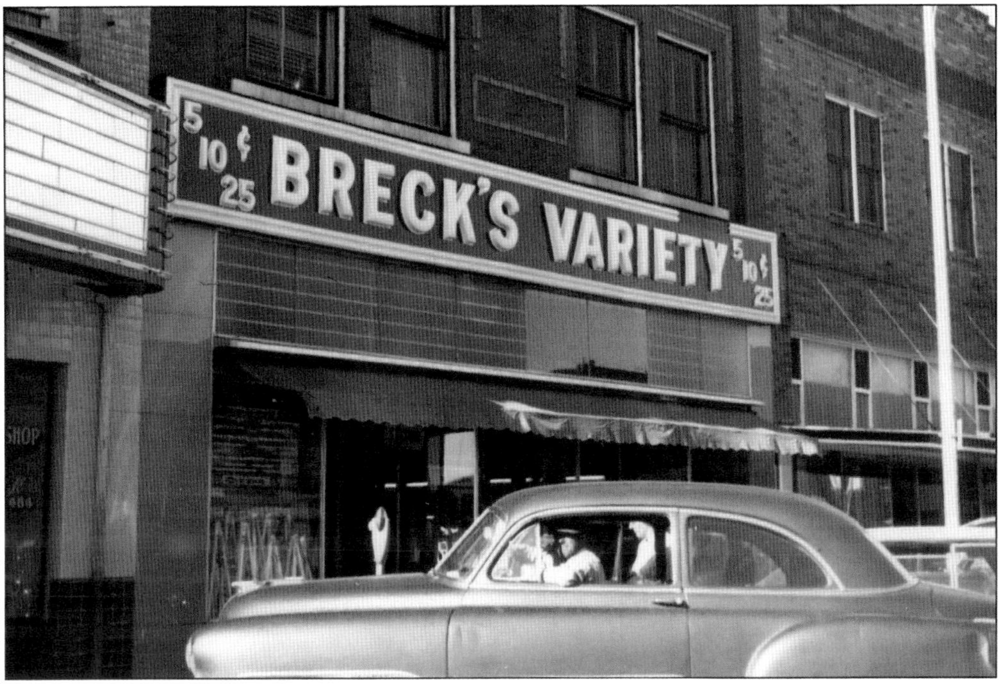

Breck's Variety store, a nickel-and-dime store, was located on Woodward's thoroughfare in the old Boehm Meat Market at 809 Main Avenue. This building is now home to the Josie Adams Cultural Centre.

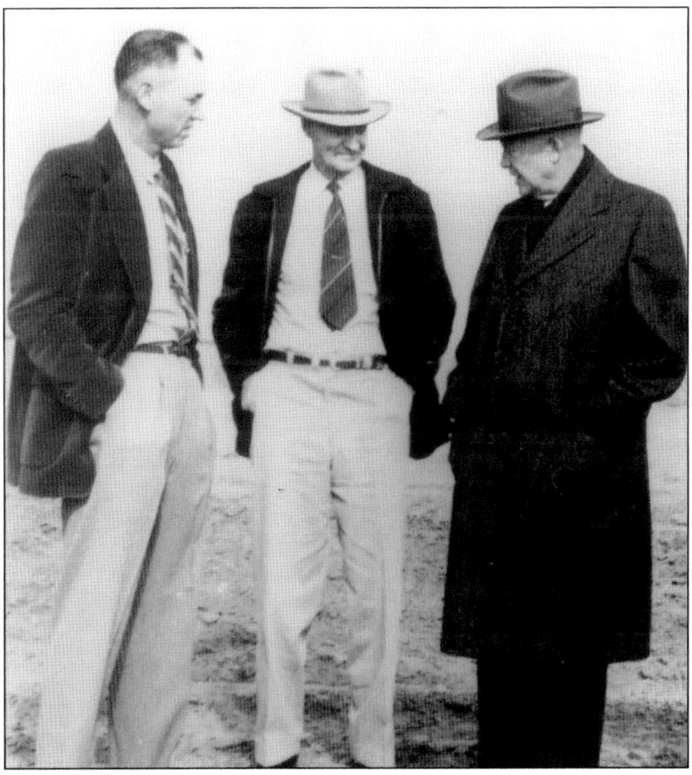

Pres. Dwight D. Eisenhower came to Woodward County during the drought of 1957. This photograph was taken on January 14, 1957, at the Carl Peoples farm north of Tangier. From left to right are Carl Peoples, C. C. Peoples, and Eisenhower.

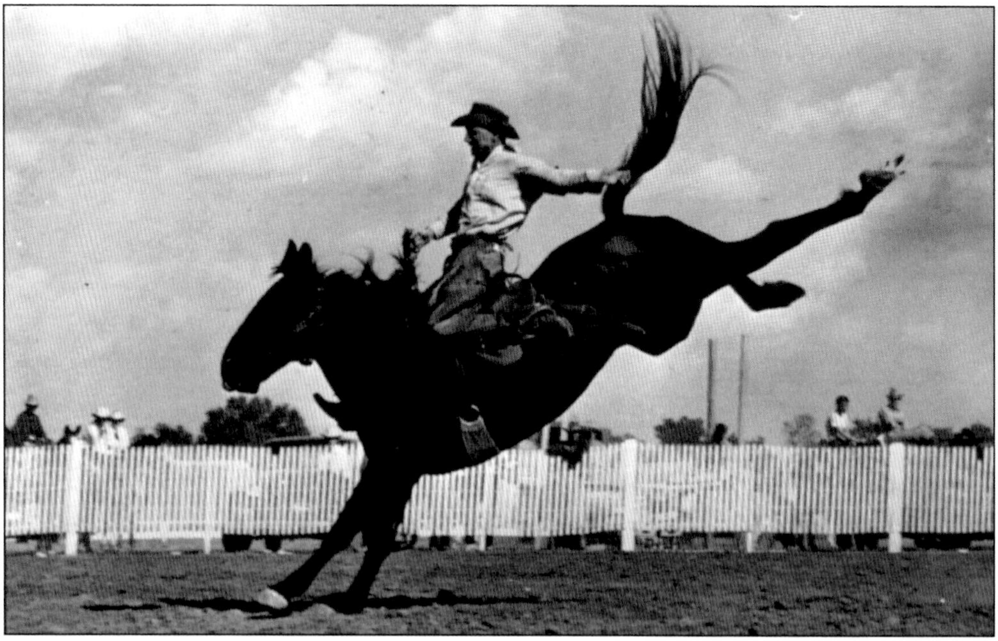

Ever since the first wild horse was tamed and ridden, there has been continuous debate about which rider rode longest and which horse bucked the best. The tradition goes back 150 years when competitions were scattered across the West. In this photograph, an unidentified rodeo participant rides a bucking bronc at the Woodward Elks Rodeo.

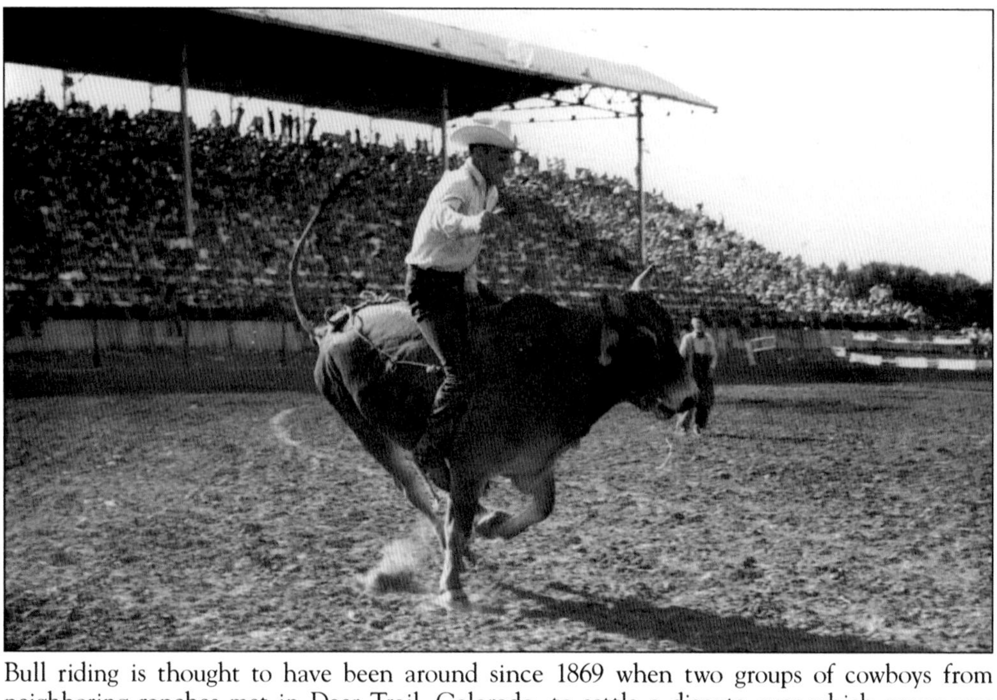

Bull riding is thought to have been around since 1869 when two groups of cowboys from neighboring ranches met in Deer Trail, Colorado, to settle a dispute over which group was better at ranching activities. It is still a main component of the modern rodeo. This bull rider is performing at the Woodward Elks Rodeo.

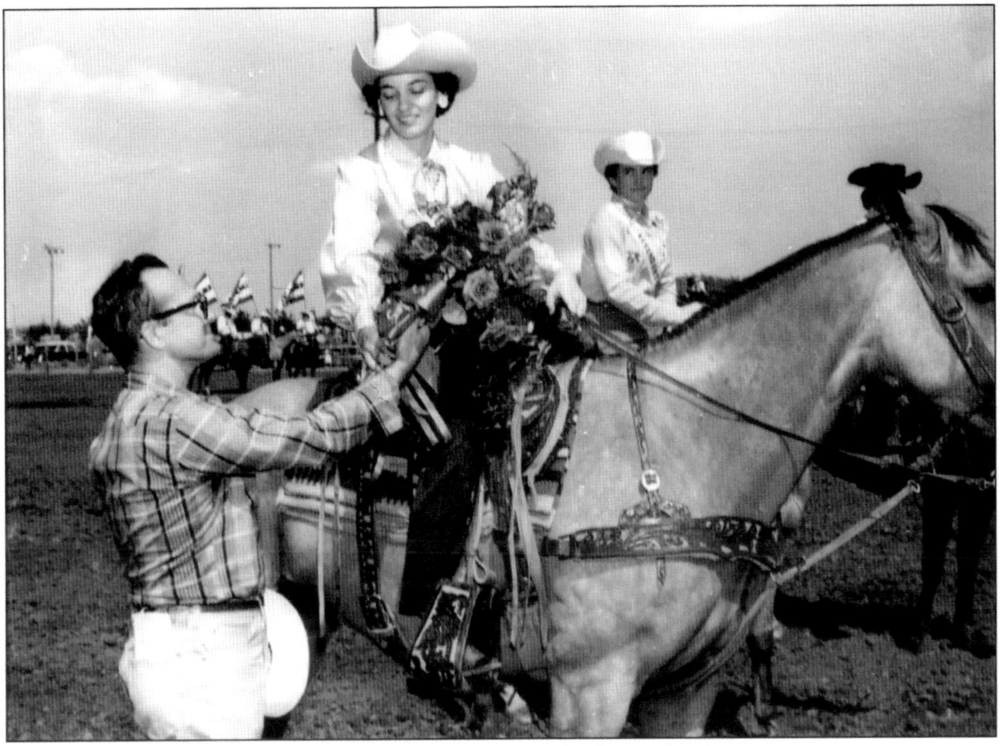

Patsy Spencer Wilson was named the 1955 Woodward Elks Rodeo Queen.

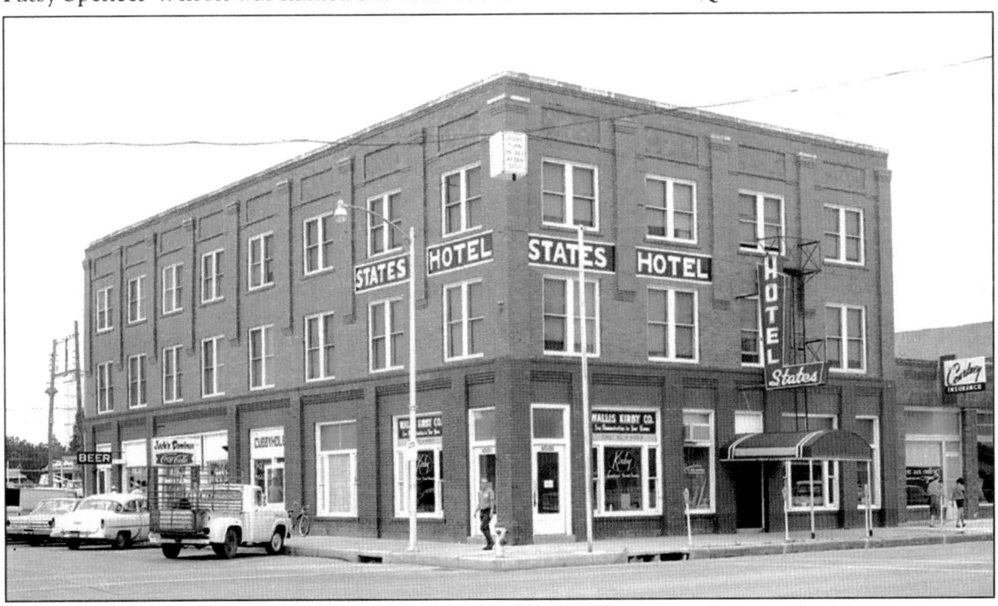

Built in 1904 by William Bolton, the owner of the original *Woodward News*, this building housed the post office until 1910. After Bolton's death, his widow installed a cafe on the first floor and later a hotel called the Ideal. During the 1920s, the hotel was known as the Bolton. It later became known as the States Hotel, named for the fact that it contained 48 rooms, the number of states in the union at the time. The hotel closed in 1983. This building now houses the Dr. Dewey Collins Chiropractic Clinic.

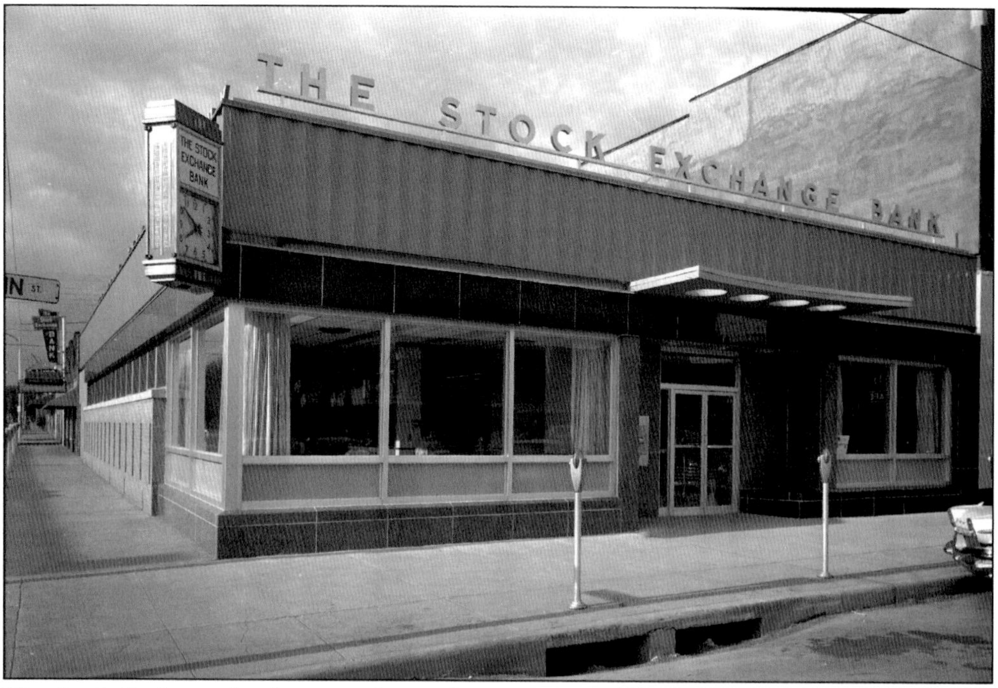

The Stock Exchange Bank sat on the southwest corner of Ninth Street and Main Avenue in Woodward. The building is now the home of Benbrook Insurance Agency. The Stock Exchange Bank moved to its present location at Tenth Street and Texas Avenue.

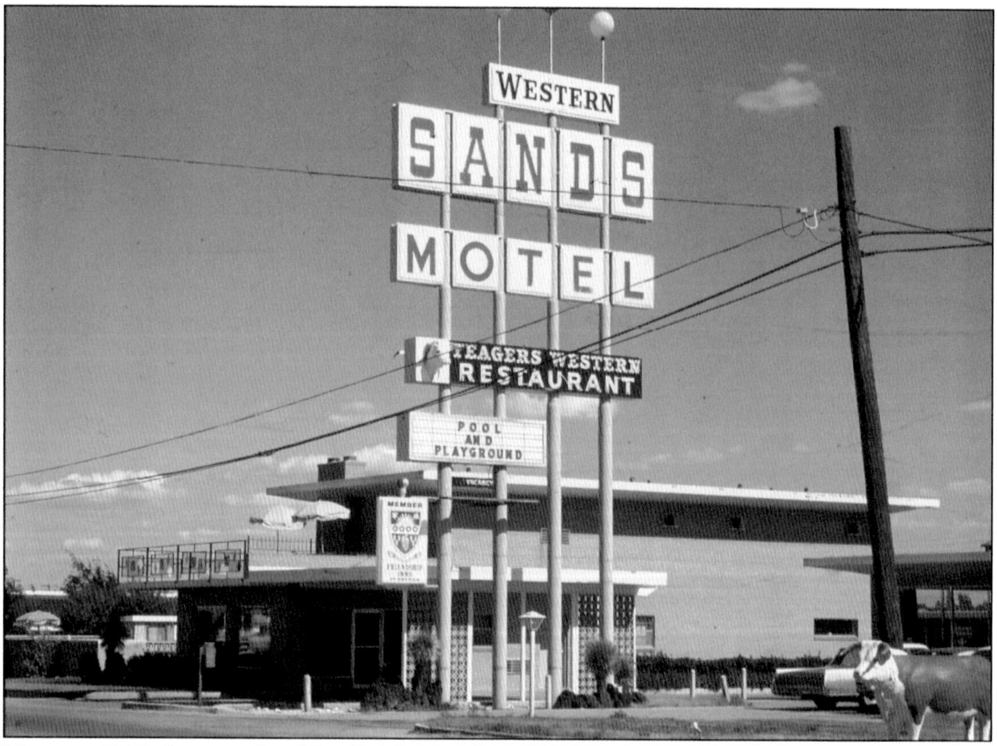

Here is a 1968 photograph of the Sands Motel on Oklahoma Avenue.

Nine

Progress 1961–2008

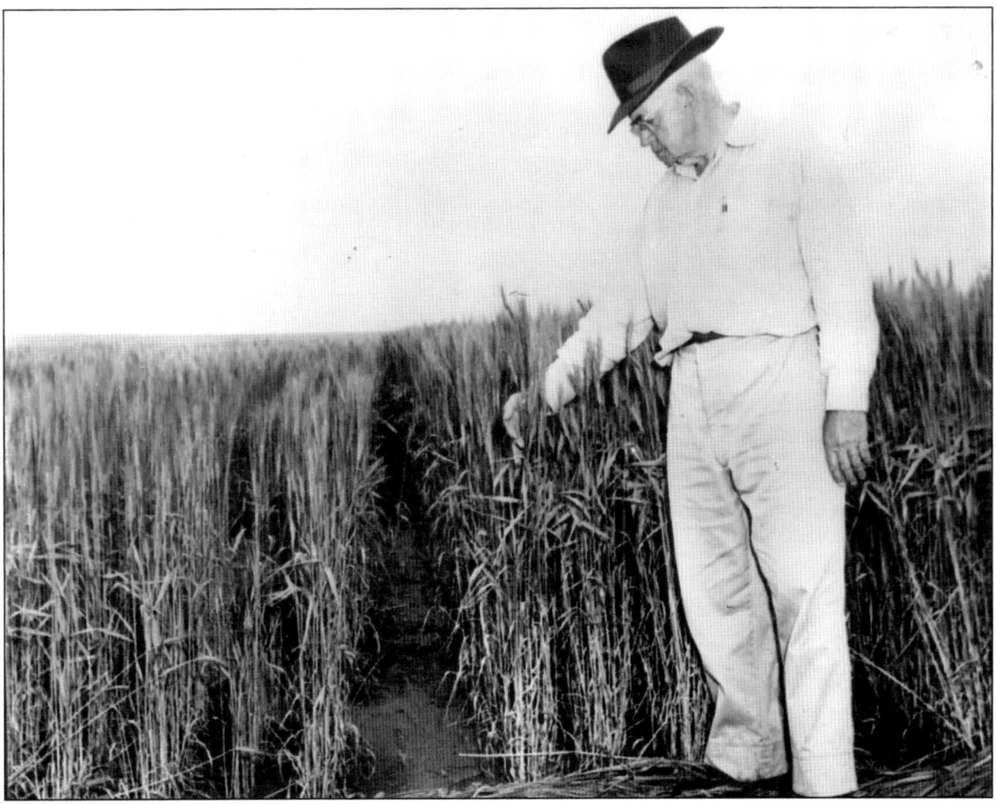

In this photograph, L. F. Locke is checking the wheat at the field station in about 1960. The field station specialized in producing many varieties of plants that yielded better harvests and were more adapted to the western Oklahoma climate.

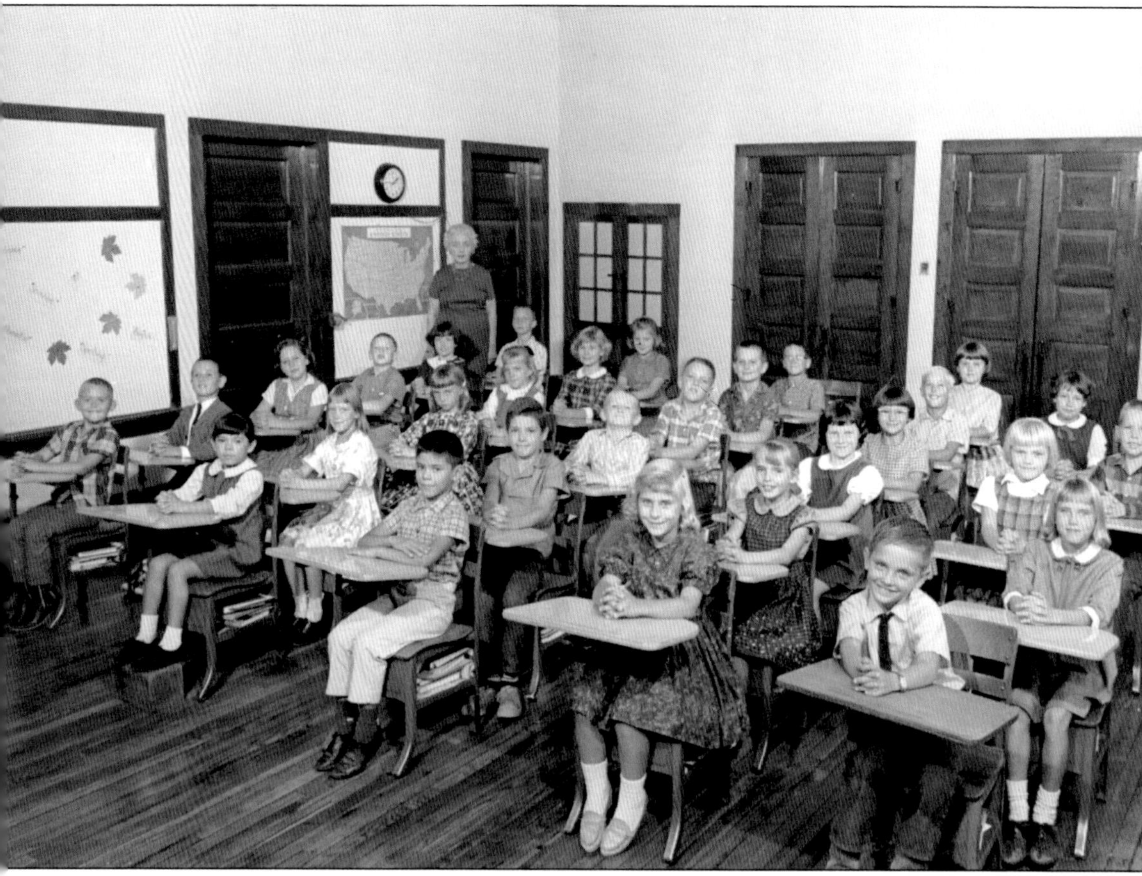

The third-grade class at Madison Park School posed in 1966 with teacher Birdie Katherine Moore. The students, from front to back, are (first row) Robert Shirley, Keith Parks, Audrey Nash, Ottis Wise, Janice Wise, and Barney Silvey; (second row) Monica Garcia, Mary Ann Clark, Honey Jean Ridenour, Sue Ann Maupin, Beverly Spivey, and Darla Swartz; (third row) Terry Garcia, Eddie Reed, Ray Dean Shepherd, Jerry Keltch, Melvin Nebhut, and Dwayne Morey; (fourth row) Dravenda Drake, Sondra Tuck, Carolyn Laxton, unknown, Jeff Dixon, and Carol Head; (fifth row) Steven Ross, Annita Foster, Debbie Stafford, Gene Karn, Cindy Barnett, and Jean Clements.

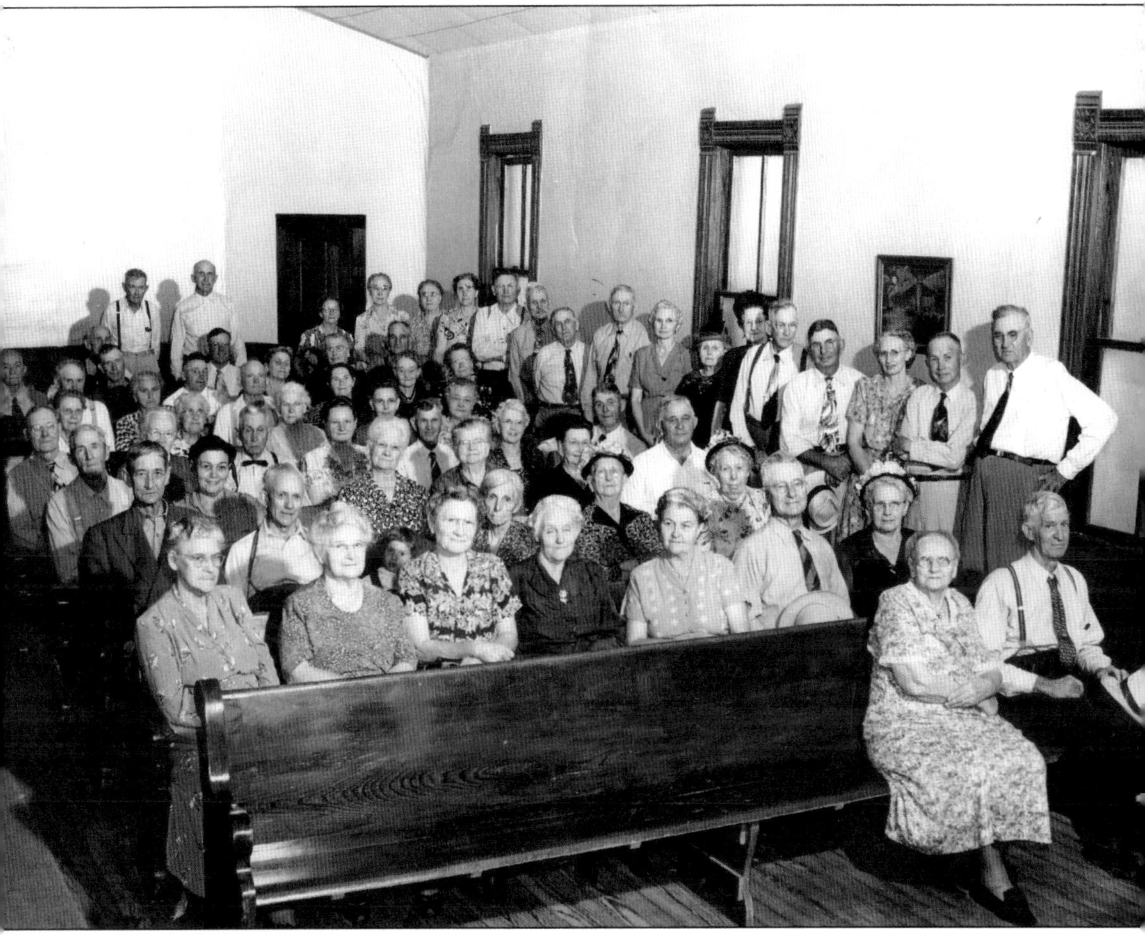

During the 1950s, an Old Settlers' Reunion was held at Mutual. From left to right are (first row) Mr. and Mrs. C. H. Kirkwood; (second row) Mrs. Jim Borden, Mary Vincent, Sarah Allison, Nellie Bertlesen, Lula Craighead, Jeff Craighead, and Violet Allison; (third row) Fred McGriff, Pink Heckart, Barbara Hall, Kate Saxton, Ada Bowen, and Rose Halderman; (fourth row) Mr. and Mrs. Delbert Simpson, Lexie League, Minnie Harper, and Mrs. and Mr. Jim Henderson; (fifth row) Charles Andrews, Mr. and Mrs. Harry McGriff, Mrs. and Mr. John Terry, and Mrs. and Mr. Enoch Hargis.

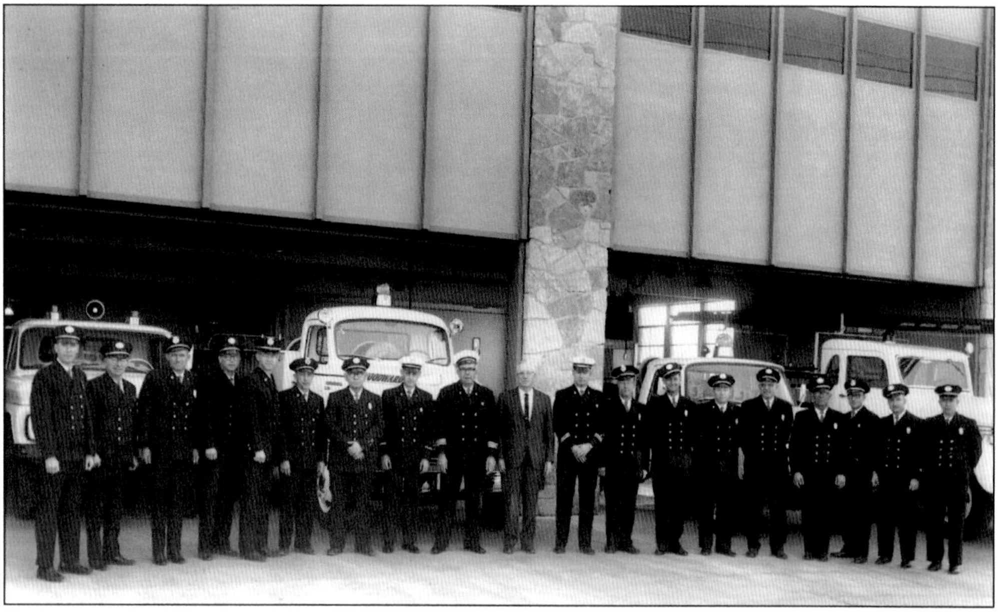

Each year, the Woodward Fire Department poses for a photograph in front of the station at Woodward Convention Hall. The 1967 department is pictured here. Shown from left to right are Rex Forrest, Carmen Barnett, Floyd Calkins, Charles W. Jones, Charles J. Gieswien, Merle A. Shore, Delford Sidders, Wilbur L. Day, John A. Lafleur, Tom Keltch, Melvin E. Gaston, Clyde L. Tower, Leonard Stocking, Bobby F. Wasson, Donald Baxter, Elmer Hosier, Roger Martin, Merritt Hunter, and Joe Maddox.

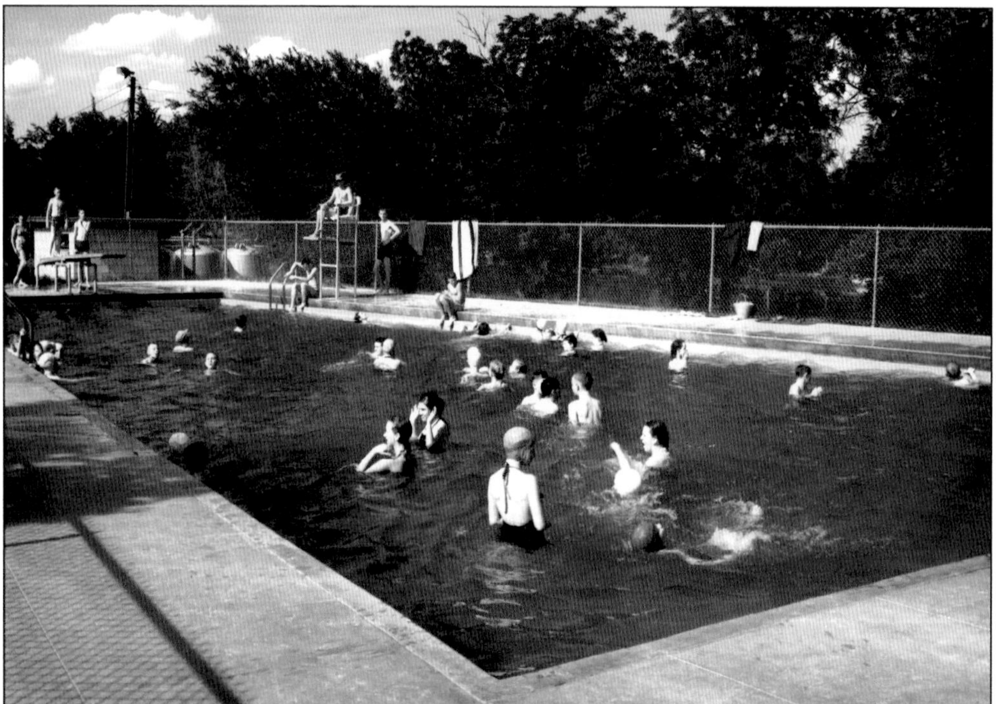

A new swimming pool was built at Boiling Springs State Park about 1964.

The Plains Indians and Pioneers Museum opened its doors to the public on September 17, 1966. The museum is dedicated to collecting, preserving, and exhibiting the history of northwest Oklahoma. It continues to provide an educational outlet for Woodward County and the surrounding area.

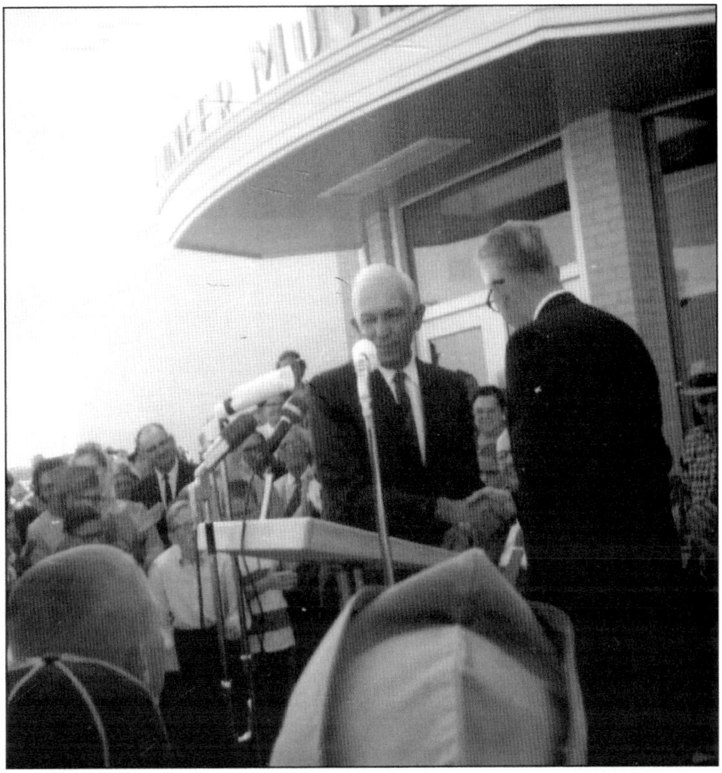

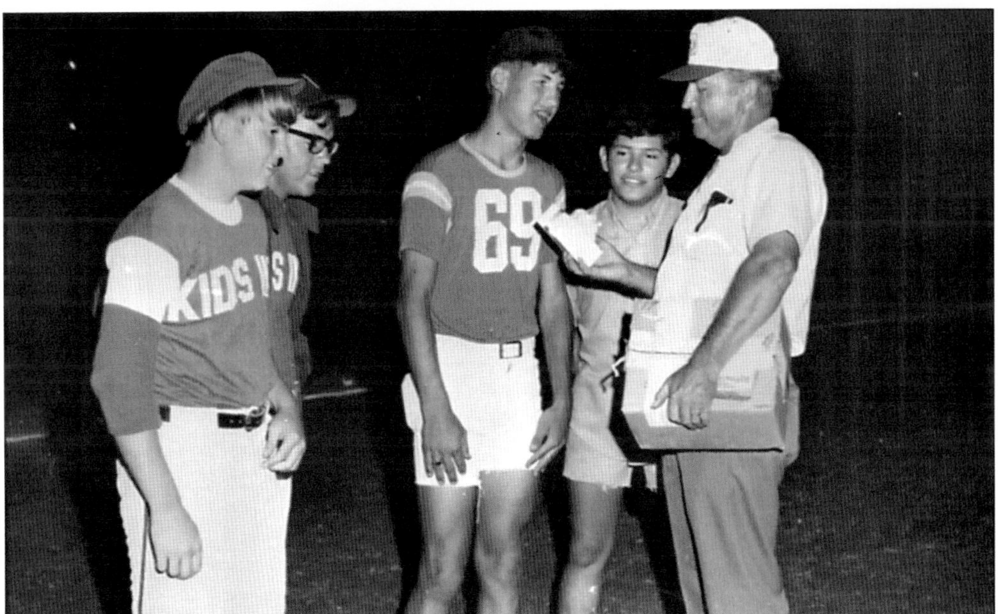

A group of teenage boys from Kids Incorporated gives coach Wendell Plank an award on February 2, 1964. Kids Inc., as it is commonly known, was created in 1948 in order to provide an organization in which children could play sports. It provided the equipment, and no fees were charged to play. The goal was to promote sportsmanship, honesty, loyalty, courage, and good citizenship by providing supervised athletic games.

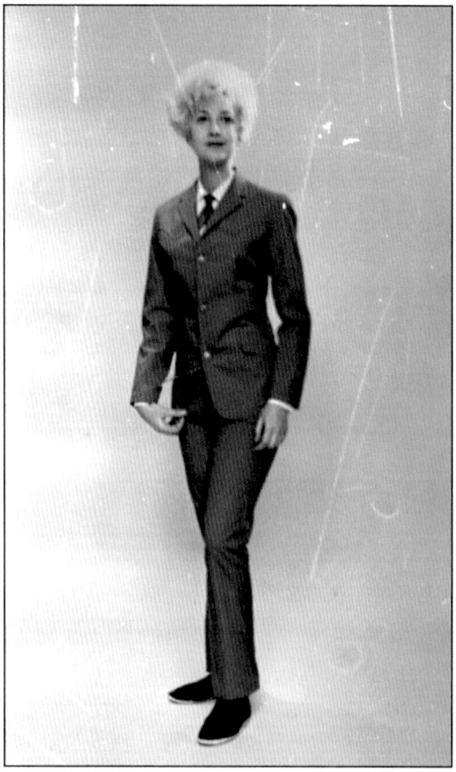

Sandy Fowler models a Western suit for Trego's Westwear in 1965. Trego's Westwear began manufacturing Western clothing in 1935 in response to a need for women's Western apparel. George Trego started the company by making women's culottes and boleros for the Woodward Elks Rodeo Booster Committee. Soon they manufactured children's and men's clothing and expanded to a national market. Trego's Westwear closed its doors in 1995 after making clothing in Woodward for 60 years.

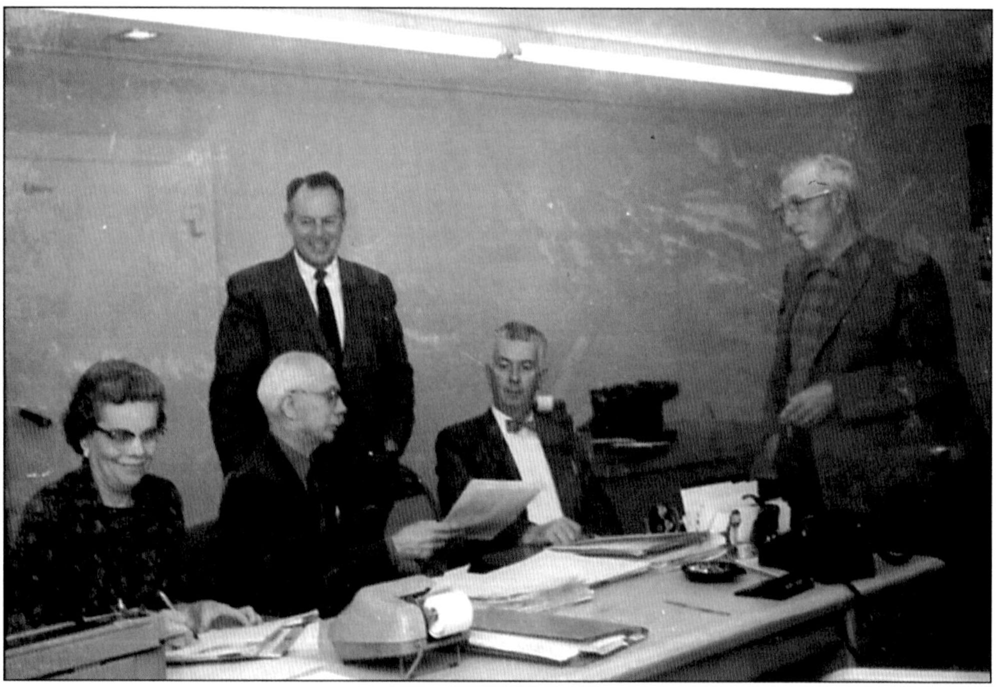

Woodward city officers posed for this photograph in 1960. From left to right (sitting) are Mary Clift, clerk; J. H. Kephart, mayor; and Cecil Campbell, commissioner; (standing) Thomas Keltch, city manager, and J. C. Homer, commissioner.

In this photograph, Woodward native Paul Laune works on one of six murals for the Plains Indians and Pioneers Museum's rotunda. With encouragement from his first art teacher, Sallie Greer, Laune gave up his early ambition to become a cowboy and decided to become an artist. Doubleday and Company published Laune's book *America's Quarter Horses* in 1973. This book is now known as the bible on the quarter horse.

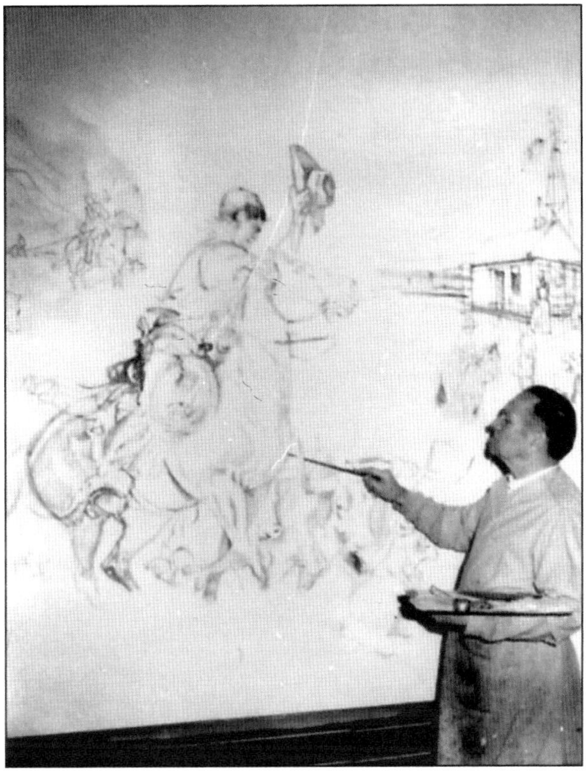

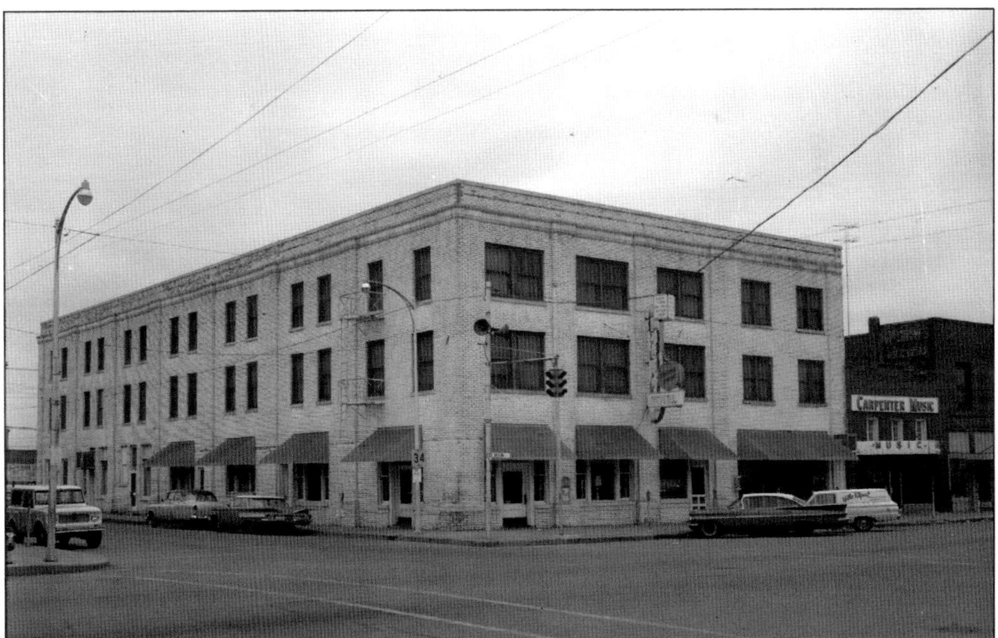

Prior to opening its doors in 1912, the site of the Baker Hotel was occupied by the Brass Rail Saloon. The 60-room Baker Hotel welcomed thousands of guests during its 52 years of service. From 1912 until 1946, it was run by members of the T. E. Baker family. It was used as a makeshift hospital following the 1947 tornado and was replaced with a modern bank building in 1967.

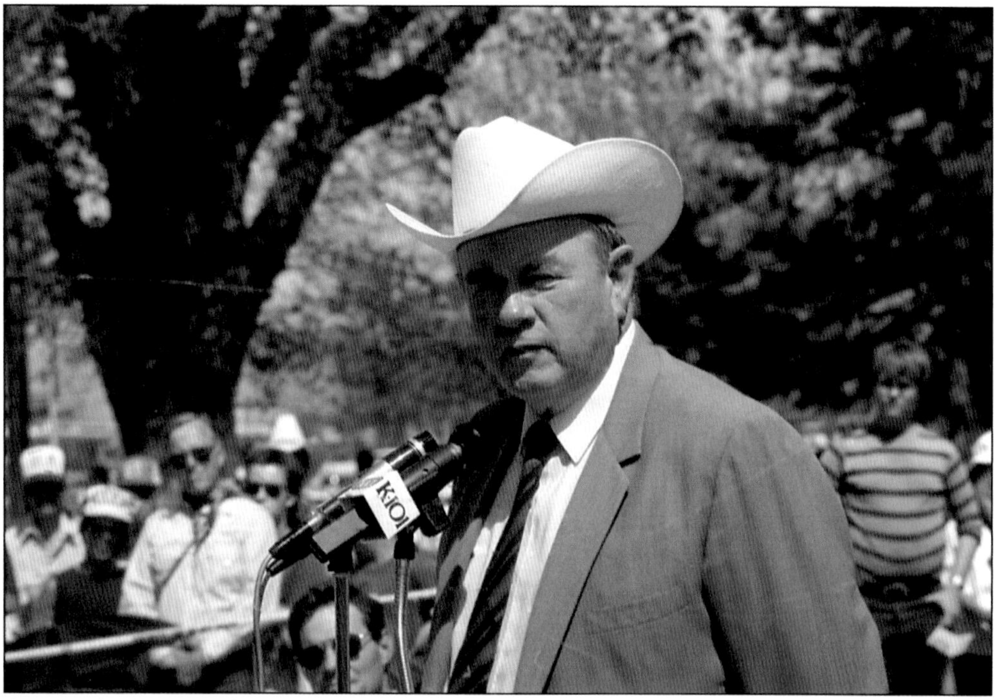

On April 25, 1987, the city of Woodward celebrated its centennial with much pomp and circumstance. In this photograph, Oklahoma governor Henry Bellmon speaks to a crowd at the dedication of the centennial marker in Centennial Park.

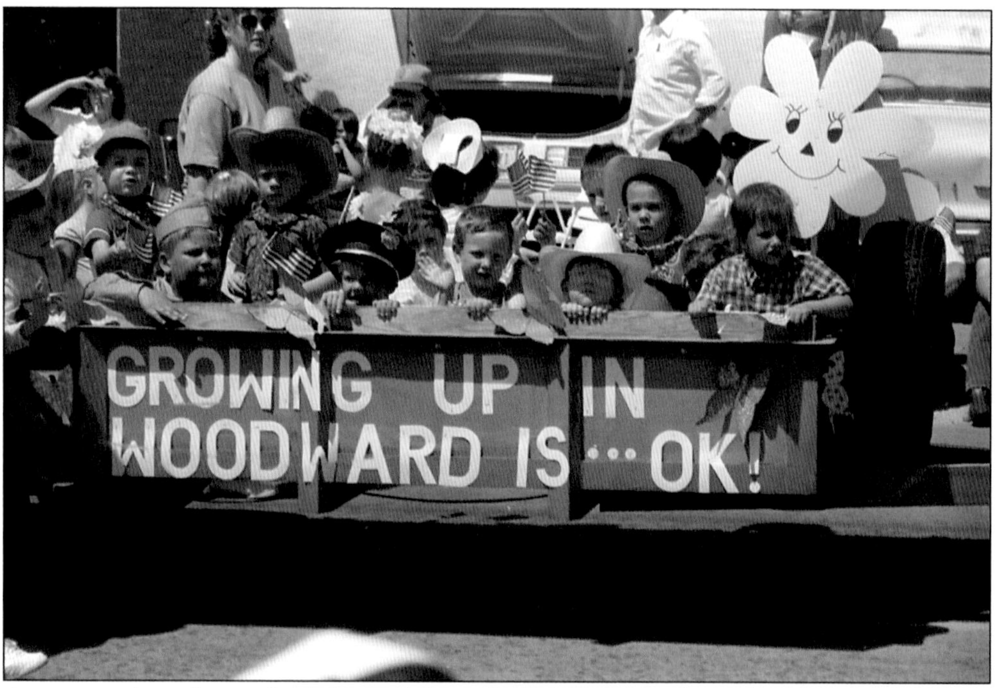

A centennial parade was also held to celebrate the first 100 years of Woodward's existence on the prairie. In celebration of Woodward's centennial, 1,987 balloons were also released.

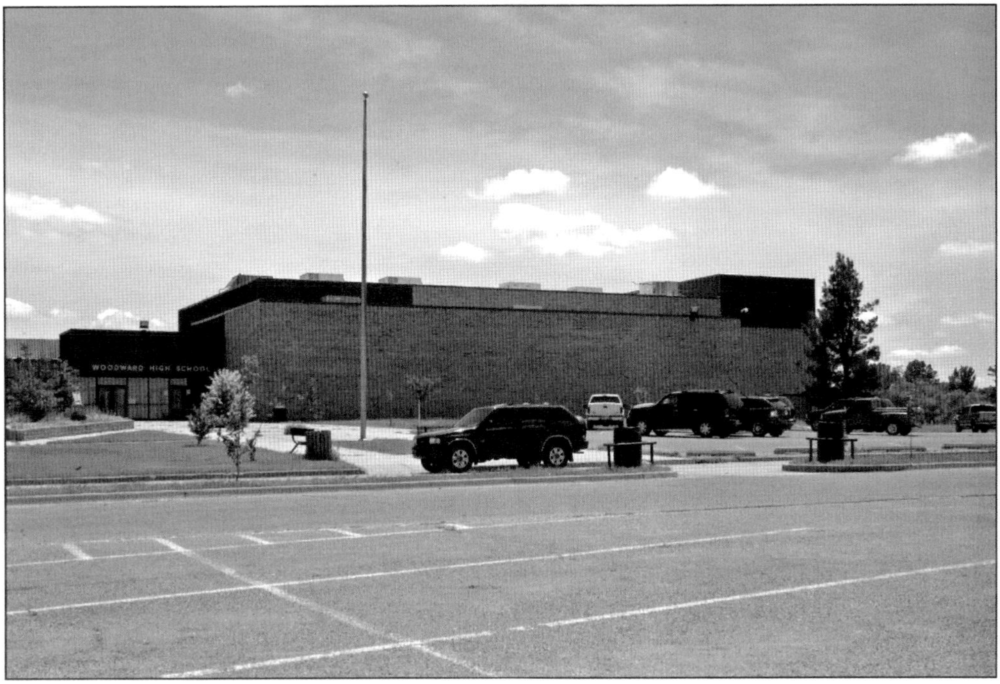

A new high school was built in Woodward in 1978 during the oil boom at the corner of Thirteenth Street and Downs Avenue. It still serves as the secondary school in the county seat.

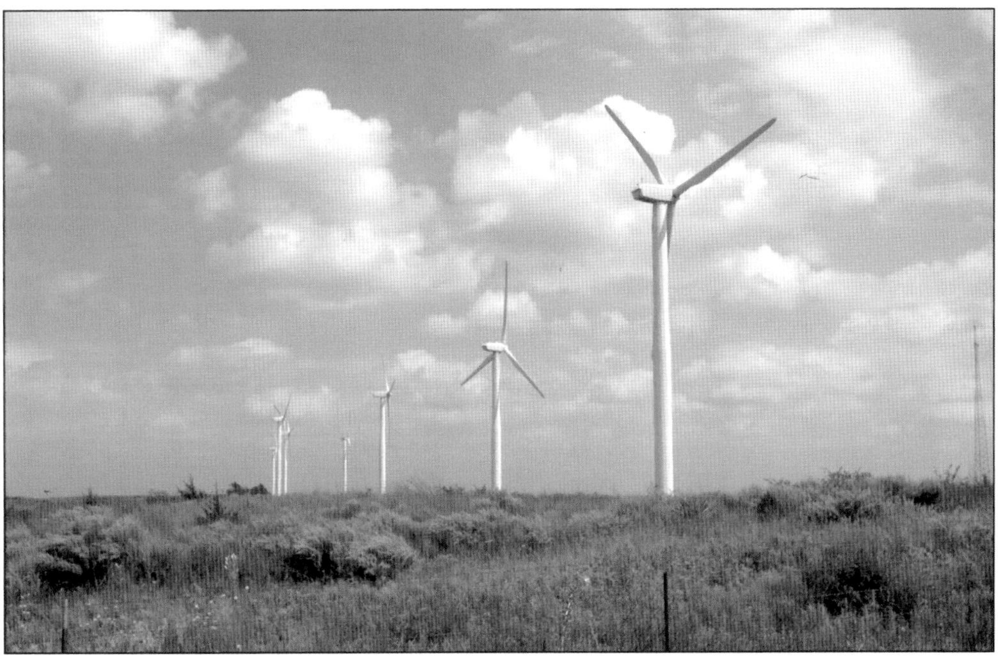

Located on 1,200 acres of ranchland 12 miles northeast of Woodward, the 68 wind turbines at the Florida Power and Light facility produce enough electricity for approximately 30,000 homes. The wind farm began operating at full power in October 2003. The windmills, which are 213 feet tall, provide a clean and reliable source of energy.

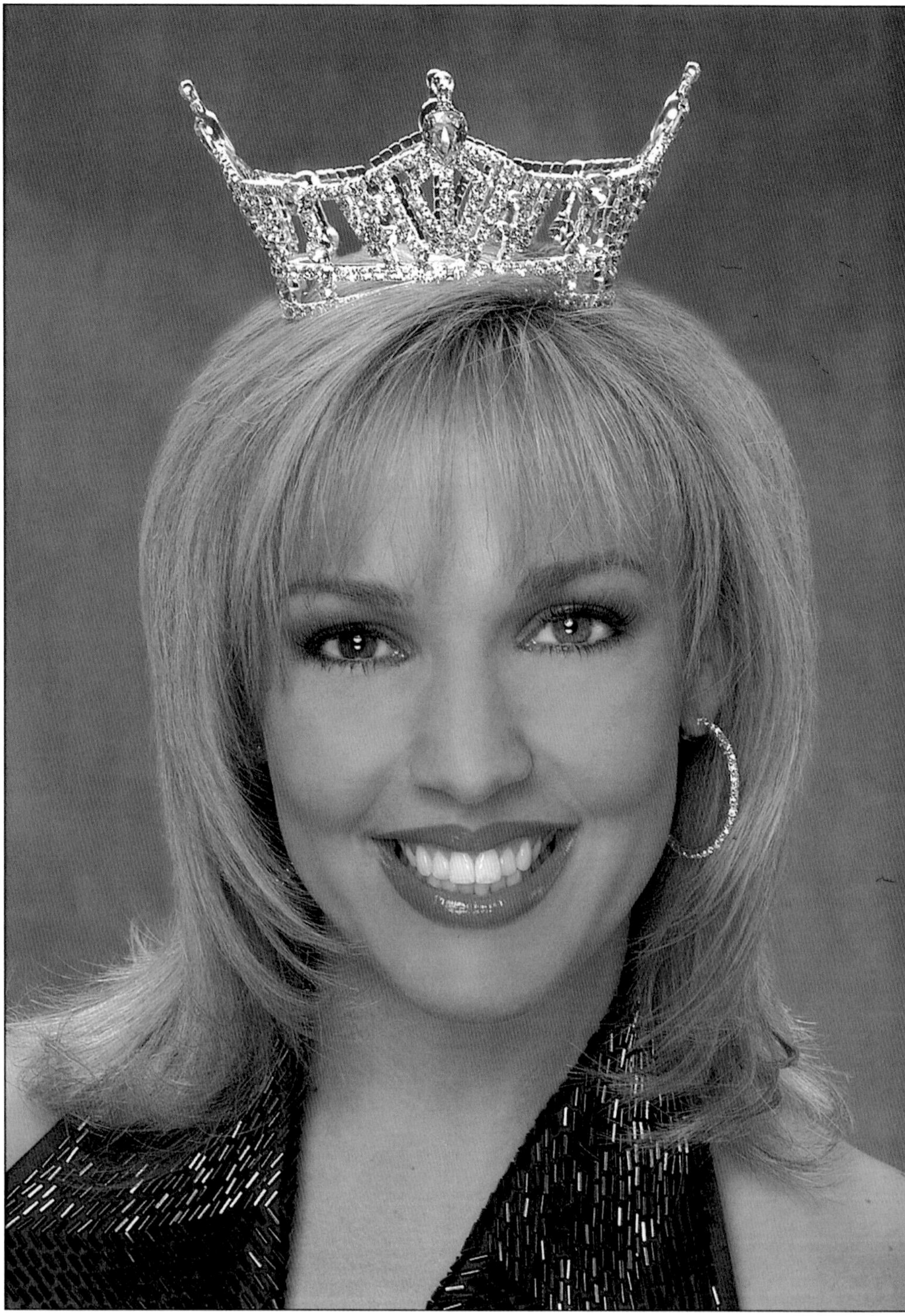

Elizabeth Kinney, a Mooreland native, became Miss Oklahoma in 2004. She is a summa cum laude graduate of Oklahoma State University with a bachelor of science degree in agricultural communications and a minor in agricultural economics. Kinney was a top-10 semifinalist at the Miss America pageant. (Photograph by Jim Grillot; courtesy of John and Melinda Kinney.)

Ten

Forgotten Places

Towns Gone by the Wayside

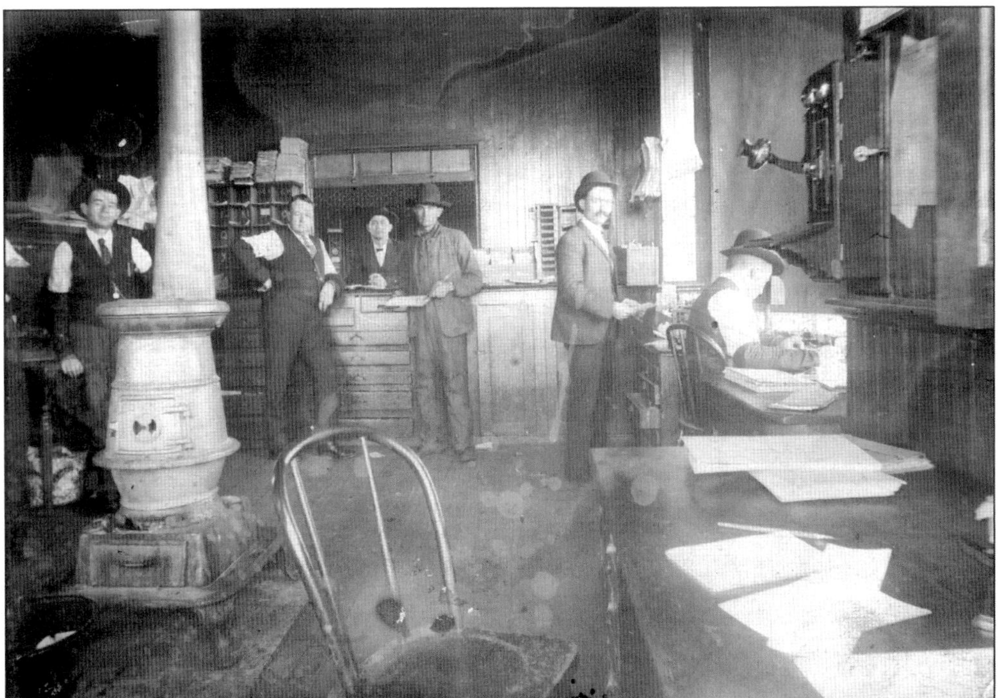

This photograph from 1906 shows the interior of the Hackberry Post Office. Ralph Gaston is fourth from left and is wearing a hat. Hackberry's post office was established on June 17, 1895. Its name changed to Sharon on February 24, 1912. It took its name from a hackberry grove on the N. Z. Rouse farm. The name Sharon comes from Alexander Sharon, the town site owner.

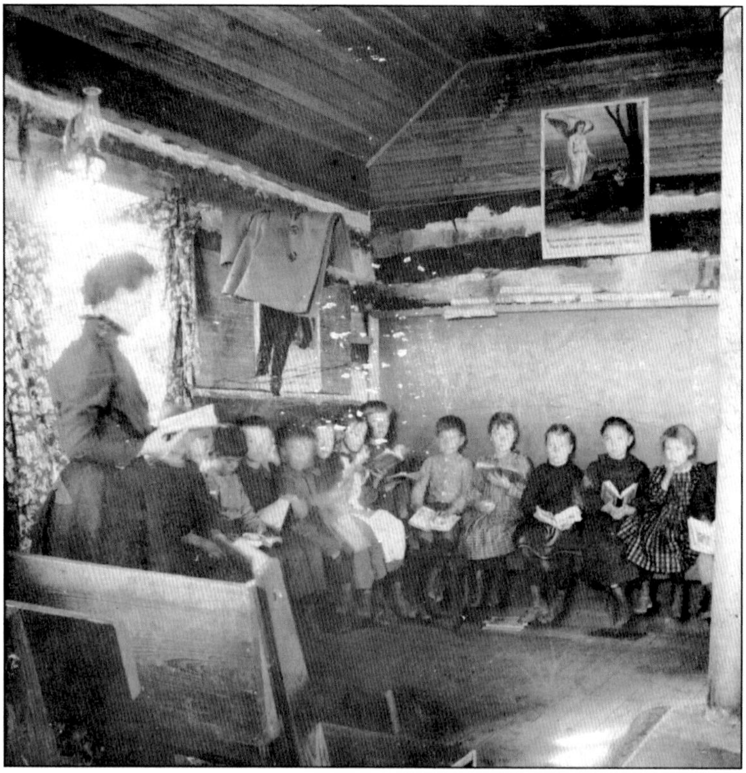

The log school at Persimmon was photographed in 1898. The town of Persimmon was located two miles west of Mutual. It no longer exists. A post office was located here from April 21, 1894, to March 30, 1907.

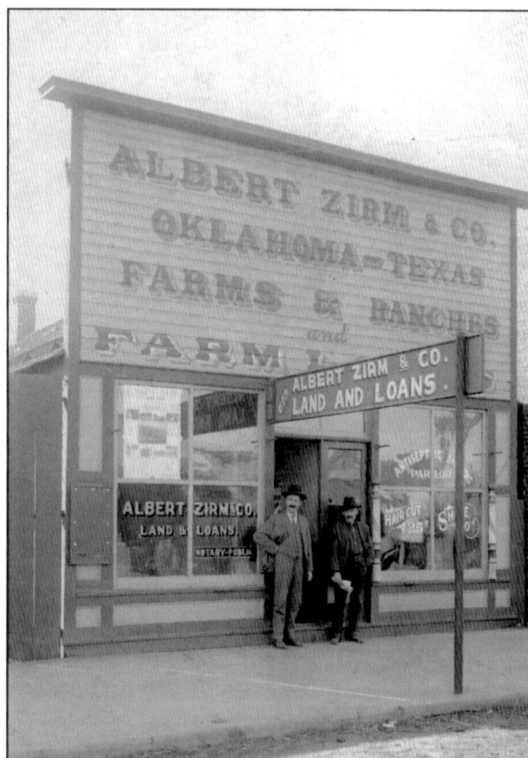

This photograph shows two unidentified men standing in front of the Albert Zirm and Company building in Quinlan. The company was a land and loan office that served Oklahoma and Texas farms and ranches. The building was also the location of a notary public and a barbershop.

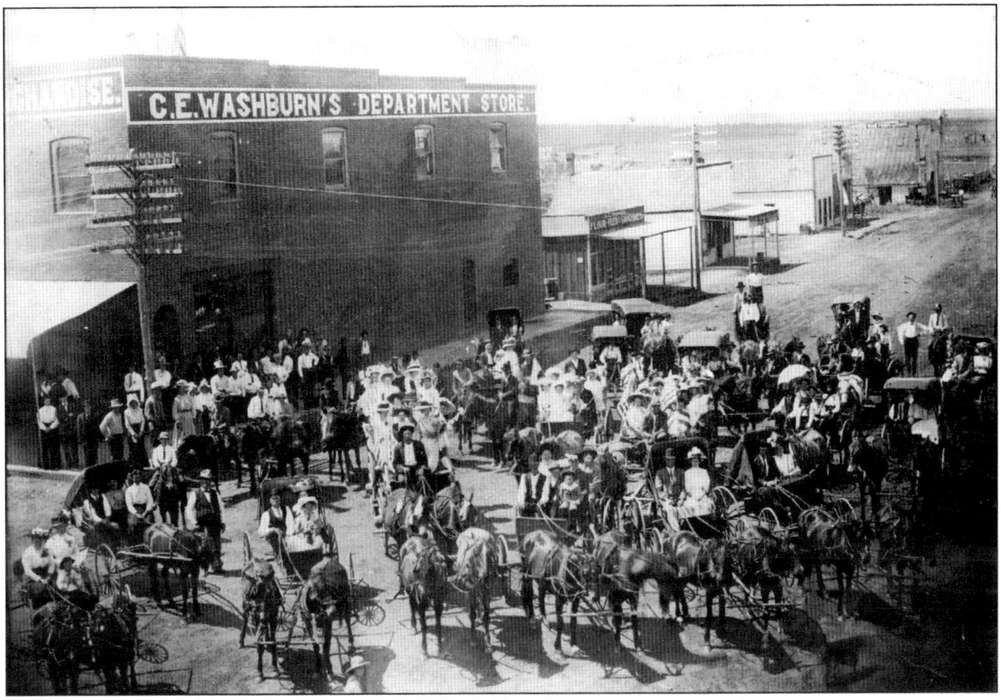

This photograph shows a celebration in Quinlan, the occasion of which has not been determined. Horse-drawn buggies filled with well-dressed men, women, and children can be seen. The C. E. Washburn's Department Store is in the background.

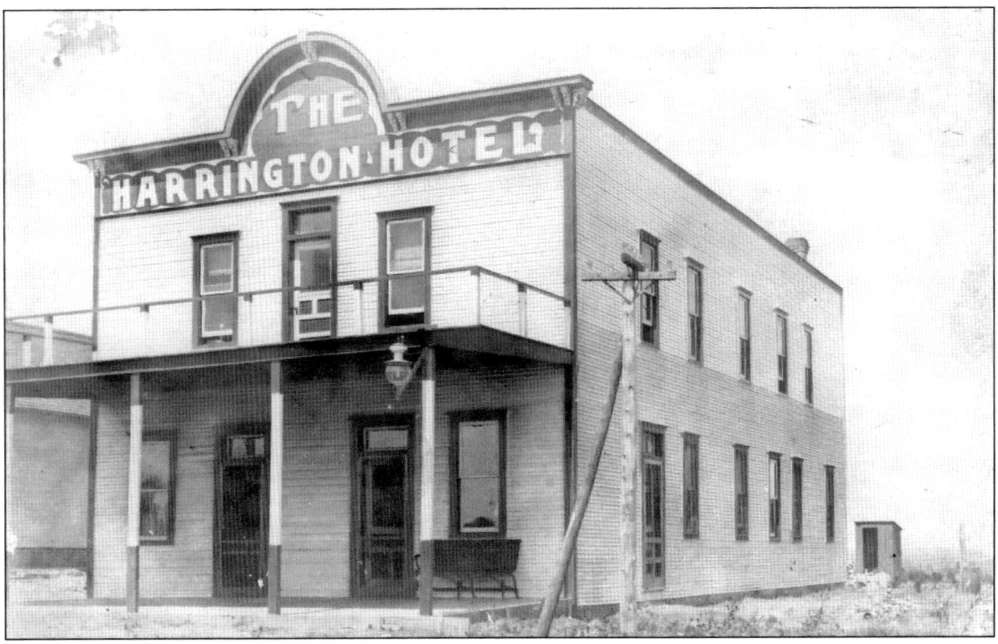

The Harrington Hotel in Quinlan is shown in this 1908 photograph. Quinlan's post office was established on April 27, 1901, and was named for Quinlan brothers William, Thomas, and Robert, who were well-known ranchers in the area.

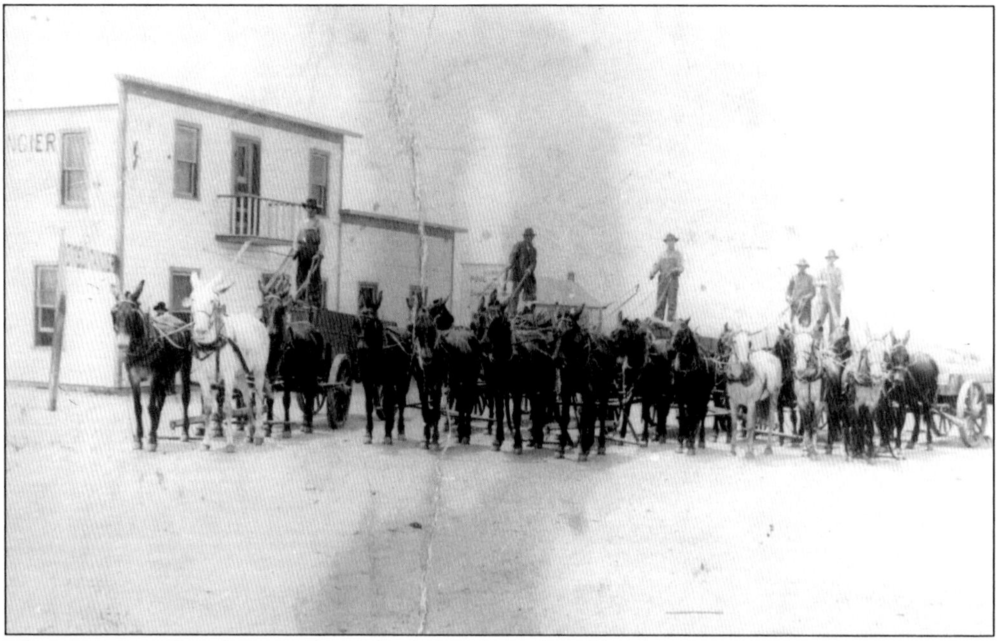

The wagons in this photograph are loaded with coal and lumber to be delivered to Fort Supply. From left to right are Orie Waller, E. C. Pearce, Allie Clanton, Bill Easteridge, and Charlie Forrest. The Tangier Hotel and Pool Hall can be seen on the left side of the street.

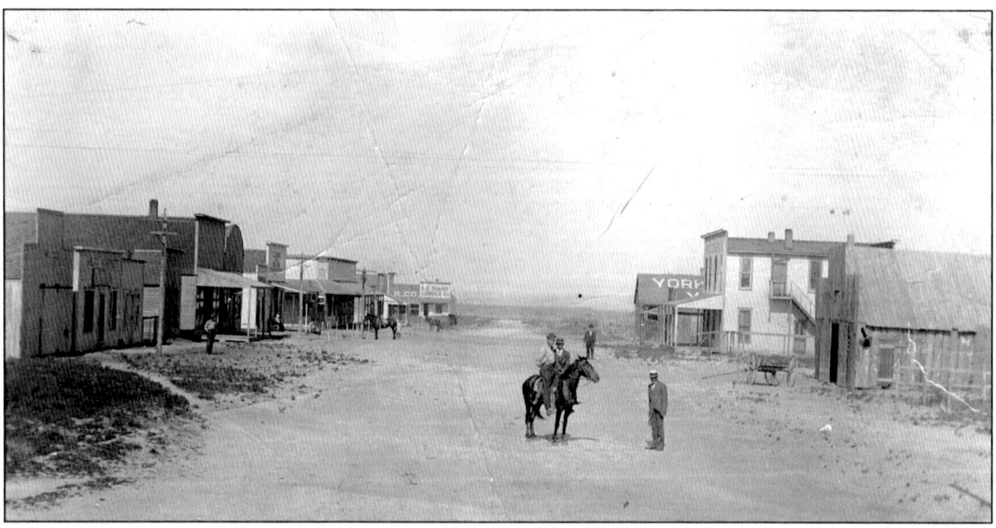

Tangier's Main Street is shown in this photograph from 1909. Tangier's name comes from a seaport city in northwestern Africa. A post office was in existence here from May 18, 1901, until August 31, 1941.

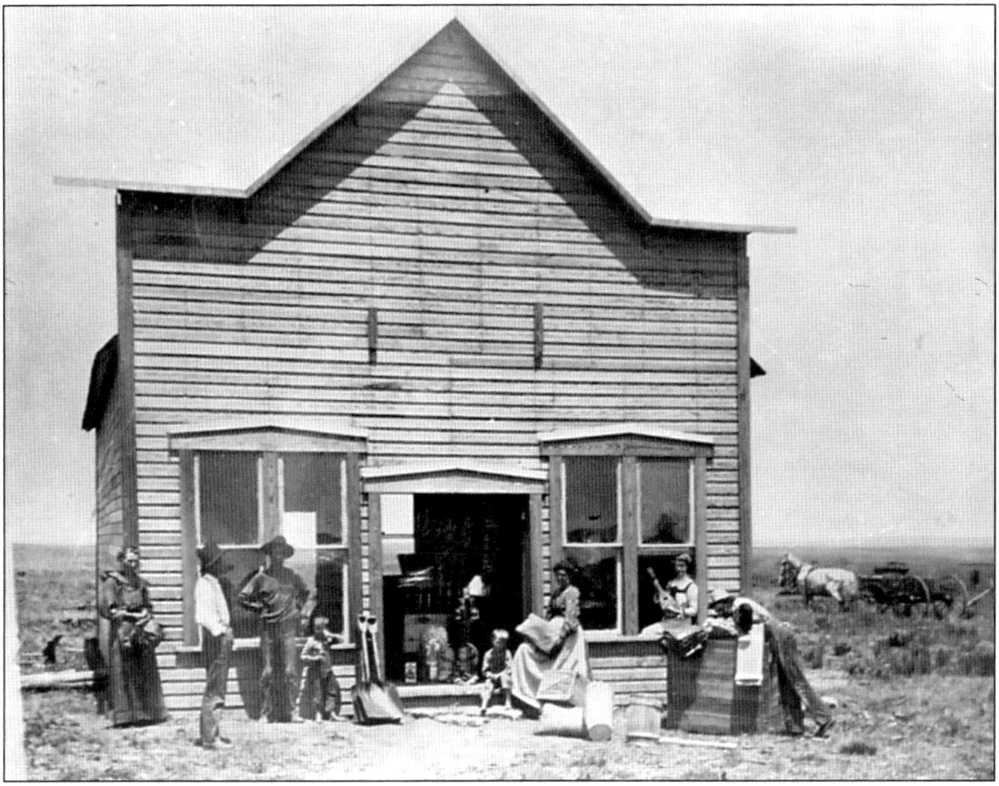

A group of people gather in front of an unidentified business in Haskew, which was located in the northern part of the county, about eight miles southwest of Freedom. Haskew had a post office from July 9, 1902, until October 15, 1921. It was named for William L. Haskew, a local rancher.

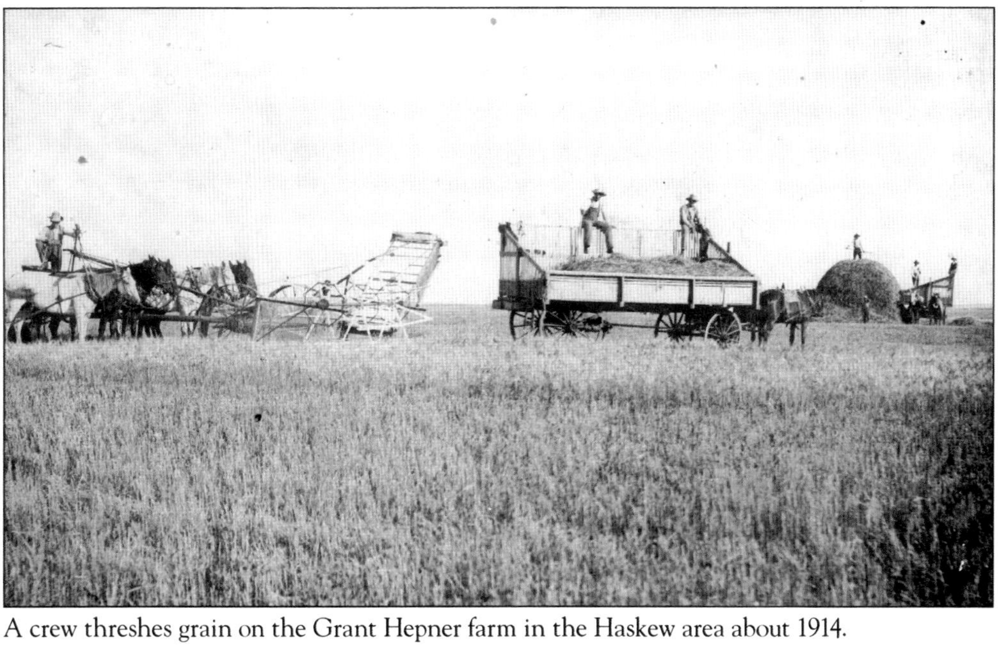

A crew threshes grain on the Grant Hepner farm in the Haskew area about 1914.

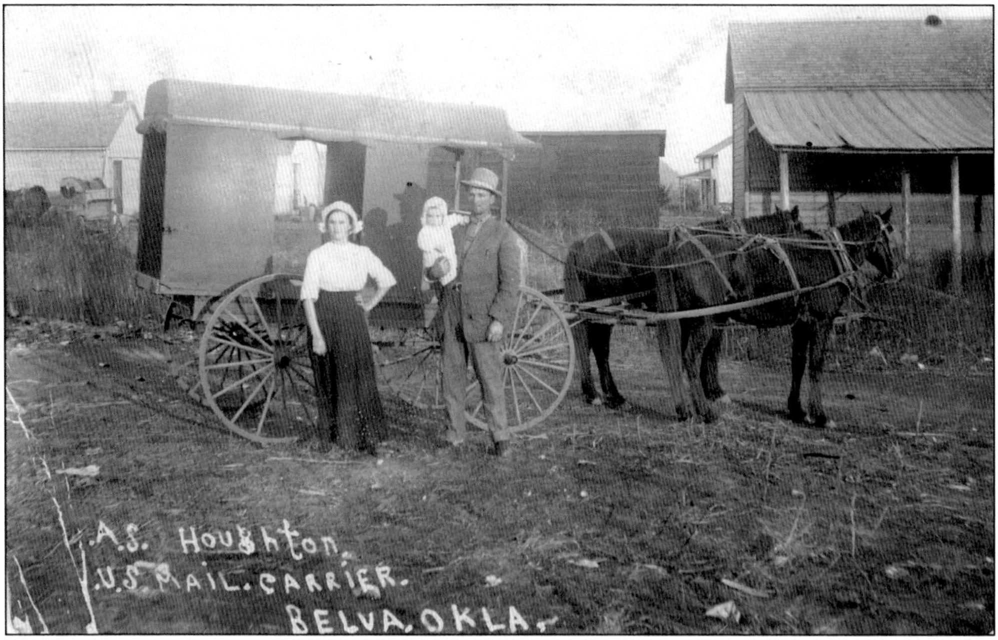

Asa S. Houghton was a United States mail carrier from Belva. His wife, Alta Washburn Houghton, and their baby Violet Houghton are also in the photograph. Houghton drove this mail hack to deliver mail from Belva to Taloga.

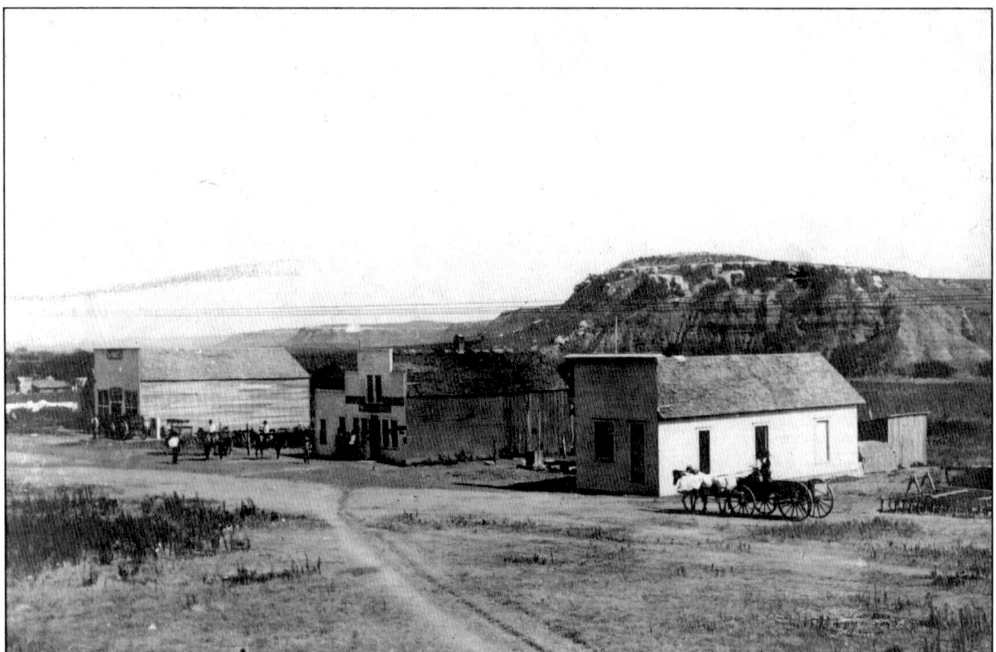

Belva, shown here in 1912, was named for the daughter of a section foreman on the Santa Fe. A post office was located here about eight miles southwest of Waynoka from August 16, 1900, until March 31, 1960. It is no longer in existence.

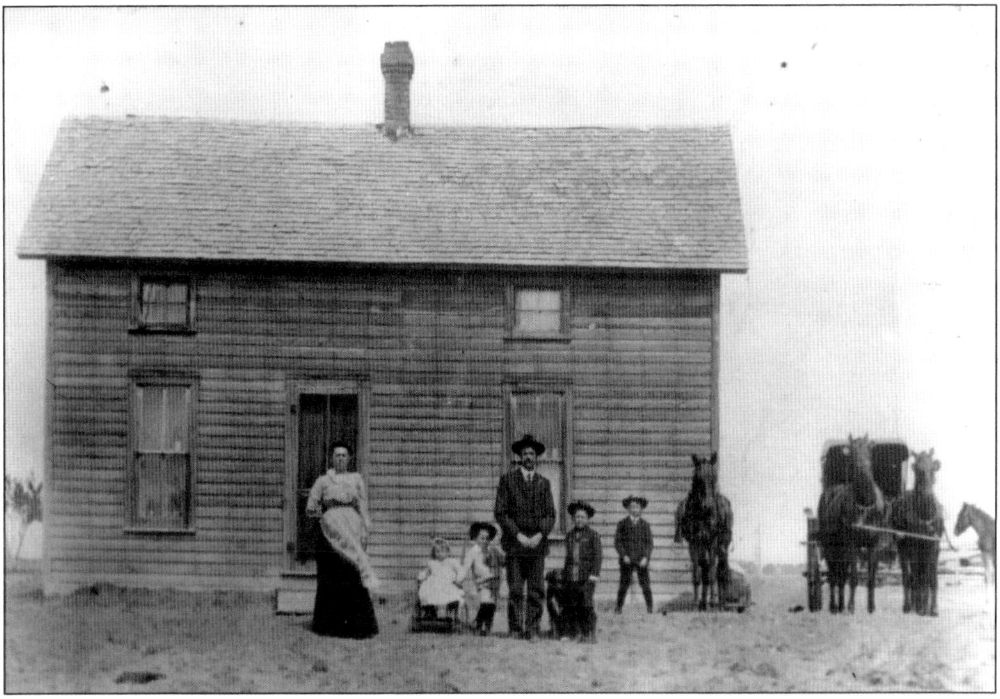

Dr. Tom C. Leachman, his wife, and children are featured in this image, which was taken in front of their home near Richmond. The small town was once located seven miles northwest of Seiling. The post office was in operation from November 6, 1893, to February 15, 1923. Its name comes from Richmond, Kentucky, the home of John White, the town's first postmaster.

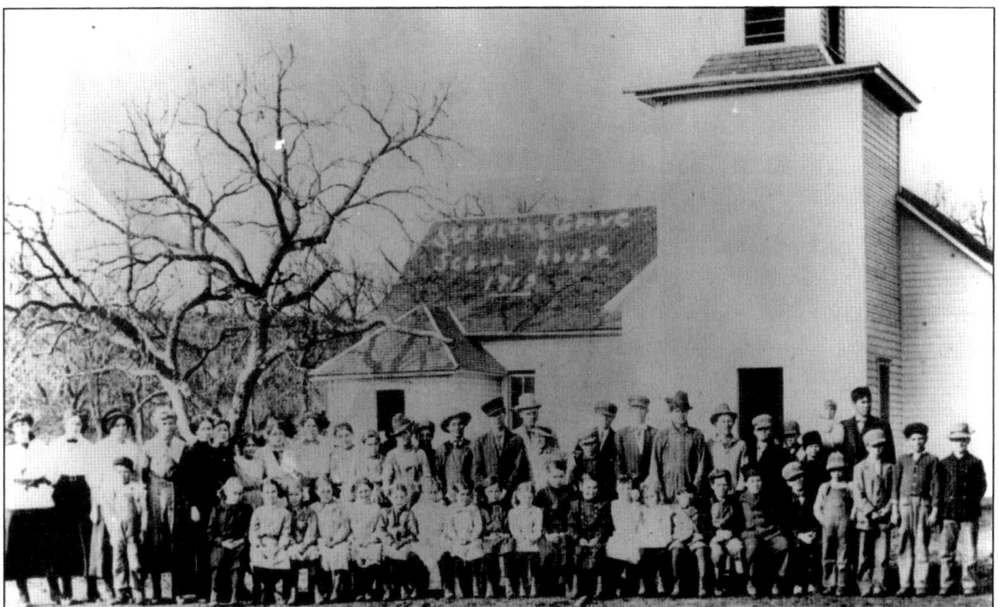

The Sterling Grove School was located near Richmond. This photograph shows a large group of schoolchildren in front of the wood-frame schoolhouse. Mr. Williams and Ada Shutt were the teachers.

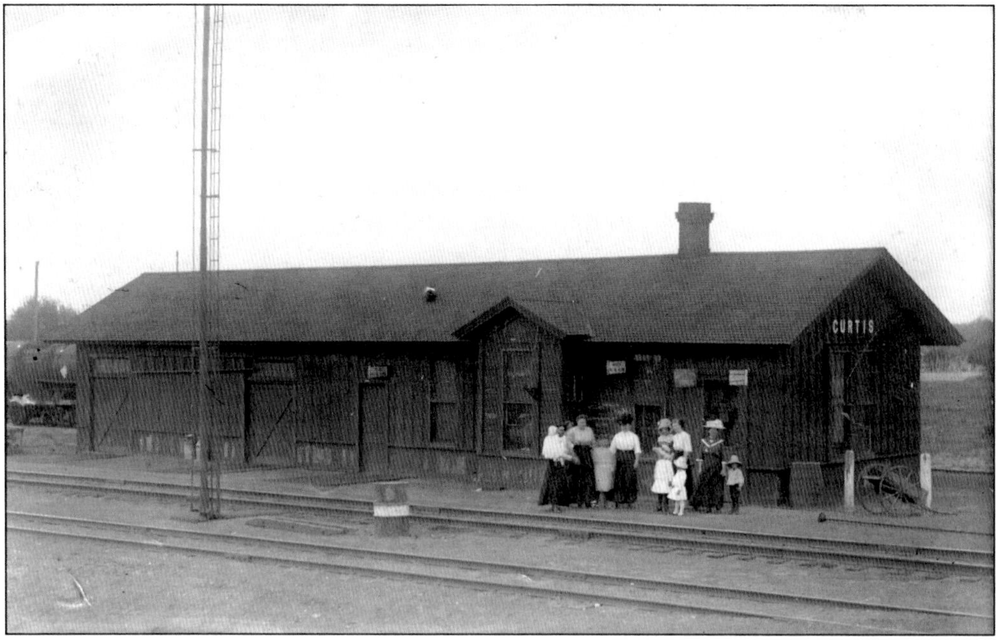

Curtis was a town about 14 miles east of Woodward along the Santa Fe. A post office existed from October 3, 1894, until October 31, 1952. The photograph shows the wooden train depot at Curtis.

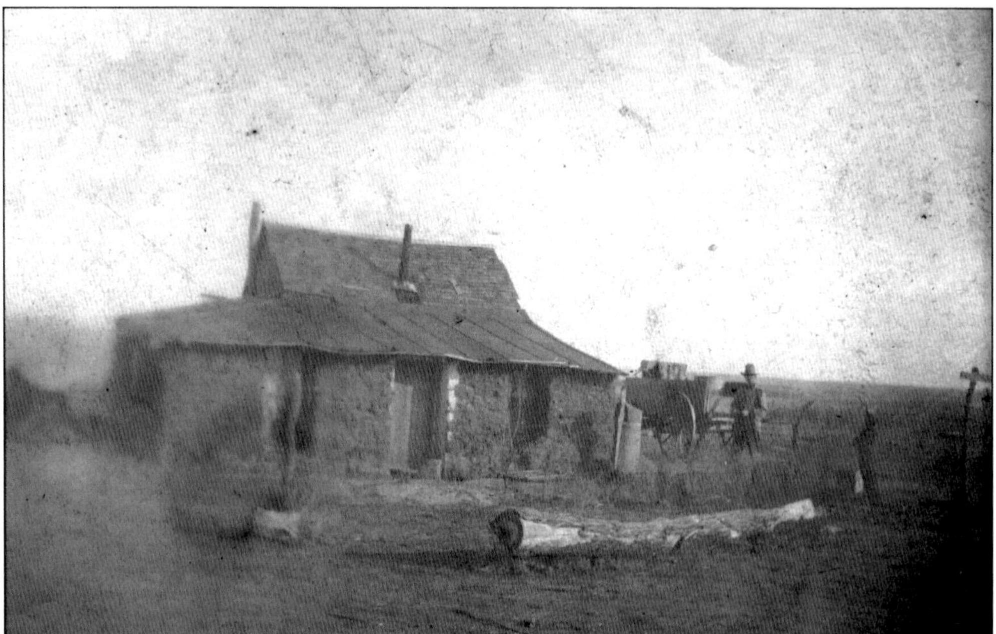

This is the only known photograph of Peace, which was located six miles north of Quinlan. The post office in the photograph is apparently made of sod bricks. The town had a post office from December 10, 1903, until February 15, 1908. It took its name from *Peacemakers*, a novel by H. E. Stannard.

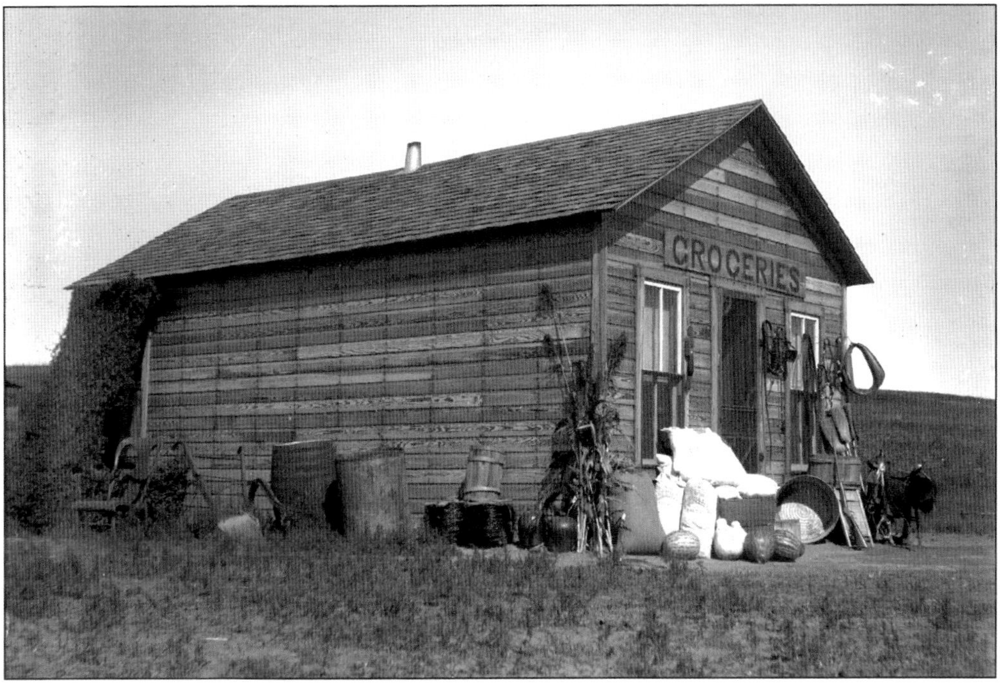

This 1901 photograph depicts the general store at Cooley in the southwestern part of the county. It is no longer in existence. Cooley was named for Beatrice Cooley, an early day resident. A post office was located here from April 17, 1902, until November 30, 1917.

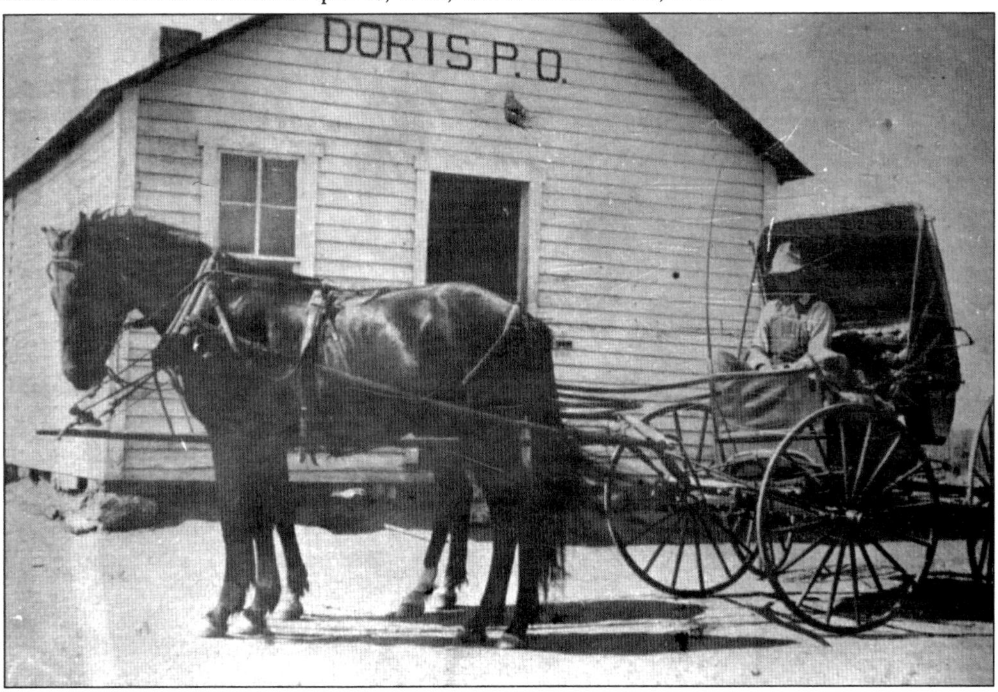

The town of Doris was located 10 miles southeast of Fargo and was established on July 6, 1901. Its name changed to Keenan on February 18, 1910. The post office at Keenan was discontinued on July 15, 1935.

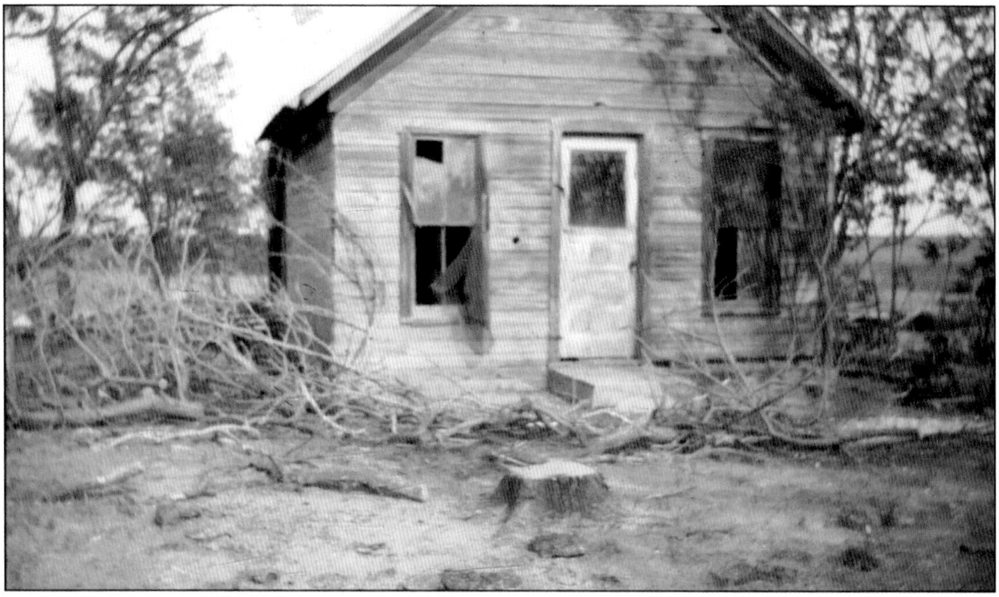

A small town named Higley once sat about eight miles northwest of Vici. A post office was established on April 24, 1901, and was named for Hubert T. Higley, the first postmaster. The office closed its doors on July 31, 1913. This 1968 photograph is of a mercantile store that was located at Higley.

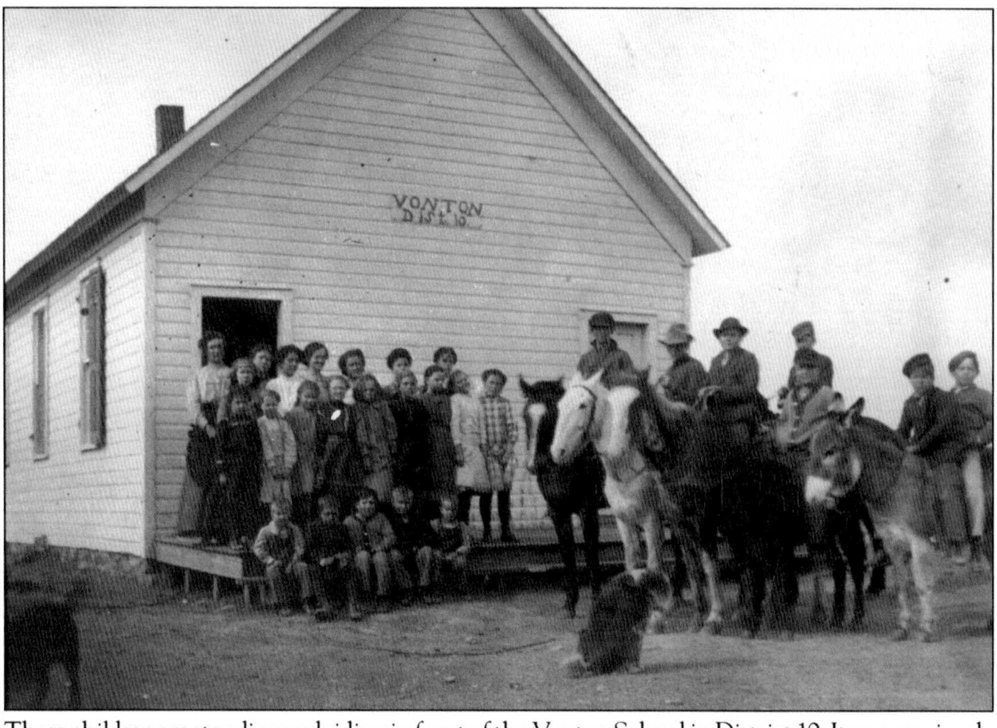

These children are standing and riding in front of the Vonton School in District 10. It was previously known as the Pleasant Hill School. Vonton was located about eight miles southwest of Woodward. The name was coined from the middle name of Wesley von Kneisley, the first postmaster. The post office was discontinued on July 16, 1906, after less than five years in existence.

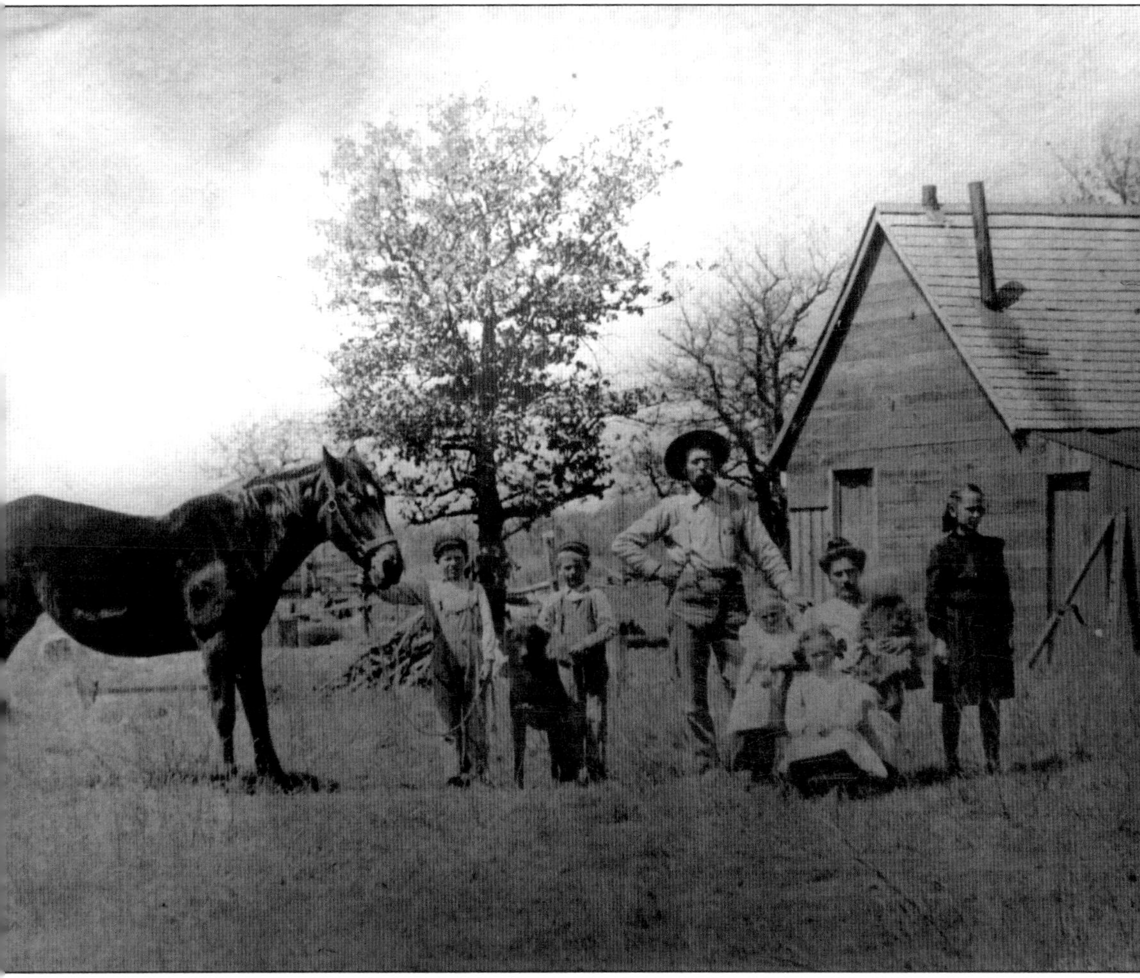

James W. Smith, a Kansan, claimed 160 acres of land west of Braman in Kay County during the opening of the Cherokee Outlet in 1893. He married Inez Gertrude Stevens on July 1, 1900. His wife had relatives living in southeastern Woodward County, so the family made the move to Pearl, arriving in about 1907. Smith ran a small general merchandise store at Pearl. They remained in the county for seven years, eventually returning to Braman. This photograph was taken in about 1911, quite possibly when Inez was pregnant with their seventh child, Lila Arvilla. From left to right are Chester Arthur, Mervin Lowell, James W., Gladyce, Althea Eunice, Inez, Frieda Argyle, and Muriel Beatrice. Pearl was located 12 miles south of Quinlan. A post office was in existence from December 16, 1897, to September 30, 1911. (Author's collection.)

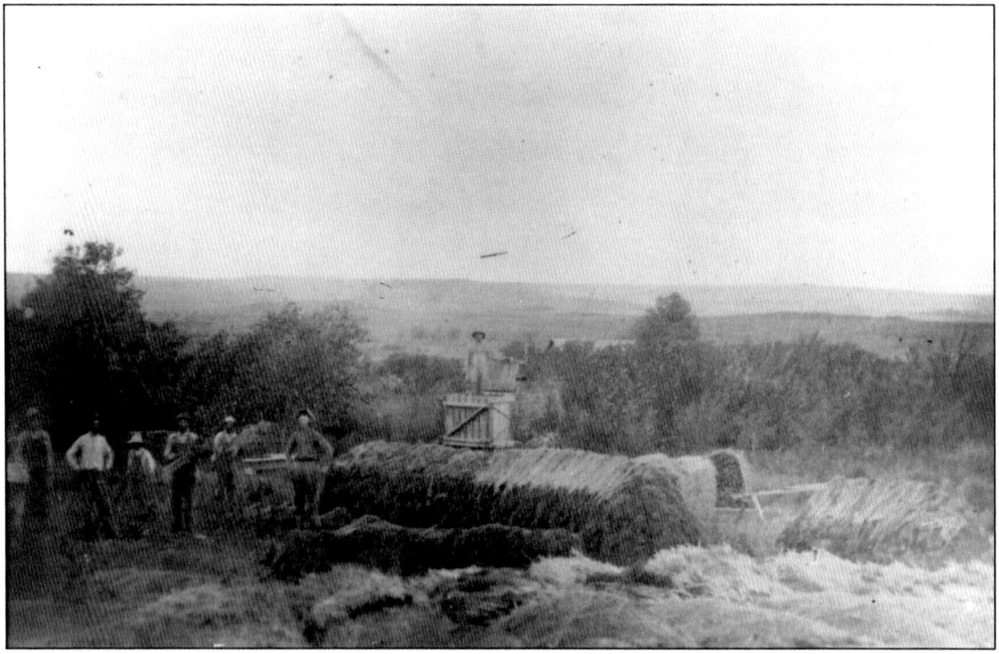

Here is a broomcorn harvest near Keenan around 1914. The town of Keenan was formerly known as Doris and was located 10 miles southeast of Fargo. The name changed to Keenan on February 18, 1910, and was discontinued on July 15, 1935. The town was named for Julia A. Keenan, the first postmaster.

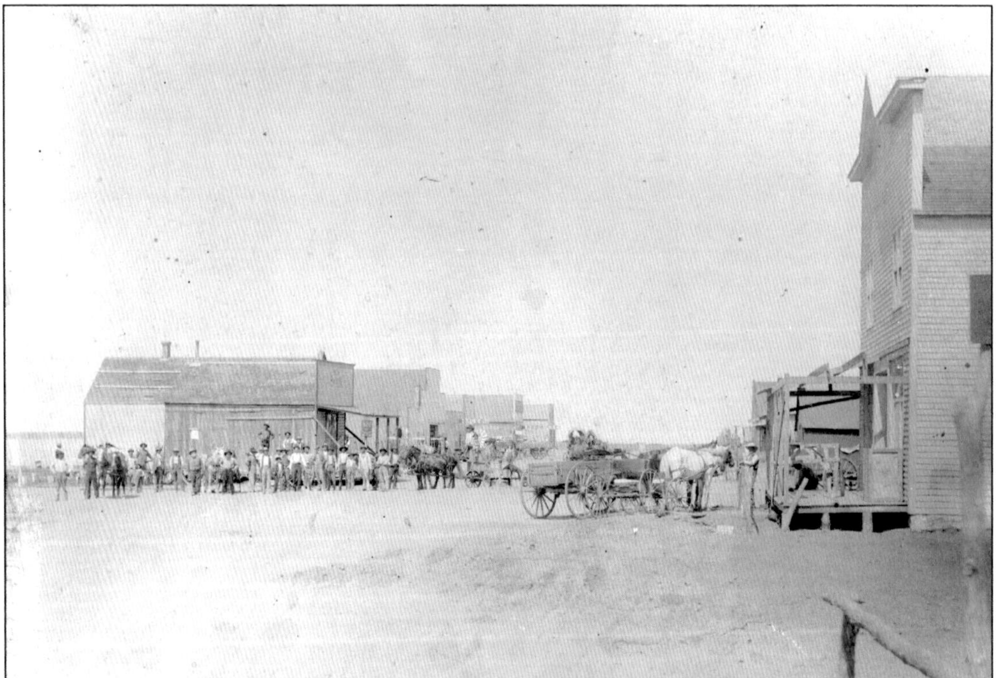

This street scene is of Curtis's Main Street, looking west, around 1900. The Masonic lodge is the large building located on the right. The B&W Saloon is one of the structures on the left.

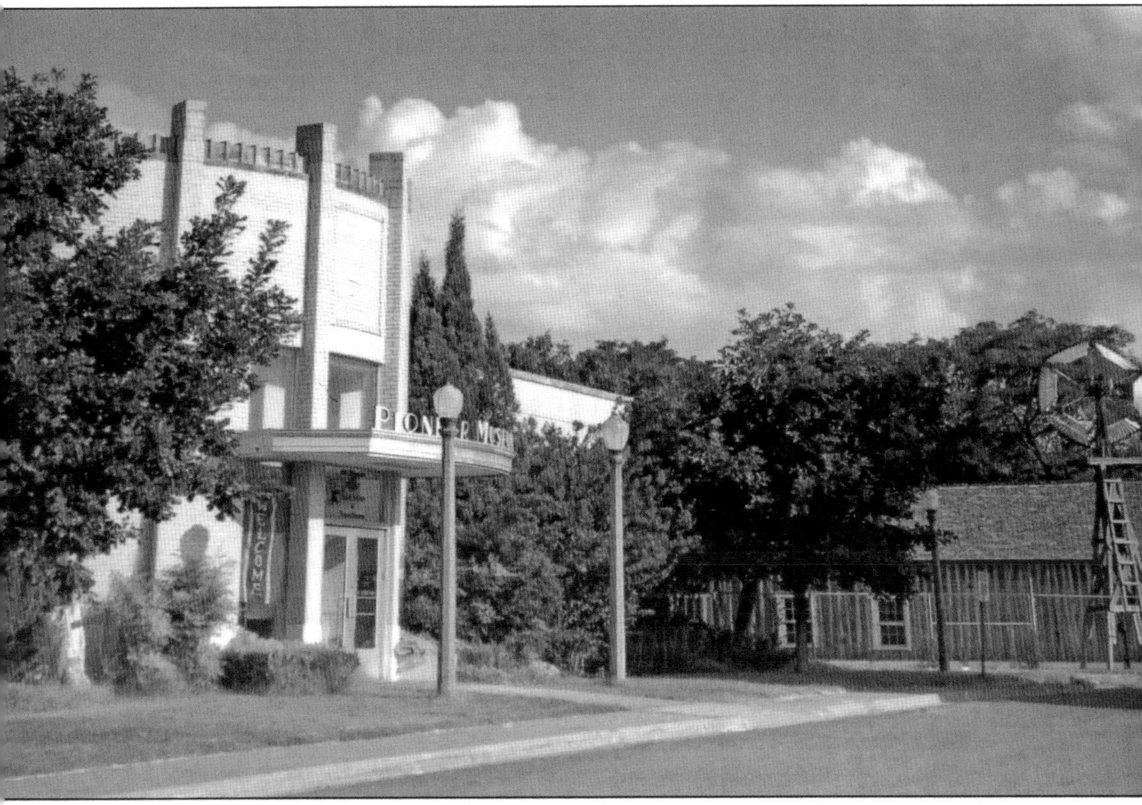

Opening its doors in 1966, the Plains Indians and Pioneers Museum serves as a permanent repository for artifacts, written and oral records, and photographs, which interpret and depict northwest Oklahoma history. The original 4,000-square-foot museum was a gift to the city of Woodward from Dr. C. E. and Anna Williams. Dr. Williams's offer to build the museum came after more than a decade of efforts by a group of concerned citizens who wanted to establish a museum in Woodward. More exhibit space and a storeroom were added to the original building in 1978. Since then, two additional buildings have also been added to the grounds. In 1984, the museum acquired the Lee-Lienemann cabin, a historic picket-style building from old Fort Supply. In 1993, an agricultural building was constructed to display farm instruments typical of the various periods depicted in the museum's murals. The museum is open Tuesday through Saturday from 10:00 a.m. until 5:00 p.m. Admission is free.